PRAISE FOR *STEINBECK'S IMAGINARIUM*

"Expansive, penetrating, and written with grace and modesty, Robert DeMott's *Steinbeck's Imaginarium* is a mash-up of delights unlike anything I've ever read. Commencing in the professor's sunlit days of youthful ardor and ambition, it's a scholar's meta-memoir—an inquiry into the nature of inquiry—that retraces DeMott's outsized role in correcting the rumor that John Steinbeck is America's most-read and least-respected author. A series of deep dives into the source material proves that DeMott chose his obsession well, which is to say it seems to have chosen him. Absorbing and revelatory— Who knew the academic life could be this much fun?—it's a truly wonderful accomplishment."—William Souder, author of *Mad at the World: A Life of John Steinbeck*

"Robert DeMott's book is a distinguished, internationally recognized scholar's professed last word on the most important literary subject of his life. In this uniquely written and entertaining confluence of creative nonfiction and scholarship, DeMott makes highly original, brilliant, and essential assessments of Steinbeck's body of work."—Brian E. Railsback, author of *Parallel Expeditions: Charles Darwin and the Art of John Steinbeck*

"*Steinbeck's Imaginarium* is a unique and wonderful book that crosses traditional scholarly boundaries into original critical spaces. There isn't anything in Steinbeck studies quite like this deeply personal book. It underscores the continuing relevance and contemporary importance of Steinbeck's artistry in an era of diverse cultural, literary, and political theories. On top of that, it is a pleasure to read."—Barbara A. Heavilin, editor in chief of the *Steinbeck Review*

"Robert DeMott is a major force in Steinbeck scholarship; *Steinbeck's Imaginarium* is his valedictory to the community and field of study he helped create. . . . A deep dive into texts, contexts, and connections, *Steinbeck's Imaginarium* is certain to become a vade mecum for serious students of Steinbeck in need of a friendly guide."—William Ray, *Steinbeck Now*

"The hallmarks of Bob DeMott's best work on Steinbeck have always been thorough archival research, love of Steinbeck's work, generosity (especially to other Steinbeck scholars), and a profound attention to the textual development of Steinbeck's ideas. . . . *Steinbeck's Imaginarium* in its own way demonstrates the same spirit of generosity to future generations of scholars. . . . In particular, graduate students and junior faculty members looking to make careers in Steinbeck scholarship could do far worse than read this book strategically for Bob's multiple hints about which large-scale projects related to Steinbeck remain unclaimed."—Kevin Hearle, *Steinbeck Review*

STEINBECK'S IMAGINARIUM

ALSO BY ROBERT DEMOTT

Works

Up Late Reading Birds of America (2020)
Angling Days: A Fly Fisher's Journals (2016; 2019)
The Weather in Athens: Poems (2001)
Dave Smith: A Literary Archive (2000)
Steinbeck's Typewriter: Essays on His Art (1996; 2012)
News of Loss: Poems (1995)
Steinbeck's Reading: A Catalogue of Books Owned and Borrowed (1984; 2007)

Chapbooks

Brief and Glorious Transit: Prose Poems (2007)
"A Play to be Played": John Steinbeck on Stage and Screen, 1935–1960 (2002)
Your Only Weapon is Your Work: A Letter by John Steinbeck to Dennis Murphy (1985)

Edited Collections

Conversations with Jim Harrison, Revised and Updated (2019)
Astream: American Writers on Fly Fishing (2012)
Afield: American Writers on Bird Dogs (2010) [with Dave Smith]
Conversations with Jim Harrison (2002)
After The Grapes of Wrath: Essays on John Steinbeck in Honor of Tetsumaro Hayashi (1995) [with Donald V. Coers and Paul A. Ruffin]
Artful Thunder: Versions of the Romantic Tradition in American Literature in Honor of Howard P. Vincent (1975) [with Sanford Marovitz]
From Athens Out (1974) [with Carol Harter]

Editions of Steinbeck's Writings

Sweet Thursday (2008)
Travels with Charley and Later Novels 1947–1962 (2007)
    [with Brian Railsback]
The Grapes of Wrath (2006)
Novels 1942–1952 (2001)
The Grapes of Wrath and Other Writings 1936–1941 (1996)
    [Elaine Steinbeck, Special Consultant]
To a God Unknown (1995)
Novels and Stories 1932–1937 (1994) [Elaine Steinbeck, Special Consultant]
Working Days: The Journals of The Grapes of Wrath, 1938–1941 (1989)

Steinbeck's Imaginarium

*Essays on Writing, Fishing,
and Other Critical Matters*

Robert DeMott

University of New Mexico Press | Albuquerque

First paperback printing 2024 | ISBN 978-0-8263-6728-0

Library of Congress Cataloging-in-Publication Data
Names: DeMott, Robert J., 1943– author.
Title: Steinbeck's Imaginarium : essays on writing, fishing, and other critical matters /
    Robert DeMott.
Description: Albuquerque : University of New Mexico Press, 2022. |
    Includes bibliographical references.
Identifiers: LCCN 2022020946 (print) | LCCN 2022020947 (e-book) |
    ISBN 9780826364289 (cloth) | ISBN 9780826364296 (epub)
Subjects: LCSH: Steinbeck, John, 1902–1968—Criticism and interpretation. |
    BISAC: LITERARY CRITICISM / American / General
Classification: LCC PS3537.T3234 Z6257 2022 (print) | LCC PS3537.T3234 (e-book) |
    DDC 813/.52—dc23/eng/20220516
LC record available at https://lccn.loc.gov/2022020946
LC e-book record available at https://lccn.loc.gov/2022020947

Founded in 1889, the University of New Mexico sits on the traditional homelands of the Pueblo of Sandia. The original peoples of New Mexico—Pueblo, Navajo, and Apache—since time immemorial have deep connections to the land and have made significant contributions to the broader community statewide. We honor the land itself and those who remain stewards of this land throughout the generations and also acknowledge our committed relationship to Indigenous peoples. We gratefully recognize our history.

Cover photograph: Erich Hartman caught Steinbeck, late 1958–early 1959, "at thought and work" necessary for the reading and writing life. This photograph appeared on the dust jacket of Library of America's third Steinbeck volume, *Novels 1942–1952* (2002). Used by permission of Magnum Photos.
Designed by Felicia Cedillos
Composed in Adobe Caslon Pro 10/14.25

Dedicated to "Old Hoss" John Ditsky (1938–2006):
poet, scholar, editor, long-distance colleague,
weekly correspondent, critical conscience,
and, most of all, esteemed friend through three decades
of traveling the Steinbeck road. . . .

Maybe it is time to . . . let all of Steinbeck—the stories and
the supposed mirror images provided by the letters and the journals and
the narrational voices—be read as a very different kind of fiction.
Only then, perhaps, will readers of Steinbeck begin to free
themselves from the tendency to judge Steinbeck on
the basis of whether or not one agrees with him.

—JOHN DITSKY, "JOHN STEINBECK:
YESTERDAY, TODAY, AND TOMORROW,"
IN STEPHEN K. GEORGE, ED.,
John Steinbeck: A Centennial Tribute (2002)

Somehow, the laws of thought must be the laws of things. . . . Thought and things are part of one evolving matrix, and cannot ultimately conflict.

—JOHN ELOF BOODIN, *A Realistic Universe* (1916)

There are some books, some stories, some poems which one reads over and over again without knowing why one is drawn to them. And such stories need not have been critically appreciated—in fact many of them have not been. The critic's approach is and perhaps should be one of appraisal and evaluation. The reader if he likes a story feels largely a participation. The stories we go back to are those in which we have taken part. A man need not have a likeness of exact experience to love a story but he must have in him an emotional or intellectual tone which has keyed into the story and made him part of it. No one has ever read Treasure Island or Robinson Crusoe objectively. The chief character in both cases are merely the skin and bones of the reader. The poetical satires of Gulliver have long been forgotten but the stories go on. The message or the teaching of a story almost invariably dies first while the participation persists.

—JOHN STEINBECK, FROM UNPUBLISHED, GHOSTWRITTEN
"INTRODUCTION BY PASCAL COVICI" (SEPTEMBER 1942),
INTENDED FOR, BUT NEVER USED, IN THE ORIGINAL
Viking Portable Library Steinbeck (1943)

How in hell do we know what literature is? Well, one of the symptoms or diagnostics of literature should be . . . that it is read, that it amuses, moves, instructs, changes and criticizes people. . . . If people don't read it, it just isn't going to be literature.

—JOHN STEINBECK, INTRODUCTION TO AL CAPP'S
The World of Li'l Abner (1953)

Imaginarium: a place devoted to the imagination.

—WIKIPEDIA

CONTENTS

ILLUSTRATIONS

DATES OF SELECTED STEINBECK BOOKS

To A God Unknown (1933)
Tortilla Flat (1935)
Of Mice and Men (1937)
The Red Pony (1937)
The Long Valley (1938)
The Grapes of Wrath (1939)
The Forgotten Village (1941)
Sea of Cortez: A Leisurely Journal of Travel and Research
    (with Edward F. Ricketts) (1941)
Cannery Row (1945)
The Pearl (1947)
The Wayward Bus (1947)
East of Eden (1952)
The Log from the Sea of Cortez (1951)
Viva Zapata! (1952)
Sweet Thursday (1954)
Once There Was a War (1958)
The Winter of Our Discontent (1961)
Travels with Charley in Search of America (1962)
America and Americans (1966)
Journal of a Novel: The East of Eden Letters (1969)
The Acts of King Arthur (1976)
Conversations with John Steinbeck (1988)
Working Days: The Journals of The Grapes of Wrath (1989)
Steinbeck in Vietnam: Dispatches From the War (2012)

ACKNOWLEDGMENTS

Long ago, at an event showcasing *East of Eden* at the Louisville Actor's Theater, Elaine Steinbeck told me an entertaining story about her husband that I have often returned to with pleasure in the past two year's seemingly endless round of lockdowns, shelterings in place, facial-mask anxiety, and long-awaited vaccinations and booster shots against COVID-19 and its insidious mutant offsprings. (And not without a certain delicious irony in recalling how often John Steinbeck wrote about public-health issues in his work, particularly in "The Harvest Gypsies," *The Forgotten Village*, and in the eerily similar effects of the influenza epidemic in chapter sixteen of *Cannery Row*.) Anyway, Broadway composer and lyricist Frank Loesser brought back a piece of stone from the Roman Coliseum and presented it to Steinbeck as a gift; concerned about the removal of an antiquity, he waited until the next time he and Elaine were in Rome and returned the stone to its rightful place.

Apocryphal stories have a way of becoming hooks on which to hang some part of our lives, so better late than never, it's easy to understand the arc of such an action, which I take to be a little parable about doing the right thing and paying back what needs to be paid back for the sake of order, continuity, and closure. It is time, then, to give credit once again where credit belongs, because— as no man is his own sire—I am happy to acknowledge that my Steinbeck passage was aided and abetted by many likeminded people who gave freely of themselves and to whom I feel warmly indebted. The journey has been long, and if I neglect to name any benefactors and/or compatriots here, I regret the omission in this registry of names, and—at nearly eighty years old—plead age-appropriate senior forgetfulness.

Every author society or lit crit fan group takes on the temperament and coloration of its studied writer, sometimes—regrettably, I should add—to disastrous, posturing, mean-spirited effect. For the most part, however, except for a couple of aberrant, attention-grabbing outliers no longer in the picture, the men and women working on and writing about Steinbeck have been among the most congenial group of scholars I have ever known, generous in sharing insights and information and in exhibiting very little one-upsmanship, jealousy, ridicule, back-biting, snobbishness, or condescension. Academic Steinbeck conferences and humanities/arts seminars, whether in Boise, Corvallis, Dallas, Hempstead, Honolulu, Louisville, Lowell, Monterey, Moscow, Nantucket, New York, Seattle, or San Jose, as well as the long-running annual Salinas Steinbeck Festival, were fun to attend, as much for the subject matter, of course, as for the quality, character, good cheer, and sociableness of the participants.

I feel acutely the loss of several mentors, colleagues, friends, and acquaintances in the Steinbeck sphere—especially my longtime compadre John Ditsky, to whose memory this book is dedicated, and two especially wise, beloved elders—the incomparable, ever-generous Warren French and the meticulous British scholar and gentleman Roy Simmonds, with whom I carried on fruitful friendships and correspondences and learned something new every time we talked. During eight years of undergraduate and graduate school, Professors John Burke, Michael O'Shea, James Farnham, James Magner, Robert Bertholf, and Howard Vincent spurred me along with their unflagging enthusiasm and passion for literature. And thanks to Peter Lisca, who, in 1970, urged me to continue writing about Steinbeck at a time when I thought I had nothing more to say. For what it is worth, I was wrong, and Peter was right. Also Preston Beyer, John Gross, Lee Richard Hayman, Joel Hedgpeth, Lester Marks, Louis Owens, Pauline Pearson, Phil Ralls, Art Ring, and Carol Robles—all gone now, and all of whom, besides helping me in a variety of personal and professional ways in my journey with Steinbeck, also fostered colorful collegial relationships.

Fifty years ago, in her brave, relentless advocacy for a frequently dismissed writer, Martha Heasley Cox, godmother of us all, for whom the San Jose State Steinbeck Center is appropriately named (now housed in handsome, specially designed quarters in the Martin Luther King Jr. Library) created a legacy that touches everyone who has ever read a Steinbeck book or written a word about him. Her monumental Steinbeck bibliography project (later carried on so capably by Greta Manville and others and accessible as an online searchable database of 12,000-plus items at the Martha Heasley Cox Center for Steinbeck Studies) created an indispensable research tool whose importance cannot be overstated. I will always be thankful to Professor Cox for having chosen me as her successor to direct the center.

In 1984 and 1985, on leave of absence from Ohio University (OU), I spent many pleasurably soulful days sequestered in the Steinbeck Center in an out-of-the-way corner at the top of old Wahlquist Library administering an enormous card catalog (which could never quite be kept up to date, despite constant manual effort in that predigital age) and superintending hundreds of books, manuscripts, documents, memorabilia, and artwork. It was a scholar's dream. After two years of visitor's status on a split contract as an administrator and a teacher, my decision to decline the permanent directorship of the center and return to OU had less to do with the nature of the job itself, which was utterly enjoyable, than with my own restlessness and the feeling that I had many other lives to live outside the confines of California.

I mourn the loss of Elaine Steinbeck, whose beneficence was unparalleled and who asked nothing in return, never once suggesting what to write about her husband or censoring or editing what I wrote but always enthusiastic and encouraging about what I did write; also Thom Steinbeck, a generous, supportive presence; Elizabeth Otis, Julie Fallowfield, and Eugene Winick, Steinbeck's agents at venerable McIntosh and Otis, who opened many doors and represented me to Viking/Penguin and The Library of America; Deborah Benson Covington (her father, Chicago's Argus Bookshop owner Ben Abramson, first introduced Pascal Covici to Steinbeck's writings, thereby setting in motion a historic publishing career) showed nothing but kindness for a wet-behind-the-ears associate editor of *Steinbeck Quarterly* in those long-gone early days when I visited her in West Cornwall, Connecticut; and Steinbeck's generous friends and acquaintances who always had time for my questions and comments and kept lines open by phone or by letter: especially Richard Albee, Chase Horton, Pare Lorentz, Virginia Scardigli, and the one and only Carlton Sheffield, to whose house in Los Altos Hills, California, I journeyed often back in the day when I was living in Los Gatos (where Steinbeck wrote *The Grapes of Wrath*) and working at San Jose State. And not a day goes by that I don't think of my late friend, incomparable novelist and poet Jim Harrison, whose abiding interest in and love for Steinbeck animated many of our conversations during the two decades of our friendship.

Thanks as well to longtime contemporaries I met along the well-traveled Steinbeck road. First and foremost, the indefatigable, visionary Tetsumaro "Ted" Hayashi, godfatherly mentor to us all, compiler of the pioneering *John Steinbeck: A Concise Bibliography* (1967) and its many succeeding offspring, creator of the

John Steinbeck Society, editor of *Steinbeck Newsletter* (1968), then editor of *Steinbeck Quarterly* (support from Ball State University funded twenty-six continuous years of publication from 1969 to 1993), and major domo behind the Steinbeck Monograph Series and Steinbeck Essay Series. For many years Ted was the engine that powered us all, a point enthusiastically agreed upon when Don Coers, Paul Ruffin, and I published *After The Grapes of Wrath* (1995), an honorary festschrift collection for Ted, with contributions by many familiar hands who felt a similar sense of indebtedness for his leadership. Hayashi and I eventually parted ways over differing editorial ideas, but there is no minimizing his accomplishments in the collective Steinbeck world.

Each of the following lent their parts in their own way to the overall effort: Dick Astro and Jack Benson, two generous compatriots and seminal, influential scholars in every sense of the term, who, along with John Ditsky, became friends from our first meeting in Corvallis, Oregon, in 1970, as did Robert Morsberger, later my roomie on a memorable and often surreal weeklong Esalen Institute–organized Steinbeck lecture tour to Moscow in October 1989, when we survived having our passports confiscated. We knew what Steinbeck meant when he wrote in *A Russian Journal*, "we had no rooms."

And these movers and shakers too, all of whom enriched my passage, whether they knew it or not: Mary Adler, Harold Augenbraum, Thomas Barden, Susan Beegel, Herb Behrens, Bernadine Beutler, Jackson Bryer, Don Coers, Jack Douglass, Thomas Fensch, William Gilly, Mimi Gladstein, Richard Hart, Stephen Hauk, Kevin Hearle, Michael Hemp, Gavin Jones, Donald Kohrs, Richard Kopley, Mike Lannoo, Cliff Lewis, Luchen Li, Audrey Lynch, Kiyoshi Nakayama, Anthony Newfield, Katherine Rodger, Gail Steinbeck, Nancy Steinbeck, Thom Tammaro, Nick Taylor, John Timmerman, Henry Veggian, and the generous bibliophiles and rare book dealers and collectors who shared their knowledge and their goods, including longtime pal Jim Dourgarian, Robert Harmon, Kenneth and Karen Holmes, Jim Johnson, and SJ Neighbors. I also extend my gratitude to Jill Lorio at Willow Transitions and Auction House (formerly Curated Estates Auctions), and to Fred C. Tom of Lamborn's Studios for many photograph and illustration courtesies. To Michael Shulman at Magnum Photos, to Zoe Bodzas of McIntosh and Otis, and to Beau Sullivan at Penguin Random House, LLC, a hearty thanks for assistance in securing permissions. Ditto to Dr. Andrew Herd, generous British angling historian extraordinaire.

At the incomparable Library of America, a deep bow to Cheryl Hurley, Geoffrey O'Brien, Max Rudin, and the late Gila Bercovitch who made working on the four Steinbeck volumes a breeze and one of the happiest ventures of my academic life. My former editors at Penguin Classics, Michael Millman and Elda Rotor, also deserve lasting praise; Michael doubly so for his enthusiastic part in finding a home for *Steinbeck's Imaginarium* at University of New Mexico Press, where he serves as an acquisitions editor and has been a cheerleader for this project from the beginning. It seems fitting that this will be the first Steinbeck title from UNMP since it published the groundbreaking anthology *Steinbeck and His Critics* in 1957, one of my favorite books in the Steinbeck critical canon, and one of the first I ever studied with attentiveness. At *Steinbeck Review*, tireless editor Barbara Heavilin, and at SteinbeckNow.com, founder and captain of the ship Will Ray, who generously supported this book from the start. At the Martha Cox Center for Steinbeck Studies, a shout-out to director Daniel Lanza Rivers, and Keenan Norris, director of the estimable Steinbeck Fellows Program, which honors and supports up-and-coming literary artists with a substantial stipend. All the aforementioned keep the Steinbeck fires fanned, as does William Souder, whose award-winning biography of Steinbeck, *Mad at the World* (2020), has lit up the skies lately and casts a long shadow.

A profound debt of thanks to Professor Susan Shillinglaw, decades-long pal, colleague, road-tripper, unparalleled Steinbeckian commentator, and the longest tenured director in the history of San Jose's Steinbeck Center, who once confessed to "seeing Steinbeck everywhere" she looked (thank goodness) and whose own marvelous, indispensable trilogy of books, *Carol and John Steinbeck: Portrait of a Marriage* (2013), *On Reading The Grapes of Wrath* (2014), and *A Journey into Steinbeck's California* (2019), among others, have helped advance and vivify Steinbeck studies in this century. Viva Susan!

I am honored, too, by the graduate students who studied John Steinbeck in my seminars at Ohio University and who went on to have exemplary professional careers of their own: Neil Browne, David Farrah, Mark Govoni, Steve Mulder, Brian Railsback, David Wrobel, Jeff Yeager, and Nancy Zane. All enriched my life in ways I can never fully recount or repay, except to offer my thanks to them for having ridden along all these years. And my gratitude includes, too, the accomplished high school teachers chosen for Shillinglaw and Gilly's semiannual National Endowment for the Humanities Steinbeck Seminar at Stanford's Hopkins Marine Station in Pacific Grove, a model of cross-disciplinary study where the currents of literature, art, science, pedagogy, and ecology merge into one harmonious stream, a Rickettsian/Steinbeckian unified field of endeavor if there ever was one.

Thanks also to Tom Carney, Nick Lyons, Paul Schullery, and Dave Smith, my literary outdoor sporting pals, for many years of good talk, sane advice, and spirited encouragement when it was needed to lift my head out of the Steinbeck universe.

My fabulous life partner Kate Fox makes all I have done or will do constantly worthwhile.

RD
Athens, OH
December, 2021

ABBREVIATIONS FOR FREQUENTLY CITED TEXTS

AASN: John Steinbeck. *America and* Americans *and Selected Nonfiction.* Edited by Susan Shillinglaw and Jackson J. Benson. New York: Penguin, 2002.

CJS: Thomas Fensch, ed. *Conversations with John Steinbeck.* Jackson: University Press of Mississippi, 1988.

JN: John Steinbeck. *Journal of a Novel: The East of Eden Letters.* New York: Viking Press, 1969.

LSC: John Steinbeck. *The Log from the Sea of Cortez: The Grapes of Wrath and Other Writings, 1936–1941.* Edited Robert DeMott, with special consultant Elaine A. Steinbeck. New York: Library of America, 1996, 693–987.

Mad: William Souder, *Mad at the World: A Life of John Steinbeck.* New York: W. W. Norton, 2020.

"Mpb": John Steinbeck. "My personal book." Autograph *Wayward Bus* Journal. New York: The Morgan Library and Museum, 1946.

SLL: Elaine Steinbeck and Robert Wallsten, eds. *Steinbeck: A Life in Letters.* New York: Viking Press, 1975.

SR: Robert DeMott. *Steinbeck's Reading: A Catalogue of Books Owned and Borrowed.* New York: Garland, 1984.

ST: Robert DeMott. *Steinbeck's Typewriter: Essays on His Art.* Troy, NY: Whitston, 1996; Bloomington, IN: iUniverse, 2012.

TAJS: Jackson Benson. *The True Adventures of John Steinbeck, Writer.* New York: Viking Press, 1984.

WD: John Steinbeck. *Working Days: The Journals of The Grapes of Wrath, 1938–1941.* Edited by Robert DeMott. New York: Viking Press, 1989.

What Went Around Came Around

Recently, while carrying out some incidental consulting and fact-checking for Curated Estates' public auction of John and Elaine Steinbeck's remaining property from their 190 East 72nd Street, Manhattan apartment (John died in 1968, Elaine in 2003; the residence was sold by heirs in 2018), I came across many intriguing items. I don't mean to wax nostalgic about this particular estate sale—I have done my fair share of buying and selling literary artifacts and memorabilia over the years, Steinbeck-related items included—but this well-publicized omnibus auction (held February 27, 2020, in Lincoln Park, New Jersey) brought with it intimations of mortality I was not expecting, by which I mean the kind of vibe one feels when the last vestiges of familiar attachment and identification are about to be dissolved.

Among the hundreds of items of furniture, bric-a-brac, household wares, letters, photographs, paintings, manuscripts, documents of all kinds, and large numbers of both John and Elaine Steinbeck's personal books in several different groupings, none was more poignant to me than Lot 214a, "Elaine Steinbeck's Personal Library." Included in her select group of fifteen books were inscribed copies of *Working Days: The Journals of The Grapes of Wrath, 1938–1941* (1989) and *Steinbeck's Typewriter: Essays on His Art* (1996). I had presented them to her heartily inscribed years earlier in gratitude for her generosity, support, and friendship above and beyond our personal connection with the first two Library of America Steinbeck volumes, for which I served as editor and she as honorary special consultant. ("Isn't our second STEINBECK beautiful? You have done a marvelous job," she wrote in one of the many gracious cards and letters I received from her over the years.) Now the books would be dispersed—to whom and at what price I did not know—but their imminent passage struck me as a melancholy but fitting finale to a long involvement in Steinbeck Studies.

———

For me, the Matter of Steinbeck—by which I mean not just his writings but the overall body of his work, the allied collection of diverse historical, personal, creative, and intellectual materials that made up his achievement and offered possibilities for sustained investigation into his life and career—was never solely a bloodless scholarly project, nor a way to mark academic time and advancement (though that came, too, in due course), but an attempt to understand and communicate one writer's important literary, social, and ecological vision that gathered strength, urgency, and relevance as the years went on. Steinbeck's gravitational pull got stronger over the decades, not weaker. The subject had vista and range, and I tried to stay true to its purpose through many varied writings and publications. Doing so lent an extra level of direction and weight to my otherwise quotidian schoolman's life.

At my age, I probably won't be training many more bird dogs or tying many more trout flies, so except for a few small items in the pipeline, this will be my last go-round with Steinbeck because I sense the circle closing and my allotment of enthusiasm winding down, especially in this age of hypersensitive and politically inspired literary discourse. (It should always be kept in mind that Steinbeck himself had little intertest in "good taste.") I hope I am not becoming one of those jaded professors Steinbeck and Ricketts accused of retiring "into easy didacticism" (*LSC* 819), but I think there is wisdom in knowing when one's given time is up on a particular subject, there is grace in knowing when the language and vocabulary of contemporary cultural criticism and literary scholarship—some of which strikes me as being overly antiseptic, accusatory, and unforgiving (I remind myself, however, that has probably always been the case, no matter the intellectual era)—are no longer comfortably one's own, and there is satisfaction in knowing that with so many gifted adepts on the scene, the field of Steinbeck inquiry will sail on in good hands, much as it always has.

It is gratifying to know that the general level of acceptance toward Steinbeck as a sufficiently complex writer worthy of extensive study has made enormous leaps forward in the past half century–plus, which I regard as a happy joint project of ongoing reclamation aided and abetted by many active, dedicated participants. Indeed, the very best scholarship of recent decades has shown that addressing Steinbeck seriously requires familiarity with the entire range of his work, utilizing all of the numerous scholarly and critical resources by and about him, being able to bring the full range of interdisciplinary and literary theory to bear, being willing to negotiate the boundaries between critical achievement

and popular acceptance, being able to balance the binaries of academic aesthet-
icism and his blend of workaday realism and myth, and being willing to view
the post-thirties work with more respect than it has yet garnered.

Having said that, John Steinbeck will probably never be a perfect exemplar
of this or that theoretical position, and there will always be aspects of his work
that don't measure up to full-blown excellence, especially for a portion of a
burgeoning skeptical "cancel culture" readership. Even so, despite not being
everybody's darling, treating Steinbeck's works through the varied lenses of
current critical theories of race, ethnicity, gender, and identity, for example,
should continue to keep him a relevant part of our give-and-take cultural
conversation for this era, and, I predict, for those to come. Every time a new
"ism" is touted as the next great thing, Steinbeck, it seems, has anticipated its
appearance in some way, shape, or form. Steinbeck's environmentalism,
inspected through the lens of eco-criticism, is a case in point. It is a significant
area of scholarly work that shows no indication of waning and continues to
set the writer apart from many of his vaunted Euro-influenced Modernist
peers. Steinbeck's attitude toward the natural environment is more akin to
Robinson Jeffers's elemental world view and Aldo Leopold's "land ethic" than
to rarefied hyperesthetic formalism. That, I suggest, is a good thing for the
sake of revising, even disrupting, the traditional lines of historical literary
descent. Steinbeck's outlier status, his fraught, uneasy relationship to
Anglo-American Modernism, is not only fitting, but well deserved, hard
earned, and necessary.

———

Plenty remains to be accomplished, however, especially from a material book-
making standpoint. John Steinbeck himself was a polymath and had a good
deal to say about many topics outside of literature, including journalism, politics, history, war, culture, science, and the arts. The Cox Center for Steinbeck
Studies has launched the Steinbeck Letters Project to create a searchable database of his correspondence, though I hope some intrepid, forward-thinking
scholar, young and energetic enough to realize it will require several years of
concentrated labor, will eventually bring forth a suitably comprehensive, uncut,
unexpurgated, *annotated* edition of Steinbeck's voluminous correspondence, for
he was a remarkably prolific, insightful, and entertaining letter writer who

deserves no less than the kind of premier treatment other Modernist writers such as T. S. Eliot, William Faulkner, and Ernest Hemingway have received.

The same can be said for a collected edition of Steinbeck's extensive writing journals; printed together they would make a substantial volume about the roller-coaster nature of the creative process and a passageway into the interior dimensions of his compositional practice. Or a production of *East of Eden* and *Journal of a Novel* bound together as Steinbeck once envisioned them being. And while I am at it, just for the sheer fascination it would create, how about an exhaustively annotated and extra-illustrated edition of *Sea of Cortez* that would appeal to both humanities and science devotees? Or a volume of Steinbeckian iconography, photographs, written and allied documents, and related artifacts that would round out the way the writer's life is historicized, curated, documented, and viewed. Luchen Li's valuable *John Steinbeck: A Documentary Volume*, volume 309 of *Dictionary of Literary Biography* (2005), is a welcome and impressive start, but I hold out hope that something jazzier and more colorful is possible. (Michael Katakis's stunning 2018 volume on Ernest Hemingway's life artifacts in the Kennedy Library collection might serve as a model for such a book on Steinbeck.) Again, the Cox Center has opened the door to such a capacious volume with its 2,300-plus–item Photo Archive. So has William McPheron, whose limited-edition exhibition catalogue *John Steinbeck: From Salinas to Stockholm* (2000) is a compelling window into Stanford University's incomparable Steinbeck collection. It too could add significantly to a comprehensive, widely available, large-format iconography volume. Furthermore, the publication in 2021 of a gorgeously produced, boxed, full-sized facsimile edition of *The Grapes of Wrath*'s autograph manuscript by Nicolas Tretiakow and Jessica Nelson's SP Books-Edítions des Saints Peres in France indicates both the feasibility and desirability of such special bibliographical offerings. Readers, students, scholars, and collectors all benefit from such inspired efforts.

In that vein, perhaps, too, a day will come when a judicious selection of Steinbeck's previously unpublished work will be made available, suitably contextualized and introduced by knowledgeable editors. Candidates that come to mind are an early mystery potboiler, *Murder at Full Moon*; an original novella, *Lifeboat*; a play, *The Last Joan*; and an English-language version of nonfiction travel pieces, *Un Américain à New York et à Paris* (*CJS* 86). These desired projects would benefit a new generation of general readers and biographical, literary, or environmental scholars, but also creative writers as well, to whom Steinbeck's obsessive struggles in his journals with issues of craft and inspiration, for example, would be as important and compelling as his themes, characters, and content are to literary traditionalists. It was not for nothing novelist Jim Harrison kept a copy of *Working Days* in his cabin in Michigan's Upper Peninsula and read it whenever he hit a writing snag of his own.

———

Meantime, as a note of warning, *Steinbeck's Imaginarium* is a set of exploratory assays, not a normal scholarly monograph with a straight-line thesis stretching from end to end. I was never handy at that kind of lockstep academic structure, preferring a digressive, random, vertical approach on a few intriguing key topics, rather than a panoramic, horizontal, chronological approach that is stock-in-trade for traditional literary criticism and biography. Which is to say, *Steinbeck's Imaginarium* is probably not a book for beginners interested in a basic overall introduction to Steinbeck's life and art, but rather a book that presupposes some prior knowledge of and interest in aesthetic dimensions of his textual world.

More accurately, I think of this late-life group of farewell personal improvisations and divagations as a narrow road to the interior of Steinbeckland, and a belated footnote to and a resonant echo of my previous work in this vein, especially to the essays that make up *Steinbeck's Typewriter*. This present book is admittedly a kind of nostalgic indulgence, a final painterly, impressionistic ramble in the Steinbeck field that has occurred after being away from full-time academic life for nearly a decade. It is belated because it resonates with some key preoccupations regarding creativity and participation that run through my earlier work on Steinbeck; it is a footnote in that it adds some new twists, tweaks, flourishes, and adornments to the larger existing critical text of inquiry. In writing about John Steinbeck I have tried to forge in my prose a personally inflected critical voice that does justice to both accurate scholarship and creative expression. My endgame was always the same: to understand Steinbeck's works from the inside out rather than imposing meaning from the top down. Process rather than product often dictated my aims. It is an engaged contextual approach I found possible by focusing mostly on his writerly practices and aesthetic preoccupations and which has generally allowed me to avoid applying the condemnatory word "failure" (the most overused term in Steinbeck scholarship) to his writings. There are many weaknesses, lapses, and missteps in his works, but I admit to being less interested in what he failed to do than in exploring the dimensions of what he succeeded in doing.

———

During the past half century I wrote many essays, articles, introductions, forewords, notes, encyclopedia entries, seminar lectures, commentaries, and book reviews that were never collected but that seemed at the time to be more than a way of just killing time and filling empty spaces. It is a dangerous and potentially embarrassing gambit to reach too far back into a scholarly past that seems murkier and murkier as time goes on. I am not even sure who I was when I produced those earlier words (some of them so long ago I had no recollection of ever having written them), except that I knew I had found a mainline subject that has kept me engaged and challenged for an astonishingly long time. So in preparing this little book I sifted through the pile and realized that, despite the generous number of pages, there were only a few pieces I wished to bring forward that fit the tone and shape of the book I envisioned. Doing so, I was reminded of Steinbeck's blurb on the dust jacket of exotic dancer Gypsy Rose Lee's *Gypsy* (1957): "It's quite a performance. I bet some of it is even true, and if it isn't, it is now." Only time will tell if *Steinbeck's Imaginarium* is anything more than a tombstone.

My introductory essay, "Half a Century with Steinbeck," appears here for the first time. The second, "The Place We Have Arrived," is suggestive and instigational, and it unpacks two important terms in Steinbeck's lexicon: "participation" and the "new." It was presented as a talk at an American Literature Association conference in Boston and later appeared in Susan Shillinglaw and Kevin Hearle's book, *Beyond Boundaries: Rereading John Steinbeck* (2002). The third, "Private Narratives/Public Texts," is patently scholarly and biographical. It was presented in earlier form as a talk at the twenty-third annual Steinbeck Festival in Salinas in 2003, then again with additions as a featured lecture at the International Steinbeck Conference at San Jose State University in 2016, then printed that same year in *Steinbeck Review* (Vol. 13, No. 2). The fourth, "Of Fish and Men," is fanciful and personal. It was given as a talk at the Silver Anniversary Steinbeck Festival in Salinas in 2005, and at a Zion Canyon (Utah) Arts and Humanities Council event, then published in the American Museum of Fly Fishing's scholarly journal *American Fly Fisher* in 2006, and later in revised form in *Steinbeck Review* (Vol. 11, No. 2, 2014), the basis for the current appearance. An illustrated iteration of the essay was presented as a lecture at Western Reserve Academy in Hudson, Ohio, in 2013, at the thirty-fifth Steinbeck Festival in Salinas in 2016, and at the Chautauqua Institute in Lakeside, Ohio, in 2017. On their way around again, the three latter pieces have been updated, expanded, and refreshed, and they are used with permission from University of Alabama Press, Pennsylvania State University Press, the American Museum of Fly Fishing, and other appropriate authorities, to whose generosity I am deeply indebted and eternally grateful. Material on *The Grapes of Wrath* that appears in my introductory chapter was presented as part of the John Howard Birss Memorial Lecture on Steinbeck at Roger Williams University in 2014, and at Columbus State Community College's interdisciplinary conference on "Protest Art During the Great Depression" in 2018. Throughout *Steinbeck's Imaginarium* I am especially pleased to be permitted to use photographs and illustrations from San Jose State University's bountiful John Steinbeck archival collection, which deserves the widest possible publicity. A special note of thanks to chief archivist Peter Van Coutren for expert help, advice, and support in navigating the center's holdings.

Chapter 1

Half a Century with Steinbeck

A Personal Retrospect

> What I always loved about Steinbeck's work was that it wasn't afraid
> of being heroic and that he . . . hung his ass out there . . . for you, for me.
>
> —BRUCE SPRINGSTEEN UPON ACCEPTING SAN JOSE STATE
> UNIVERSITY'S JOHN STEINBECK AWARD (1996)

> Steinbeck made a lifetime of writing seem possible.
>
> —BARRY LOPEZ, "STEINBECK'S INFLUENCE" (2002)

John Steinbeck saved my life. I mean that metaphorically, of course, which
doesn't make the statement any less true. In the autumn of 1964, at the start
of my senior year at Assumption College (now University) in Massachusetts,
I was challenged by John Burke and Michael O'Shea, my two favorite American Lit professors, to consider writing about Steinbeck for my required
senior thesis. A one-time biology major turned English major, I was floun-
dering at a loss about how to proceed. I loved to read, but I had no critical
writing skills. A book was merely a collection of words on a page, and I had
no sense of such technical, formal qualities as point of view, modulation of
voice, narrative structure, and rhythmic timing, or other further niceties of
tone, style, and language. Producing an extended formal academic essay
seemed beyond my meager abilities. Utterly intimidated, I hardly knew where
to turn. One afternoon, on my way to hockey practice at the Worcester ice
rink, I stopped in the college's library and checked on its Steinbeck holdings.
The first title my eye fell on was *Travels with Charley in Search of America*,
published two years earlier, in 1962. I had only vaguely heard of the book,

didn't know if it was fiction or nonfiction, but as a lifelong dog owner and fledgling seeker myself, I was intrigued.

I read its opening pages and discovered something I had never experienced in my willy-nilly career as an English major. Early in Part I, Steinbeck describes riding out Hurricane Donna, a powerful category-three storm with ninety-five-mile-an-hour winds and ten-foot storm surges that swept up the East Coast in August and September of 1960 and delayed the departure of his cross-country trip. Never mind the famous British and American literary places I'd read about but never visited—this was the first time in my life I had ever encountered an event, a place, a time in a book that I too had personally experienced. I grew up in southwestern Connecticut on the north shore of Long Island Sound, west and north across the Sound from Steinbeck's Sag Harbor summer home. In the early days of my senior year in high school, I witnessed the devastation and upheaval Donna's swath caused in the mid-Atlantic, New Jersey, New York, and lower New England region, and the way its brutal force changed people's lives, among them relatives of mine.

For the first time I could recall, a book created a visceral response rather than a merely intellectual one and felt like something had actually "happened to me," as Steinbeck once famously said about the effects of reading (*SR* xx). I was hooked. And though *Travels with Charley* did not figure in my senior thesis and never became one of my go-to Steinbeck books during the following years, discovering it at that moment was enough to spark my interest, though at that time I had no idea where my fascination would lead or how far it would go or how deeply Steinbeck's message would influence my life. All I wanted to do was get through hockey season (we lost more games than we won), write the damn thesis (a thoroughly forgettable one, as it turned out, on Steinbeck's biologist heroes), and graduate the following spring (successfully but hardly with flying colors).

There were immediate effects, however. I came away with an abiding love for *The Grapes of Wrath*, *The Log from the Sea of Cortez*, and *East of Eden*. (So much so, I should add, that I confess to still having my original paperbacks of the latter two works; familiar, well-worn talismans of my initial attraction that I have kept close at hand for what seems like forever. They were supplemented by two inspirational totems: an Air Mail envelope hand-addressed by Steinbeck to his Viking Press editor Pascal Covici, postmarked January 18, 1941, in Los Gatos—which I bought and framed during my Steinbeck Center days in the mid-1980s and which has hung on the wall of my work study ever since—and a small framed quartet of US Postal Service John Steinbeck stamps issued in 1979.) More importantly, sentimentality and fetishism aside, discovering Steinbeck turned me into an attentive reader and student of literature. Aided by E. W. Tedlock and C. V. Wicker's invaluable anthology *Steinbeck and His Critics: A Record of Twenty-Five Years* (1957) and Peter Lisca's *The Wide World of John Steinbeck* (1958)—still two of my favorite foundational academic books on Steinbeck—I gained some semblance of evaluative, critical know-how, which in turn convinced me to take my own life as a student, teacher, and writer more seriously than I ever had before.

Those two books in particular gave compelling reasons for considering Steinbeck a complex thinker and artist. It was a view of Steinbeck decidedly in the minority back then as he was more often than not considered the writer critics loved to hate. But Tedlock's, Wicker's, and Lisca's combined message was one I needed to hear, because even at that juncture I realized Steinbeck added something enriching to my life and I sensed I would go on needing his words as a tonic, as I hope this retrospective chapter will show. As often happens, however, even in a ho-hum life, one thing led to another: my participatory journey with Steinbeck kept stretching farther and longer, and eventually colonized large portions of my academic and personal existence. I broke away now and then to write on T. S. Eliot and W. H. Auden for my master's thesis and Henry David Thoreau for my doctoral dissertation, as well as other topics, genres, and writers in the ensuing years as a teacher of American literature and creative writing, but Steinbeck always found ways to pull me back in, and not necessarily against my will.

Half a century–plus goes by quicker than I could have imagined on that autumn day in 1964 when time seemed to stand still and a door opened that I walked through. There always seemed to be one more element of Steinbeck's work to address, then one more after that, and so on. Now, nearly six decades later, my lengthy preoccupation is wrapping up with this modest honorific gathering of loose ends, by which I mean a quartet of previously uncollected essays of a particular ilk, each of them loosely concerned with the theme of creativity, a topic that remains close to my heart as a student of literature, a scholar, and a writer.

———

My first two academic Steinbeck-related publications, instigated by mentorly Tetsumaro Hayashi, were a review of Joseph Fontrenrose's *John Steinbeck: An Introduction and Interpretation* (1963) in the fledgling, hand-cranked, mimeo-graphed *Steinbeck Newsletter* (precursor of *Steinbeck Quarterly*) and a review of Warren French's *The Thirties: Fiction, Poetry, Drama* in Japan's *Kyushu American Literature* (1967). The reviews appeared the month Steinbeck died in December 1968, when he was sixty-six years old. From then until now, half a century–plus later, he has been an integral part of my professorial life, and I confess that laboring in the Steinbeck vineyard gave me an additional measure of purpose and direction beyond the routine of my daily teacherly existence, which I loved exceedingly and honored with my best primary efforts. Teaching always came first, as I believe decades of former students would attest, but I needed my sustaining academic avocations as well, which is where studying Steinbeck came in.

In our current intellectual climate, single-author studies are risky enterprises, but I came up in an era in American humanities scholarship when the model of approach favored drilling down on a single author. I am admittedly old school in that regard. Going deep rather than going wide was a commonly accepted posture that gripped me with special urgency. That was because How-ard Vincent, a renowned Melville scholar, was my major professor at Kent State University in the late 1960s, where I specialized in the American Renaissance period (as it was then known) and oversaw my doctoral dissertation on Henry David Thoreau. His landmark book, *The Trying-Out of Moby-Dick* (1949), with its emphasis on transformative reading and adaptive creativity, and his exhaus-tively annotated edition of *Moby-Dick* (1952), exerted an enormous influence on my critical development and scholarly bearing. I found in Vincent's writings, in his lively seminar sessions, in his warm personal cheerfulness, and in his inspir-ing dissertation directorship an abiding concern for the creative dimensions of literary production that went beyond the normal reaches of then-current New Critical formalism. Vincent made reading and writing about literature an excit-ing personal adventure rather than a routine intellectual exercise. He was one of a line of blessed former teachers who made sparks fly, who demonstrated why great teaching matters so much and cannot be divorced from scholarly pursuits. Naturally, I trace a direct connection from Vincent's work in establishing the importance of the books Melville hungrily drew upon while writing his mas-terpiece, to my later efforts in reconstructing Steinbeck's own library and detailing his textual borrowings in my annotated *Steinbeck's Reading: A Catalogue of Books Owned and Borrowed* (1984), a thirteen-year-long project, and from there tracing the influence—or better yet, presence—of certain books on his own art.

From the outset I took to heart Emerson's pronouncement in "The American Scholar" that there is "creative reading as well as creative writing." Steinbeck, a self-confessed "shameless magpie" (*SLL* 95), often read to write, and the fruits of his studiousness and his allusive and/or referential habits appear in many places, from the unpublished novel, *Murder at Full Moon* (1930) and onward, including *The Grapes of Wrath* (1939), *Sea of Cortez* (1941), *Sweet Thursday* (1954), and his posthumous *The Acts of King Arthur* (1976). Also *East of Eden* (1952), which got a huge shot in the arm from the 1951 centennial of *Moby-Dick* (Steinbeck wrote sections of *East of Eden* while summering in Nantucket that year where the centennial was being celebrated). Writing an essay on *Moby-Dick*'s presence in *East of Eden* for a conference on "Steinbeck and the Environment," held in Nantucket in 1992 (collected in *Steinbeck's Typewriter* as "'Working at the Impossible': The Presence of *Moby-Dick* in *East of Eden*" in 1996 and in the volume of conference proceedings in 1997) brought me back around to Professor Vincent, my beloved former teacher, adviser, and Melville scholar extraordinaire (who had died a few years earlier), and in a way completed a vital circuit of piety. So I have come to think of my long arc of work on Steinbeck not at all as a dutiful, lockstep grind but as a kind of gift, a joyful presence of its own, and a serendipitous journey, which Steinbeck bequeathed to me—and to all of his readers—in return asking only that we pay attention as fully and scrupulously as possible. It is not for nothing that "participation" looms so large in his canon.

Reading Steinbeck, we live into his words and become coconspirators in a text that is somehow larger than all of us combined: "And they listened while the tales were told, and their participation made the stories great," he says in chapter twenty-three of *The Grapes of Wrath* (556). Participation is a key concept in Steinbeck's artistic lexicon. Author, text, and audience add up to a needful triad, a circle that remains unclosed until the "trinity" of "the writer, the book, and the reader" are present. He purposefully sought to achieve a strong participatory effect by reaching a common ground between text and audience in a liminal site, a contact zone, where a reader can take from his book as much as they can bring to it emotionally or psychologically. His view, that there is no single absolute truth and that we are all highly subject to our own individual perspectives and warps, resonates throughout his body of work. No one, Steinbeck believed, reads objectively. The story fades, but the sense of participation persists. I am proof of that.

The breakthrough empathetic effect he sought encourages people to understand each other by inhabiting the lives of his characters without first making biased, teleological, a priori judgments. Around the time Louise Rosenblatt published her pioneering reader-response book, *Literature as Exploration* (1938), and altered the way people thought about the act of reading, Steinbeck was working on his own transactional writing/reading dynamic. In many cases he staked out an area at the shifting borderland between group dynamic and individual identity, history and textuality, fiction and nonfiction, linear plot and digressive hooptedoodle, where interrelatedness outmuscles absolutism every time. It is a border geography, an in-betweenness, I find attractive and congenial to my interests, which have always had a quality of waywardness to them.

It follows, I suppose, that for better or worse we remake writers in our own image, according to our own intuitive demands and unconscious desires. Or perhaps it is that we are drawn to writers who reflect something of ourselves in their makeup. I have never been certain which assessment is most correct, but this late in the venture it probably doesn't matter. Some strange, weird alchemy of identification has taken place that I cannot fully explain and cannot deny. I give thanks for that and choose not to look the gift horse in the mouth. What does matter is that I got just what I deserved, because I found Steinbeck to be an ideal subject and a welcoming, sustaining fit for my working-class, middle-brow tastes and my public, state university sensibility. It might have been otherwise, but it wasn't, and I have not regretted one moment of the travels that have brought me to this place.

———

Among the many photographs of John Steinbeck in the public record, there is a less widely circulated one that has always commanded my attention. It reveals Steinbeck in unusual deportment, and for that reason it strikes me as an intriguing symbolic icon that represents hidden or unsuspected aspects of his life. I speak of a photograph of John Steinbeck by Robert Capa taken in a hotel room in Moscow in August or September of 1947. Because it is personal and self-reflexive and not objectively journalistic, the photo never made it into the published version of their joint project, *A Russian Journal* (1948). As far as I can determine, it was not available in even limited circulation until it appeared in James Swenson's *Picturing Migrants: The Grapes of Wrath and New Deal Documentary Photography* (50), then in the January 2, 2018, issue of *The New Republic*, and a week later in the January 8, 2018, edition of Will Ray's informative SteinbeckNow.com website, and most recently on the dust jacket of Gavin Jones's *Reclaiming John Steinbeck: Writing for the Future of Humanity* (2021). There isn't anything else quite like the Capa picture in Steinbeck iconography. It is an arresting, unsettling photograph that immediately grabs a viewer's attention and holds it. You can't look away. Steinbeck is staring slightly upward into a large wall mirror; Capa, reflected in the mirror, is behind him, head down, concentrating on his camera and focusing the image. We see the back of Steinbeck's head in the foreground, but we also see a frontal view. From that angle, Steinbeck seems to be scowling.

And though I don't wholeheartedly embrace the proposition that Steinbeck

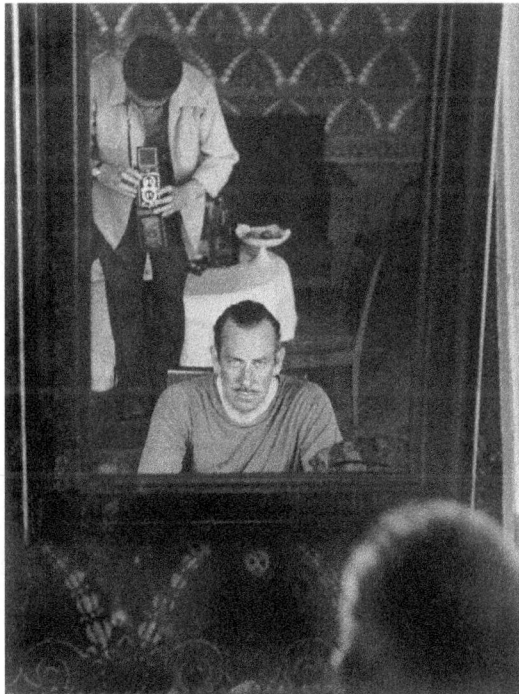

Figure 1. Portrait of Steinbeck by Robert Capa, Moscow, August or September 1947. Used by permission of International Center for Photography/Magnum Photos.

was eternally angry and overarchingly, consumingly mad at the world to the exclusion of all other emotional registers, here anyway he does look the part of the brazen, steely eyed, resolute, perhaps even pissed-off, and put-upon writer, as though he is challenging us to meet his piercing gaze, daring us to imagine what is on his mind. "If you think you know me, guess again," I imagine him saying. Among the many artifacts of his life that I have found intriguing and resonant, this compelling photo, with its equal traces of artifice, emotion, reflection, and mystery, has become a favorite touchstone that focuses my own quest for illusive and elusive Steinbeck. "Photographs," Susan Sontag wrote, "are inexhaustible invitations to deduction, speculation, and fantasy." Amen! Encountering Steinbeck, in print or art, we never quite know what we will get, though it most assuredly will be more than or different from what we imagined or have been told to expect.

As with all parts of the vast Steinbeck Archive (much of which is still sequestered in public and private institutions and not likely to gain wide currency), this photo suggests hidden depths and secret recesses, a shadow Steinbeck, an unknown Steinbeck, whose interior dimensions are often unrecognized or unacknowledged. Attending to Steinbeck's interiority, or "dramas of consciousness," in Warren French's phrase (borrowed from Henry James) in *John Steinbeck* (40), strikes me as wholly worthwhile path to pursue for a revised and revitalized view of his achievement. There is always more to Steinbeck than meets the eye at first glance.

Which is to say, Capa's stark photo has haunted me and so became a kind of focal trope for my own two-step with Steinbeck. I think the image helps illuminate the single recurring tenet that has guided my interest for many years: John Steinbeck was a better, more complex, and much different writer than he was ever given credit for being. There, I've said it, and my overarching rationale is exposed for good. But then some ventures begin with the simplest, least high-falutin' instigations. I devoted a good part of the past half century to studying John Steinbeck's career because I felt that he was a far more challenging, accomplished, sophisticated, varied, and prophetic writer than the world at large admitted. The contrarian in me wanted to talk back to the likes of cynics and naysayers Edmund Wilson, Arthur Mizener, Alfred Kazin, Leslie Fiedler, Harold Bloom, Robert Gottlieb, Jonathan Yardley, and Keith Windschuttle, those imperious cultural and critical tastemakers whose top-down critiques kept Steinbeck pigeonholed as a lesser (for which read "sentimental," "populist," "trite," "simple," "contrived") novelist compared, say, to his major high literary art contemporaries F. Scott Fitzgerald, William Faulkner, and Ernest Hemingway, all of whom—different as they were from each other—got out of the gates early and never looked back, hastened along the way, for the most part, by a more admiring, approving, elite critical chorus than Steinbeck received. Steinbeck "never quite seemed to make the mark," the compilers of an indispensable collection of his contemporary reviews claim (McElrath, Crisler, Shillinglaw x). Years ago, Donald Noble posed The Steinbeck Question: "Why has Steinbeck not received the intense academic scrutiny awarded his peers?" Noble dubbed him the "Lawrence Welk of American Literature," whose achievement will always be beset by "issues, mysteries, and conundrums" (2). Instead I've often thought he was the Rodney Dangerfield of American letters, because he got "no respect," or at least not of the kind and quality commensurate with his abilities. Whatever, he was no one-note Johnny.

Given the increasing acceptance of straightjacketed formalist norms that came to mark the era of academic New Criticism in the post–World War II period (my era as an undergraduate and graduate student in the 1960s), Steinbeck was not always judged on his own merits but rather was held up to a yardstick that favored other, more dyed-in-the-wool Modernist writers who exhibited vaunted degrees of technical wizardry, stylistic influence, or lyric sophistication. That was an authorial model that didn't look much like straw man Steinbeck, whose detractors always seemed to want him to write like those other guys, a desire which struck me as being not just nonsensical, but beside the point. Steinbeck, often suspicious of the highly ramified writerless book, chafed at being made an example of how not to write a novel (*CJS* 57). He was not averse to redefining the fictional contract every time out, not afraid to stray outside the lines of normative realistic fiction, for example.

All writers have their detractors, but in assessing Steinbeck there is often a special tone of exasperation—ranging from righteous outrage to gleeful condescension—by an elite cadre of critics who seemed bent on countering Steinbeck's popularity with accusations of the author's middlebrow philosophy, shameless sentimentalism, inadequate style, and concocted characters. Edmund Wilson seems to have initiated the formula: slap one cheek, kiss the other. In his chapter on Steinbeck in *The Boys in the Back Room*, Wilson's parting words were: "Yet there remains behind the journalism, the theatricalism, and the tricks of his other books a mind which does seem first rate in its unpanicky scrutiny of life" (53). No wonder Steinbeck harbored a lifelong animosity toward Wilson (*TAJS* 984).

Indeed, in *Reclaiming John Steinbeck*, Gavin Jones rightly discerns a marked "degree of animosity" toward Steinbeck in some of these critiques (1). Harold Bloom, Emperor of the Western Canon, claimed that nothing after *The Grapes of Wrath* bore rereading and that the "people in Stockholm ... seem to have a dusty file on people no one ever heard of that they pull out when making the [Nobel] awards" (quoted in Li 344). In Leslie Fiedler's terms, critics found Steinbeck guilty of the "four cardinal literary sins—didacticism, sentimentality, stereotyping, and melodrama" (57). Like Fielder, whose 1989 speech at San Jose State University's fiftieth anniversary *Grapes of Wrath* celebration could only be considered "graceless patronization" (Ditsky 99), Steinbeck's severest critics were almost gleeful in their denunciations of his sentimentality (one of the most grievous flaws a writer could possess in that Modernist age), though I could never quite understand how shooting a companion in the back of the head to save him from a lynching or castration, or putting a stillborn baby's corpse in a box and dumping it in a flooded freshet, or witnessing a grown man—a scientist, no less—moved to tears by the sight of a drowned woman in a coastal tide pool, could be construed as sentimental, saccharine, or smarmy.

Anyway, it struck me that a strictly formalist orientation toward Steinbeck's work was needlessly limiting because that generation of influential critics often neglected larger issues, such as the way, for instance, all of Steinbeck's work seems to be a commentary on the necessary but uneasy and fraught search for home and family, which reflected his longstanding belief in the ecology of humans, or the way his alleged fascination for animality was not a capitulation to base Darwinism, but an indicator of deep ecological patterns and species relationships that back then were simply not being heeded or widely appreciated.

In the late 1950s and early 1960s, an earlier group of scholars, including Joseph Fontenrose, Warren French, and Peter Lisca, were among the first wave (behind Joseph Henry Jackson and Harry Thornton Moore) to go against the grain by treating Steinbeck's work seriously and with respect, and they set a high mark in doing so. Then, in the late 1960s and early 1970s, along with some other congenial, likeminded scholars just starting out—notably Richard Astro, Jackson Benson, Martha Heasley Cox, John Ditsky, Tetsumaro Hayashi, Lawrence William Jones, and Robert Morsberger—I, too, hoped the level of critical discourse on Steinbeck could be upped several notches yet again. That was to be done by meeting his work on its own terms, not by approaching it with blinders, predisposed by a set of prior convictions and outmoded value assessments that kept Steinbeck in his place below the salt. In *Thematic Design in the Novels of John Steinbeck* (1969) the late Lester Marks, my longtime Ohio University colleague, spoke for many of us then when he highlighted the positive allure of Steinbeck's "versatility," "craftsmanship," and "wide range of techniques and subjects" (137). There was clearly more to be reckoned with in Steinbeck's writings than many earlier critics acknowledged, and we were hell-bent on proving that by disrupting the parochial hold of rote criticism.

In 1966, with bibliophile Preston Beyer, Tetsumaro Hayashi founded the John Steinbeck Bibliographical Society and became a moving, instigating force in promoting and nurturing Steinbeck studies here and abroad. In his stellar history *John Steinbeck and the Critics* (2000), John Ditsky devoted an entire chapter to Professor Hayashi and the Steinbeck Society (43–71) and claimed it wasn't possible to "overemphasize" their "significance." Hayashi, he concluded, was "a tsunami in Steinbeck Studies." The society changed its name in 1967 to The John Steinbeck Society of America. It resided for a few years at Kent State University, where Hayashi was finishing his PhD in English. That was where I first met him and helped launch *The Steinbeck Newsletter*, which, after five hand-typed and hand-cranked mimeographed issues in 1968, became the commercially printed and professionally vetted *Steinbeck Quarterly* (1969–1993). In 1969 the society and its journal eventually found regularly funded support at Ball State University in Muncie, Indiana, when Hayashi took a tenured position in its English Department, which he held until his retirement in 1993. (The historical archive of Hayashi's remarkable mover-and-shaker tenure regarding John Steinbeck is available in seventy-six boxes totaling thirty-four cubic feet in the Hayashi Steinbeck Collection housed in the Special Collections Department at Ball State University's Alexander M. Bracken Library.) Since 2015, after moving to San Jose State's Martha Heasley Cox Center for Steinbeck Studies, the group was renamed the International Society of Steinbeck Scholars, with Professor Luchen Li at its helm. The current president is a distinguished Slovenian scholar, Danica Čerče, of the University of Ljubljana, who works closely with members of worldwide groups, notably the venerable and energetic John Steinbeck Society of Japan whose heroic efforts deserve their own book.

———

While the Steinbeck Society was undertaking a practical identity of its own, organized academic conferences began to showcase critical, biographical, and theoretical dimensions. From 1969 to 1973, four such conferences devoted to Steinbeck were held at University of Connecticut, Oregon State University, and San Jose State College (later University). Taken together, that quartet of landmark gatherings helped initiate serious scholarly study on John Steinbeck, aided and abetted, of course, by the timely founding of *Steinbeck Quarterly* around the same turn-of-the-decade era. A new era had begun.

The first ever Steinbeck conference, organized at the University of Connecticut by the noted Americanist John Seelye and held April 29 to May 3, 1969, in Storrs to celebrate the thirtieth anniversary of *The Grapes of Wrath*, was highlighted by three eminences: Malcolm Cowley, Granville Hicks, and Carey McWilliams, all of whom were integral, respected, even legendary observers of the American cultural scene from the 1920s onward. McWilliams's great book, *Factories in the Field (1939)*, which came out a few months after *The Grapes of Wrath*, is a major sociological study of migrant labor in California and is a work often compared to *Grapes* for its impact and savvy insight. When McWilliams spoke on "California in the Thirties," we sat upright and listened attentively, because we were in the presence of an eyewitness to its history and a living contemporary of Steinbeck's.

The same was true for talks by Cowley and Hicks. Pascal Covici, Jr., the son of Steinbeck's longtime editor, Pat Covici, and rumored to be the silent editor of Steinbeck's *Journal of a Novel: The East of Eden Letters* (1969), spoke on "Work and the Texture of *The Grapes of Wrath*." Well-known professors Hyatt Waggoner (Brown University) and James Cox (Dartmouth College) spoke on various Americanist themes. Ted Hayashi gave an address on the formation of the Steinbeck Society, and Peter Lisca and Warren French—both of whom I met for the first time—concluded the formal series of conference lectures prior to a showing of John Ford's film version of *Grapes*. Amid the late 1960s campus tensions and unrest popping up everywhere across the country, that gathering showcased Steinbeck's relevance to the unsettled social sphere of the thirties and the divisive political scene of the sixties. In an embattled time, I came to understand dimensions of *The Grapes of Wrath* I might never have otherwise appreciated, though I had plenty more to learn about abusive power in the wake

of the Kent State shootings in May of the following year. It was a stark prophecy about the myriad ways Steinbeck's greatest novel spoke to successive decades
and to progressive generations of outraged readers. Anyway, I regret to say that
when Hayashi and I wrote up a brief account of the Storrs conference for the
summer 1969 issue of *Steinbeck Quarterly*, we hardly did the seismic event justice, though we did conclude with "our hope that a conference of this kind will
be held regularly."

In terms of widespread effect on what was coming to be known as "Steinbeck Studies," the second conference, "Steinbeck: The Man and His Work,"
organized by Richard Astro at Oregon State University in Corvallis on April
17–18, 1970, was the confab that really got the ball rolling because it generated a
valuable, well-received anthology of original conference proceedings, *Steinbeck:
The Man and His Work* (1971), ably edited by Astro and Hayashi. The conference
and the volume, now a collector's item (which featured contributions by maverick Rickettsian marine biologist Joel Hedgpeth and Steinbeck's longtime pal,
confidante, and attorney, Webster "Toby" Street) were enthusiastically received
for their boldness, originality, and quality. The collegiality and shared sense of
effort at that gathering had a profound influence on my decision to keep working on Steinbeck at a time when I thought I had little more to say on the subject. Peter Lisca was generous in his appreciation of my essay on *Sweet Thursday*
as a fabular parable of art and the creative process and urged me to deepen my
commitment to further study, which I found easy to do once I had met and
spoken with other attendees, especially Astro, Jackson Benson, John Ditsky, and
Robert Morsberger. Scholarly and personal bonds were formed that would
prove mutually enriching and sustaining for decades to come.

The third of the four early conferences was "Steinbeck Country: A Conference and Film Festival," organized by Martha Heasley Cox at San Jose State
College on February 26–28, 1971. It was the first to set up shop on the author's
native ground and the first to feature tours of its relevant, Steinbeck-related
sites, places I'd only read about but never visited. Gwyn Steinbeck, the novelist's
second wife, was a featured guest. The conference, with 800 attendees, was part
of Professor Cox's effort to get the fledgling Steinbeck Research Center (as it
was then called) off the ground as a legitimate scholarly enterprise. (The center
was formally opened in March 1974). Peter Lisca and I cochaired an afternoon
session devoted to comparative discussions of Steinbeck's lean and brittle elegy
to human frailty, *Of Mice and Men* (1937). I confess that although I was dutifully

conversant with both his novella and with Lewis Milestone's riveting film, up until that time I had not yet attended to either one with anything approaching a deep dive.

The conference was another learning experience for me. Thankfully, something happened that weekend to kick my interest into high gear and enlarge my view about *Of Mice and Men*; in my ramped-up enthusiasm and wider embrace I once again became one of Steinbeck's intended participatory recipients. "To read an objective novel is to see a little play in your head," Steinbeck wrote in an essay that appeared in the January 1938 issue of *Stage*. Seeing the "play in your head" required "visual imagination and an unconscious awareness" (*AASN* 155) for full investment and placed the task of making meaning on the observer's initiative. *Of Mice and Men*'s terse, sparse minimalism (simple, not simplistic, as some early critics claimed), erected on a hidden foundation of background, is its most bountiful, generous attribute. It is an example of the "at-onceness" of paradox: looking into the text we see both what is there and present, but also glimpse what is beyond and latent.

I have thought of that San Jose State conference many times in the intervening years because besides widening my critical tastes, it also booted up my growing fascination for visiting the physical places that inspire literary and artistic works, a habit that remains unabated even today, as I have willingly traveled thousands of miles (often out of my way) to view firsthand the sites made famous by writers, from Melville's Nantucket to Thoreau's Walden Pond to Aldo Leopold's Wisconsin shack to Willa Cather's Red Cloud to Jim Harrison's Upper Peninsula of Michigan to Nick Lyons's Montana spring creek near Ennis, and on and on. The portrayal in words is oftentimes only an approximation of the actual physical place, but I have never found the disparity to be disappointing. There is always something valuable, even transformative, to be learned from standing in the spirited spot where an individual artist's creative juices started flowing.

Which is to say, traveling northern California's so-called The Steinbeck Country, first named and graphically mapped in 1939 by Harry Thornton Moore, then subsequently replicated in various ways by numerous later artists, is an exciting prospect for any student, scholar, or aficionado, because geography/landscape/place made up Steinbeck's ground of being, the root stock of his "'hunger for there,'" as Susan Shillinglaw reports him saying in *A Journey into Steinbeck's California* (ix). Steinbeck told Moore that "maps don't work [as

absolute depictions of locales] because I mixed up the topography on purpose."
To which Moore noted, his map "is intended to be only a guide, in a general
sort of way, to readers . . . interested in tracing the relationship between his life
and his work. There is no exact parallel between some of these places as they
exist, and as they are imaginatively reflected in his stories" (104). And so was
born an imaginatively inflected representation of cultural real estate no less
significant than William Faulkner's famous mapping seven years later of Mississippi's fictional Yoknapatawpha County that appeared in Malcolm Cowley's
1946 edition of the *Portable Faulkner*. Where Faulkner's vision, turned inward,
pinpointed a small enclosed postage stamp of local soil as a way of wrestling
with a complex cultural and racial history, the Steinbeck cartography opened
outward and suggested a whole geographical region with permeable boundaries
and a fluid history in the making.

In today's parlance Steinbeck can be considered a cultural or human geog-
rapher and his books examples of literary cartography because you can't cruise
around Salinas or drive the Monterey Peninsula or walk the streets of Pacific
Grove without coming face-to-face with this or that iconic site where reality
and imagination, factuality and narrative, humans and story intersect and, in
some cases, collide. In her pioneering essay on the many physical waypoints and
factual determinants of Steinbeck's California geography, Martha Heasley Cox
wrote that "the sights, sounds, and scents of this land inform Steinbeck's fiction
and give it meaning as he depicts the relationship between man and the world
he inhabits—and creates or destroys" (41). This layered, overlapping geographical, cultural, and literary dimensionality, which Lowell Wyse aptly calls "ecospatiality," holds true for *Tortilla Flat* (1935), *The Long Valley* (1938), *Of Mice and
Men*, *Cannery Row* (1945), *Sweet Thursday*, and especially *East of Eden*, wherein
it is still possible to employ Kate's walk in that novel as a guide to sections of
historical downtown Salinas (Cox 45–47; Pearson 3–4).

I did not attend the fourth conference. "Steinbeck and the Sea" was organized by Richard Astro and Joel Hedgpeth and held at Oregon State University's Marine Science Center in Newport, Oregon, on May 4, 1974. The
gathering resulted in a booklet, *Steinbeck and the Sea* (1975), that once again, with
Jackson Benson's brilliant centerpiece essay, "John Steinbeck: The Novelist as
Scientist," took commentary in a new and promising conceptual direction away
from the tired caveats of earlier critics. Richard Astro's introduction announced
in no uncertain terms that the critical times were changing regarding

Figure 2. Map of The Steinbeck Country in Harry Thornton Moore's *The Novels of John Steinbeck: A First Critical Study* (Chicago: Normandie House, 1939), p. 4.

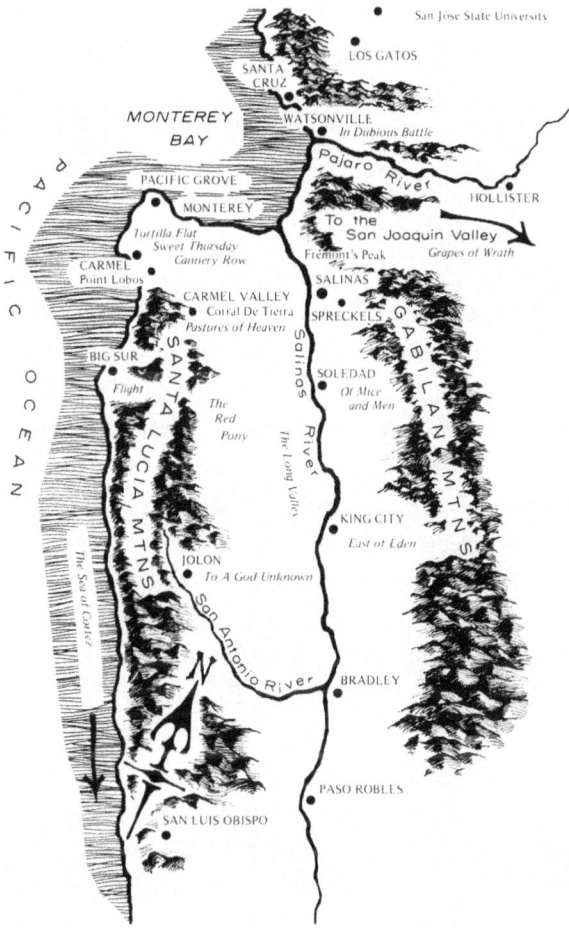

San Jose State University

LOS GATOS

SANTA CRUZ

MONTEREY BAY

WATSONVILLE
In Dubious Battle

Pajaro River

PACIFIC GROVE

MONTEREY

HOLLISTER

To the
San Joaquin Valley

Tortilla Flat
Sweet Thursday
Cannery Row

Fremont's Peak   *Grapes of Wrath*

CARMEL
Point Lobos

SALINAS

CARMEL VALLEY
Corral De Tierra
Pastures of Heaven

SPRECKELS

GABILAN MTNS

BIG SUR
Flight

SANTA LUCIA MTNS

SOLEDAD
Of Mice
and Men

Salinas River

The Long Valley

The
Red
Pony

PACIFIC OCEAN

KING CITY
East of Eden

The Sea of Cortez

JOLON
To A God Unknown

San Antonio River

BRADLEY

N

PASO ROBLES

SAN LUIS OBISPO

Jessie Ericson

Steinbeck Research Center

Steinbeck Country

Figure 3. Jessie Ericson's map of Steinbeck Country that illustrated the printed flyer announcing San Jose State College's Steinbeck Conference and Film Festival, February 26–28, 1971, organized by Martha Heasley Cox. James Clark, and Robert Woodward. It was reprinted in a special Steinbeck issue of *San Jose Studies* (November 1975) to accompany Professor Cox's essay, "In Search of John Steinbeck: His People and His Land." In this later version San Jose State College has been amended to San Jose State University in upper right-hand corner. Courtesy of Martha Heasley Cox Center for Steinbeck Studies, San Jose State University.

Steinbeck's reputation and forecast the opening of a new era that considered him "a major American writer who in his own tempo and with his own voice defined and gave meaning to the complicated nature of human experience" (6). It was the kind of bold intellectual assertion that many of us found timely, compelling, and necessary.

The effect of those four conferences can't be overstated. After them, a gathering of one kind or another on Steinbeck continued to be held nearly annually at one national or international venue after another, from New York to Honolulu, Moscow to Kyushu, Nantucket to Monterey, Salinas to San Jose (site of the most recent international gathering, in 2019, "Steinbeck and the Twenty-First Century"), all of which, aided and abetted by various publishing outlets— notably *Steinbeck Quarterly* and The Scarecrow Press in the early days and *Steinbeck Review* in our era—created a shared forum for knowledgeable scholars working on Steinbeck. Even Upland, Indiana, home to Taylor University, weighed in with a Bicentennial Steinbeck Seminar on May 1, 1976. Warren French, the president of the John Steinbeck Society of America, made a compelling case for Steinbeck's place in Modernism. Kenneth Swan, a conference organizer, presented a judicious, evenhanded overview of the previous four decades of contested critical debate about "The Merit of John Steinbeck" and concluded that a better day was dawning, when, "despite his flaws," Steinbeck would be considered "one of America's great writers of fiction" (80).

I should add, too, that along the way there were various other welcome infusions that moved the needle and upped our momentum. When Elaine Steinbeck and Steinbeck's main agent, Elizabeth Otis, attended a Steinbeck Society panel session at the December 1976 Modern Language Association convention in New York City, the whole venture got an unexpected nudge forward and a degree of legitimacy it might not otherwise have had. It was a pivotal moment for me as well. Someone in the audience asked a question following my presentation on *To a God Unknown*. I don't recall now what my answer was, but Elaine approached me afterward and said, "That's what John would have said." I was honored by her generosity.

In that same vein, it is perhaps anecdotal on my part, but it strikes me that the general level of acceptance toward Steinbeck as a sufficiently complex writer worthy of extensive study made enormous leaps forward thirty-plus years ago. Pulitzer Prize–winning novelist William Kennedy's laudatory review of both *Working Days* and the fiftieth anniversary edition *of The Grapes of Wrath* (with an introduction by Studs Terkel) that appeared on the front page of the *New York Times Book Review* on April 9, 1989, set the tone for numerous other positive assessments in major news and media outlets across the country in the following weeks and gave Steinbeck vivid popular national exposure (McElrath, Crisler, Shillinglaw 544–53), a familiarity certainly helped along by Viking Press's energetic publicity campaign (Li 329). Kennedy's praise for Steinbeck's "mighty, mighty" novel (44) and Hemingway biographer Kenneth Lynn's claim that *Working Days* makes "*The Grapes of Wrath* and its author more complex and interesting" (Li 330) were welcome words to Steinbeckians everywhere. (At Viking's launch party for *Working Days* I had a Warholian quarter hour of fame when I rubbed elbows with honored guests Douglas Fairbanks, Jr., Elia Kazan, Arthur Miller, and Pare Lorentz.)

Another move of the needle occurred in March 1990 when Chicago's Steppenwolf Company brought Frank Galati's 1988 dramatic version of *The Grapes of Wrath* (with Gary Sinise as Tom Joad) to Manhattan's Cort Theater. Besides winning a Tony Award for Best Play, it also garnered universal acclaim, ran for 188 performances, and was adapted for television by PBS's *American Playhouse*, introduced onscreen by Elaine Steinbeck. Yet another lift came in May 1992 when Elaine attended the "Steinbeck and the Environment" conference in Nantucket (she later wrote a foreword to the conference proceedings, published in 1997). Then in August she attended that year's Steinbeck Festival in Salinas. It isn't an earthshaking scholarly insight or critical plum, but it is a pleasing memory to recall that several of us at the latter conference celebrated her seventy-eighth birthday at a dinner for her at the Pine Inn in Carmel, the place where she and future husband John had their first date in 1949 ("I'm sure John's spirit was hovering over us," she wrote me a few weeks later.) By the mid-1990s, then, the editors of *John Steinbeck: The Critical Reviews*, and Jay Parini, author of *John Steinbeck: A Biography*, agreed that while no unqualified consensus was probably possible on many of Steinbeck's individual titles, overall, his was a literary career worth studying seriously. The "purity and wholeness of [his] vision will haunt, inspire, and move readers for years to come," Parini concluded (488).

By the close of the twentieth century, numerous polls conducted by a wide range of focus groups showed that while John Steinbeck's overall reputation was still being debated (DeMott, "Status" 22), one significant consensus had emerged. *The Grapes of Wrath* appeared prominently on every one of the

Figure 4. Author with Elaine Steinbeck at Viking Press fiftieth anniversary celebration of *The Grapes of Wrath* and publication launch of *Working Days: The Journals of The Grapes of Wrath*, April 13, 1989. "21" Club, New York. Guests included Douglas Fairbanks, Jr., Elia Kazan, Arthur Miller, and Pare Lorentz. Author collection.

half-dozen or so lists, from the Modern Library Editors' straight-laced compilation on the right to Larry McCaffery's experimental fiction list on the left. In attempting to establish a reasonably definitive corpus of twentieth-century fiction in English, Stanford University's Literary Lab crunched the numbers from those turn-of-the-century polls and lists (and added results from a more recent Postcolonial Studies Association finding) and concluded that *The Grapes of Wrath* is "the most central work in our corpus" and "the only book . . . that is both deeply respected as an important critical, and to some degree experimental, work and popular (and perhaps approachable) enough to be a number one bestseller" (Algee-Hewitt, McGurl 17–18). Polls of course are susceptible to personal and institutional warps and biases, but the collective findings about *The Grapes of Wrath* indicates that something more is at work than commercial brand recognition or special pleading by a cadre of rabid aficionados. The merits of the novel spoke for itself across a wide audience spectrum. Even at that, however, it was rare to see any Steinbeck book being taught at elite American research universities, proving once again, I suppose, that in some intellectual arenas, the tale of Steinbeck's critical reputation is a tale of two differing sets of values, often at odds with one another.

Yet another, even more vigorous surge took place twenty years ago in the wake of the 2002 National Steinbeck Centennial "Bard of the People" event, an ambitious yearlong, coordinated effort to encourage Americans to read and discuss his work and raise awareness of his place and value in the US literary canon. It was "the largest single author tribute in American history," according to Anne Keisman (473). Spearheaded by codirectors Harold Augenbraum at New York's Mercantile Library and Susan Shillinglaw at the Center for Steinbeck Studies at San Jose State, the project was partly funded by the National Endowment for the Humanities. Free instructional reader's guide pamphlets and short handbooks on starting a Steinbeck book club were widely disseminated. Many cities, towns, libraries, and cultural centers across the country got on board and gave Steinbeck a participatory airing not witnessed on behalf of many other American writers. At the University of Texas, the Harry Ransom Center mounted "John Steinbeck in His Time: A Centennial Exhibition" that ran for five months. In New York City, the mayor decreed February 27, 2002, as "John Steinbeck Day." That evening, at the Lincoln Center Barnes and Noble in Manhattan, Penguin Books and Library of America sponsored a reading by Steppenwolf actors Terry Kinney (Jim Casy) and Lois Smith (Ma Joad). Jack Benson and I joined the stars on a four-way panel discussion in front of a very receptive audience.

The following month, an international academic conference on "John Steinbeck's Americas" cooperatively organized by Hofstra University's Cultural Center, San Jose State's Center for Steinbeck Studies, and the John Steinbeck Society of Japan convened at Hofstra from March 21–23, 2002. Distinguished cultural critic Morris Dickstein's keynote address on Steinbeck in the 1930s gave the audience an early glimpse of his important book *Dancing in the Dark: A Cultural History of the Great Depression* (2009). Addresses by Warren French, John Seelye, Jackson Benson, John Ditsky, Kiyoshu Nakayama, Robert Morsberger, Mimi Gladstein, Danica Čerče, Luchen Li, Brian Railsback, Susan Shillinglaw, Louis Owens, Thom Steinbeck, and other veterans (myself included) and newcomers highlighted the most intense and varied Steinbeck conference yet assembled. Interest and momentum surged like that for several years, and it felt as though the tide was definitely shifting

and attitudes toward Steinbeck were beginning to alter toward greater understanding and acceptance. He wasn't every critical identity group's favorite
writer, but at last, a sustained revisionary effort seemed to be under way (Li
335–51). It was a point not lost on the late Stephen George, coeditor of a new
annual, *Steinbeck Yearbook*, who prophesied stridently in his closing address at
the Sixth International Steinbeck Congress in Kyoto, Japan, in 2005 that "the
end of Steinbeck apologetics is at hand" (197).

In addition, the choice of my Penguin Classics edition of *The Grapes of Wrath*
as one of the initial text offerings for the National Endowment for the Art's Big
Read program, launched in 2006, was another momentous push for Steinbeck.
(*Grapes* was once again among six text choices for the 2021–2022 season.) The
heralded seventy-fifth anniversary of *The Grapes of Wrath* in 2014 was yet another
boost and received considerable media attention, as did Susan Shillinglaw's
timely, indispensable *On Reading The Grapes of Wrath*, a sprightly, informative
contextual companion to the novel. A year later, art historian James Swenson's
scrupulously researched *Picturing Migrants: The Grapes of Wrath and New Deal
Documentary Photography*, one of the most impressive books in the entire Steinbeck critical canon, appeared to much-deserved acclaim. Such widespread cultural popularity and exposure, no doubt aided and abetted by a vigorous
American studies approach rather than a strictly formal lit-crit approach, found
its way into increased academic attention, so that ample scholarship of the past
two decades, for instance, much of it published in the Barbara Heavilin–edited
Steinbeck Review (2004–), besides impressing with its diverse and innovative
qualities, suggests a remarkable continuity of effort now and into the future.
During his lifetime, Steinbeck often disparaged literary critics and criticism,
but in a twist of irony, some of his most fair-minded, deep-diving, evenhanded
commentators and advocates hailed from the academic world.

Recently, in reading Professor Heavilin's comprehensive, annotated, online,
Oxford University Press Steinbeck bibliography (2022), I was reminded again
(pleasurably, I should add) of the range and quality of the critical record. For
example, given Steinbeck criticism's ninety-year history, the relatively recent
large-scale application of ecological criticism and environmental studies to
Steinbeck (linking him to pioneering contemporary naturalists Aldo Leopold,
Rachel Carson, and E. O. Wilson) and the increasingly detailed relevance of his
rich intellectual partnership with polymath marine scientist Edward F. Ricketts
(pioneered by Richard Astro's groundbreaking *John Steinbeck and Edward F.*

Ricketts: The Shaping of a Novelist in 1973) are fruitful instances of scholarship trending in contextual cross-disciplinary directions.

Seven fine cases in point are scholar and novelist Brian Railsback's *Parallel Expeditions: Charles Darwin and the Art of John Steinbeck* (1995), literary scholars Susan Beegel and Susan Shillinglaw and marine biologist Wesley Tiffney's indispensable anthology *Steinbeck and the Environment: Interdisciplinary Approaches* (1997), Rickettsian scholar extraordinaire Katherine A. Rodger's superbly introduced and expertly curated editions of *Renaissance Man of Cannery Row: The Life and Letters of Edward F. Ricketts* (2002) and *Breaking Through: Essays, Journals, and Travelogues of Edward F. Ricketts* (2006), environmental journalist Eric Enno Tamm's informative *Beyond the Outer Shores* (2004), anatomy professor/field biologist Michael Lannoo's elegant monograph *Leopold's Shack and Ricketts' Lab: The Emergence of Environmentalism* (2010), and fisheries scientist Kevin M. Bailey's *The Western Flyer: Steinbeck's Boat, the Sea of Cortez, and the Saga of Pacific Fisheries* (2015), all of which enact a continuity with past scholarship and herald a path for the future. In that vein, the new Richard Astro and Donald Kohrs study, *A Tidal Odyssey: Ed Ricketts and the Making of Between Pacific Tides* (2021), and Gavin Jones's critically nuanced understanding of some key Steinbeck texts in *Reclaiming John Steinbeck: Writing for the Future of Humanity* (2021), carry us beyond the tepid, often rote critical accounts of earlier years and provide ample proof that Steinbeck remains our contemporary who continues to matter to an engaged audience.

Overall, the collective effort, with some exceptions then and now, became a persistent push to see Steinbeck not solely as a workaday journalist or a writer of Depression-era naturalism and documentary realism, but rather as a literary novelist, an engaged tactician of letters, committed to a fully conscious artistic project. With varying degrees of success, he addressed the artful dimensions and bittersweet paradoxes of American life, language, and speech and challenged issues of scriptive representation by writing (and sometimes mixing) fiction, journalism, plays, filmscripts, and essays. His constant, varied experimental searches for suitable narrative form, as well as his deep concerns about the nation's myriad political, historical, cultural, environmental, and moral/ethical intentions, goals, and shortcomings drove his art. "At his core," James Swensen notes, "Steinbeck was a storyteller" (51). For Steinbeck, strict adherence to genre mattered less than narrativity.

John Steinbeck was a writer who prized the shaping power of imagination and the rigors of craft (however tenuous and imperfect that proved to be), yet he also realized how indebted he was to a welter of historical particulars, unconscious desires, contextual determinants, and social relations. "A novelist is a kind of fly-paper to which everything adheres," he admitted in 1958. "His job then is to try to reassemble life into some kind of order" (*SLL* 591–92). It wasn't a case of either/or but rather both/and; the best of the emerging new scholarship reflected that synchronous duality, that fluid tension and debate between the tide pool and the stars, where the laws of thought and the laws of things coincide.

———

It has always been intriguing to me that some lengthy ventures begin with the simplest instigations, the most basic urges of curiosity. In addition to Steinbeck being routinely undervalued by mainstream critics, I was also spurred on by thousands of pages of his unpublished writing that had rarely if ever seen the light of day, sequestered in various public and private repositories. The major collections of Steinbeck's first editions, memorabilia, correspondence, journals, manuscripts, typescripts, and galley proofs of his published and unpublished fiction, essays, and plays, as well as other related documents, are housed at Ball State University, Princeton University, Stanford University, the Harry Ransom Center at the University of Texas at Austin, Columbia University, University of California at Berkeley, Harvard University, University of Virginia, San Jose State University, New York City's Morgan Library and Museum, the John Steinbeck Library in Steinbeck's hometown of Salinas, and later its National Steinbeck Center (the most elaborate research center/museum dedicated to any single American author). Over a period of many years, starting in the mid-to-late 1970s, with financial support from research awards at Ohio University, and with generous letters of permission from the Steinbeck Estate, I spent considerable time at every one of those collections.

That was like finding a trout stream that had rarely been fished. The effect was heady and narcotic. The allure of the Steinbeck Archive was immediate, constant, and gratifying, and I admit to becoming something of an archive junkie, utterly happy to dive into the dusty enclaves and byroads of literary history. Spending time in so many reclusive collections, frequently in the undisturbed quiet of this or that archival reading room, I often experienced deeply felt "connections between what was and what is," as poet and Emily Dickinson archivist Susan Howe asserts in *Spontaneous Particulars* (43). What I found in those quiet enclaves—evidence of the shadow Steinbeck, the hidden Steinbeck, the unknown (and sometimes unsuspected) presence behind the public and commercial brand of "Steinbeck, Inc."—found its way into my research and writing activity. In tracing threads of literary genesis and developing what I realize now is a kind of textual biography of creativity, the collective Steinbeck Archive did not explain everything nor provide all answers (as Archive skeptics, like Michel Foucault, have rightly claimed all along), but, illusions of intimacy and completeness aside, its plenitude and diversity opened many paths of inquiry I might otherwise have missed or neglected, and helped round out, in my mind anyway, a fuller view of Steinbeck's life and career than was available elsewhere.

Educating myself to decipher Steinbeck's notoriously tiny, eye-straining handwriting lent a degree of immediacy to and appreciation for the creative act, the moment when, as French poet Rene Char once said, the bread came fresh from the oven. Steinbeck could wedge 500 words on a single side of a normal-sized postcard, so learning to read Steinbeck's compressed handwriting required a slow, deliberate puzzling over nearly every figure until a more or less complete picture emerged. (Even at that, there were always individual words impossible to decipher). If reading his original documents and unedited first drafts fostered patience and deliberation, it also created a sense of awe and respect. Plus, aura and halo effect aside, I loved the spirited, jazzed feeling of working with one-of-a-kind documents that few if any other readers had encountered. Selfishly, I felt as though there was no one else looking over my shoulder, and I had the field to myself. Luck was involved, too, as my situation was a result of being in the right places at the right times.

I came into a field made up of thousands and thousands of pages of unpublished material that seemed at times almost trackless and endless in their reach and expanse, with very few signposts and way stations. In those laborious pre-internet days it was a matter of hands-on prowling, and I often felt like I was a character in Richard Altick's classic, *The Scholar Adventurers* (1950). On the hunt, I was especially enamored of Steinbeck's voluminous correspondence, much of it either unpublished or published only in edited form, so there was always something new to glean from reading his letters. Then there were various journal ledger books he kept while writing this or that novel and, of course, intriguing unpublished fiction and drama.

My first extended research junket was to the Humanities Research Center (HRC), as it was then called, at University of Texas, where I spent a week in December 1976 buried to my eyeballs in the vast Pascal Covici collection (Covici died in 1964). It was a memorable experience and can stand in as representative of all my road trips to research collections. The HRC collection held many choice items that were foundational in my evolving study of Steinbeck's creativity. The *East of Eden* materials (novel and journal manuscripts, typescripts, galleys, etc.) generated a good deal of later scholarship on that novel, which has always been one of my leading favorites among Steinbeck's works (*ST* 55–106, 206–32, 265–317). Steinbeck's letters and documents were key, too, including an archival gem—his ghostwritten "Introduction by Pascal Covici" (intended but never used for the first Viking Press *Portable Steinbeck*), which has figured prominently in a number of my discussions on participation, including in the following chapter of *Steinbeck's Imaginarium*.

Diving into HRC's bounteous collection was always a delightful surprise, characterized by a certain unmapped random quality. I never knew what I would find from day to day. Often my snooping led me well off the beaten path and into unknown thickets. It was there I found the typescript of Steinbeck's *Grapes of Wrath* journal. Another such pleasurable discovery—worth a little riff here—was *Murder at Full Moon*, a complete 230-page apprentice murder mystery, a bit over 60,000 words in length, with a werewolf twist and thematically reliant on Carl Jung's *The Psychology of Dementia Praecox*. It was written by Steinbeck in nine days in 1930, under the pen name of "Peter Pym" (a melding of Dirk Peters and Arthur Gordon Pym in Edgar Allan Poe's 1838 novel *The Narrative of Arthur Gordon Pym*). It is a shameless tongue-in-cheek, burlesque parody of pulp detective fiction of the kind written by the popular Frank L. Packard, J. S. Fletcher, Edgar Wallace, and especially S. S. Van Dine, whose "Twenty Rules for Writing Detective Stories" (1929) may have provided something of a spur to the eager Steinbeck. Van Dine is mentioned several times in the text. Maximillian Sergius Hoogle, a main character, tells Egg Waters, the narrator, that he gets "a little bored . . . what with S. S. Van Dine getting so terrible that I can usually figure out the murder from the title page" (35). Steinbeck, desperate to have a commercial success at that early juncture of his career, was witheringly harsh in his self-evaluation of the manuscript; it made him "sick," he told Ted Miller, as it was full of "all the cheap rackets I know of" (*SLL* 32), but he hoped it would sell anyway, his "artistic integrity" overridden by his commercial desire. "The trouble with it," he later admitted to Robert van Gelder in 1947, "was that I satirized detective stories and my detective. I tried to use the formula and kid it at the same time. No one wanted it" (*CJS* 47).

The book was rejected by publishers, no doubt for what they thought were valid reasons, but that's not to say the creaky sleuthing narrative didn't have interesting facets that show Steinbeck in his apprentice phase utilizing first-person point of view, impactful geographical setting, wry humor and social satire, irony, and especially self-reflexive literary playfulness—all elements that would resurface to one degree or another in his later fiction but that were not as common in his earlier, more rigorously objective work. More than anything else, reading the manuscript reinforced my fledgling conjectures about how deeply Steinbeck read to write and gave me confidence that tracking down and registering his bookish proclivities and obsessions was a useful intellectual labor. Compiling the 900-plus titles that make up the bulk of *Steinbeck's Reading*—a project that took thirteen years of off-again, on-again work—was a task that depended for entries and annotations on research in just such unpublished sources as the *Murder at Full Moon* manuscript at HRC, and of course plenty of other collections as well.

Speaking of other archival collections, there are a number of unpublished manuscripts in the various repositories. The superb Annie Laurie Williams collection at Columbia University's Butler Library (Williams was his drama and film agent at McIntosh and Otis) includes *The Wizard of Maine* and *The Last Joan*, two plays from the 1940s, and a terse unpublished 1950s-era short story called "Burial at Sea," a humorous, ribald tale about Fartin' Jenny (a brothel owner who appears in *East of Eden*) and her husband Jerry Donovan. And of course personal journals and compositional ledgers from the 1940s and 1950s housed at the Morgan Library and Museum (noted in the third chapter of *Steinbeck's Imaginarium*). Imagining unpublished documents in print puts a gleam in the eye of all of us who take literature seriously, and even if the works don't hold up as accomplished, full-fashioned achievements, they will inevitably have any number of technical, stylistic, biographical, or thematic elements that appeal to literary biographers, scholars, and general readers. Thomas Barden's comment in the preface to his intelligently curated collection *Steinbeck in Vietnam: Dispatches From the War* (2012) is telling: it's important, he writes, that Steinbeck's "entire body of written work be available in print" (viii). We want transparency and some kind of real or digital access to these rare documents, but deciding—particularly in the case of unfinished manuscripts—whether they enhance a writer's reputation or detract from it is often the conservatorial province of the administrators or agents of the author's estate, whose lives are sometimes far from the precincts of progressive academia. In the case of turning Steinbeck's raw, sometimes cryptic daily journal he kept while writing *The Grapes of Wrath* into a companion text, *Working Days*, I was able to persuade McIntosh and Otis that it would be a worthwhile addition to Steinbeck's canon if it were historically contextualized and annotated for scholars and general readers alike. As literary tastes change from era to era and what one reader considers juvenile or shameless another reader might consider appropriate and valuable, the future of other unpublished archival items might hinge on similarly persuasive and reasoned curatorial approaches.

In all instances, thanks to Elizabeth Otis and Elaine Steinbeck, I was fortunate to receive a letter from them (April 16, 1977) granting blanket permission "to make Xerox copies of any John Steinbeck unpublished manuscripts" I needed for my pursuits, which reduced the amount of anxiety I might otherwise have felt over tight travel budgets and copyright restrictions. Over the years I assembled a home file cabinet stuffed with copies of primary materials that fueled my pursuit and made checking sources less painless and onerous than usual. In short, I had a field day exploring archival holdings and writing narratives that linked process and product. And at least once I also added to the archival store. When I directed San Jose State's Steinbeck Research Center in 1984 and 1985, I purchased $85,000 worth of primary items for its collection, including manuscripts and correspondence. Those acquisitions, supported generously by Maureen Pastine, SJSU's director of Libraries, led eventually to a limited-edition chapbook, *Your Only Weapon Is Your Work: A Letter by John Steinbeck to Dennis Murphy* (1985). Intended to serve as a fund-raising publication to celebrate the eleventh anniversary of the Steinbeck Center, *Your Only Weapon* was the first separate Steinbeck letter publication in more than a decade and caused a stir among scholars, bibliographers, collectors—and Elaine Steinbeck, too, who was deeply appreciative ("I shall treasure it," she wrote me on March 14, 1985). Best of all, it was gratifying to give something back, so to speak.

————

I am not embarrassed to admit that most of us only have half a dozen or so truly

Figure 5. Author (left) with Jack Douglass and Bernadine Beutler of Wahlquist Library's Special Collections Department in original Steinbeck Research Center (1985), examining newly purchased archive of Steinbeck correspondence. Over their shoulders an oil portrait of Gwyn Steinbeck by Vittorio Borrielo and a drawing of Steinbeck by Barnaby Conrad. Courtesy of Martha Heasley Cox Center for Steinbeck Studies, San Jose State University.

good ideas in our whole lives. My run of good critical ideas was probably over a long time ago, but one of them was my belief that Steinbeck was more deeply immersed in the conjoined reading and writing life than most of his earlier critics were willing to admit. It turned out to be a propulsive belief that I attempted to line out in an early essay called "The Interior Distances of John Steinbeck," published in *Steinbeck Quarterly* in 1979. Influenced by Gaston Bachelard's *The Poetics of Space* (1964), I mused in an amateurish phenomenological kind of way about Steinbeck's recurring use of an analogous group of interior elements—including symbolic landscapes, as well as images of enclosures, dreams, and creativity—that taken together comprise a kind of imaginative architecture or textual habitation in his true home, by which I meant his fiction and nonfiction. Tracing out implications of Steinbeck's imaginarium, broadly considered, and following the trail of the gilded figure in his carpet, so to speak, became an abiding theme and ongoing process that was furthered in that essay and eventually ran through just about everything else that followed.

This was especially true of *Steinbeck's Typewriter: Essays on His Art*, kick-started one day in early 1984 when Thom Steinbeck gave me his father's baby Hermes portable typewriter as a token of friendship. I learned later that the elder Steinbeck bought it in Geneva, Switzerland, in June 1952 so he could type his own dispatches to *Collier's*, and that he later carried it on his GMC pickup truck Rocinante as he made his way across the United States with Charley. (Eventually Steinbeck replaced it for regular use with a portable Olivetti, which he felt had a better-looking typeface.) But as I was visiting Thom that day in Carmel Highlands on behalf of San Jose State's Steinbeck Research Center (as it was then called), where I was serving as acting director, I declined his generous offer for myself and instead gladly accepted his gift for the center. (The little writing engine that could is still displayed there and has recently found its way into blogs, news reports, and even a movie about famous typewriters.) When I saw that Steinbeck scratched "The Beast Within" on the rear of his portable's cover, it wasn't long before that otherwise utilitarian mechanical contrivance took on a life of its own and became for me a trope of his writerly life, with all its attendant drama, blessings, and curses. The chapters in *Steinbeck's Typewriter* constellated themselves around that magnetic focus and drew into relief a preoccupation in his life (and in mine) that demanded attention.

As befits Steinbeck's ideas of participation, he was utterly correct when he claimed on numerous occasions that criticism is subjective and personal, not objective and universal. I'm in those pieces and I don't pretend not to be. Which is to say, accurately or not, I have come to think of *Steinbeck's Reading*, my edition of Steinbeck's *Working Days: The Journals of The Grapes of Wrath, 1938–1941*, and *Steinbeck's Typewriter* as a loosely federated trilogy. They are all linked in my mind by their concern with various aspects of writerly imagination and authorial creativity (however fraught and controversial that may be), and all resulted from a big "slug of work" (to use Steinbeck's phrase) that took up much of my time and energy from the 1970s through the first decade of this century.

In my newcomer's exuberance, I was especially fascinated by Steinbeck's lesser-known works that I felt had been unfairly slighted or neglected. In doing

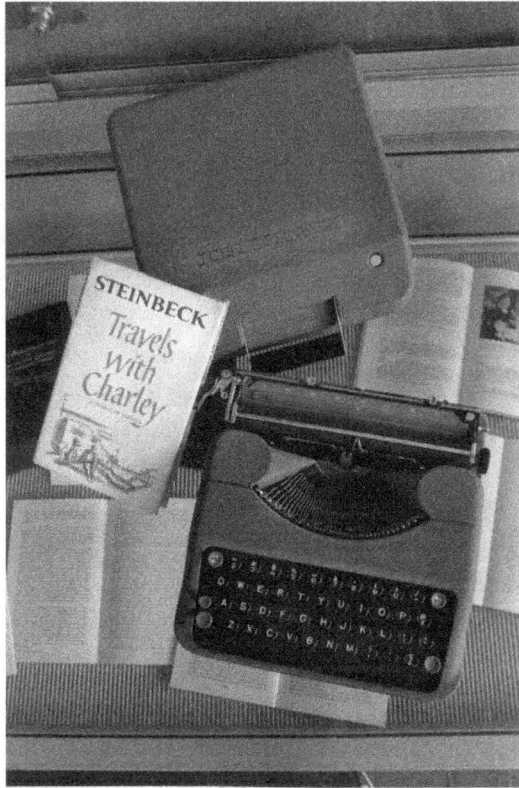

Figure 6. John Steinbeck's Hermes portable typewriter. Gift of Thomas Steinbeck to San Jose State University's Steinbeck Center, 1984. A cropped version of this photo appeared on the cover of *Steinbeck's Typewriter: Essays on His Art* (1996). Courtesy of Martha Heasley Cox Center for Steinbeck Studies, San Jose State University.

so, those early critical studies became a kind of signature for my way of approaching all aspects of Steinbeck's career. The long stretch of reclamation started with a playful essay called "Steinbeck and the Creative Process: First Manifesto to End the Bringdown Against *Sweet Thursday*," delivered at the aforementioned 1970 Oregon State conference (later published in *Steinbeck: The Man and His Work* in 1971) and was followed in 1973 with "Toward a Redefinition of *To a God Unknown*," published in the John Ditsky–edited *University of Windsor Review*. There were others along the way, including a one-off piece on Steinbeck's previously unknown love poems to Gwyn, his future second wife, "'The Girl of the Air': A Speculative Essay on Steinbeck's Love Poems" (collected in *Steinbeck's Typewriter*). The exploratory stretch culminated decades later with "Prospects for the Study of John Steinbeck," a detailed summary review of the history of Steinbeck criticism, including numerous suggestions for future scholarship, I wrote with Brian Railsback's invaluable authorial help for *Resources for American Literary Study* in 2009.

At forty-plus pages in length, that latter essay was the last of my sustained, concentrated efforts at understanding and situating Steinbeck in the largest way possible by treating a number of key substantive areas of practice and theory in the scholarly record of his work. "Prospects" drew inspiration from Warren French's critical recap of Steinbeck criticism for an earlier generation in *Sixteen Modern American Authors* (1973) and had its foundation in much of my earlier research and writing, especially the introductions and explanatory notes to three Twentieth-Century Penguin Classic editions—*To a God Unknown* (1995), *The Grapes of Wrath* (1994; 2006), and *Sweet Thursday* (2008)—and the 429 annotations that accompany eighteen of his books included in the uniform Library of America's four-volume John Steinbeck publishing project (1994–2007). The goal of those explanatory notes was to create a "wall of background" (Steinbeck's phrase in his 1936 *Long Valley* ledger) to inspire readers to look behind the pages of his texts and develop a broader understanding of his voracious interest in and dialogue with various fields of historical, cultural, scientific, and literary discourse. That, I hoped, might be an answer to decades of critics who considered Steinbeck a member of the dumb ox school of writing, and instead show how deeply he was a citizen of and participant in a capacious intellectual world. The annotations were intended to provide readers with a thick description of his cultural and ideational geography and put him on a similar referential footing with other notable Modernist writers, who had been exhaustively researched, analyzed, annotated, and footnoted.

More than that, the addition of Steinbeck to the Library of America's celebrated nonprofit publishing venture of uniform authoritative omnibus editions, launched in 1982, was a perfect fit from every point of view, fully in concert with the cultural vision of American pragmatist critic and Library of America President Richard Poirier (who invited me to edit the Steinbeck volumes) and other members of the original founder's board. By early 2021 the Steinbeck volumes (numbers 72, 86, 132, and 170 in the series) had sold close to a quarter of a million copies and joined more than 300 other individual volumes that help secure the legacy of an open and fluid American literary canon and anchor our diverse cultural and intellectual heritage. It is the most ambitious, meticulous, and important noncommercial publishing venture in American literary history, thanks to many prescient, committed, expert people and organizations who have carried out its work for the past four decades.

The corrected text of *The Grapes of Wrath* in Library of America Volume 86 is of particular value. In-house editor Gila Bercovitch performed an exhaustive combinatory collation by examining the original manuscript, Carol Steinbeck's typescript, and the Viking Press galley sheets. The edition corrects typing errors, including accidental omissions of sentences, misreadings, and mistypings. It also restores censored words (notably several instances of "fuck," "fuckin,'" "fucked," etc.). The corrected final text of 1996 is also the version Viking/Penguin used for the second edition of *The Grapes of Wrath: Text and Criticism*, edited by Peter Lisca and Kevin Hearle (1997). Taken together, the four Library of America volumes are the closest thing to a complete English-language Steinbeck we are likely to get.

So, like the proverbial fly on the wagon axle, I want to shout, "see what a dust I raise," but the truth is I was only along for the ride and had plenty of help along the way. As it turned out, Steinbeck probably did not need me—or any of us, for that matter—as a commentator; but, vanity of vanities, that did not stop me from adding my two cents' worth whenever I was asked to do so. My efforts were probably akin to shoveling sand against an incoming tide, but in retrospect the exercise itself has been enough of a reward, because I've enjoyed what I've done and found it endlessly interesting and sustaining, like a long, spirited conversation with adept and sympathetic friends. If I facilitated some part of the general ongoing critical dialogue about Steinbeck, so much the better. I am happy to have been a useful part of the scholarly phalanx.

———

In the spring of 2007, I was a talking head on two documentaries. One appearance was for a segment discussing *The Grapes of Wrath* and Theodore Dresier's *Sister Carrie* for a PBS *American Masters* television series called *Novel Reflections on the American Dream*. The other appearance—the more exotic of the two—was in a Russian documentary film about John Steinbeck coproduced by Olga Zhgenti and George Santulli. Zhgenti and her crew had come to the United States from Tbilisi, Georgia, on the occasion of the sixtieth anniversary of Steinbeck's *A Russian Journal* (1948). The two-hour-long film, *John Steinbeck and a Russian Journal After 60 Years*, was being underwritten by a competitive grant from the United States Department of State's Office of Broadcast Support, directed by Santulli.

The setting that day was Steinbeck's former Tower East Manhattan apartment at 190 East 72nd Street (sold by Steinbeck's heirs in 2018). After my interview session was over and the camera stopped rolling, my hosts and I wandered around the apartment, marveling at the spectacular omnidirectional city views from the thirty-fourth floor and *oohing* and *aahing* at this and that intriguing Steinbeckian object and artifact before making our way into the small room that served as Steinbeck's study. I admit to a compulsive fascination about writers' studies, studios, and libraries—the places they sit down to their daily craft chores and where they perform the imaginative work that keeps people like me busy for decades. It is probably dumb luck, but I always seem to come away from such visitations with new insight and renewed enthusiasm for the bookish life.

Joyous Garde, Steinbeck's hexagonal writing studio at his Sag Harbor house, is a good deal more famous, but this little apartment nook held its own surprising charms and gifts as well. There was Steinbeck's Presidential Medal of Freedom, awarded in 1964 by Lyndon Johnson. The framed citation read: "A writer of world-wide influence, he has helped America to understand itself by finding universal themes in the experiences of men and women everywhere." One corner of the room was occupied by a floor-to-ceiling bookcase whose shelves were filled with volumes and put me in mind of Steinbeck's pronouncement that there are never enough books, and his confession to his old pal Carlton Sheffield that "home" is "that place where the books are kept" (*SLL* 798). Time was short and there were a bunch of us shoehorned into that cramped space, so I only had time to take down one volume: Carl Sandburg's novel *Remembrance Rock* (1948). Inside, Sandburg had written, "For John Steinbeck, in Fellowship." (Had I seen it years earlier it would have become entry #706a and joined the other ten Sandburg entries in *Steinbeck's Reading*, a list that includes all six volumes of Sandburg's biography of Lincoln.)

On the same wall, hung at eye level, there was a framed 10" × 8" color lithograph portrait of Abraham Lincoln after one taken in 1863 by Alexander Gardner. According to Elaine Steinbeck's March 1994 "Household Inventory" that accompanied the lithograph, "John said he had never written in a room where this didn't hang" (Lorio Item 211). The portrait was sold in February 2020 as part of the Curated Estates auction sale. Steinbeck writing under the signifying visage of Lincoln is an appealing trope; whether it was an urban myth seemed

Figure 7. Steinbeck's talismanic lithograph portrait on
glass of Abraham Lincoln
after one taken in November
1863 by Alexander Gardner.
Courtesy of Curated Estates
Auction, 2020.

beside the point because the parts fit together so well. Lincoln's grave face as iconic metaphor for Steinbeck's democratic enthusiasm resonates powerfully and underscores his vibrant advocacy of heartfelt, right-minded humanism; that Steinbeckian spirit of engagement that vivifies so much of his writing. In that vein, Steinbeck's fiction, Robert McParland states in *Citizen Steinbeck*, opens "our awareness to the hopes and needs of our common humanity" (196).

———

My Lincolnian fantasy leads me to a serious and needful digression, whose indulgence I hope will be accommodated, and which I also hope will prove useful in this otherwise random, higgledy-piggledy retrospect. I can go only so far in my account without needing to speak urgently of *The Grapes of Wrath*, whose big-heartedness and soulfulness makes it a worthwhile candidate for that mythical beast, the Great American Novel (Buell 415–21). In this section, I don my professorial lecturing hat to comment on what I consider to be a central book in Steinbeck's career and in my life as a reader. This I-to-We moment is part of the personal journey recorded in this chapter of *Steinbeck's Imaginarium*, and it begins a reflective turn toward focusing on what's at stake in his writing and what its message is for all of us on the planet. Think of this divagation as a transition toward the larger implications of not simply studying Steinbeck but heeding his words in true participatory fashion.

So whether *The Grapes of Wrath* is read as straight historical fiction or artful metaphoric vehicle, like many of our other cultural mainstays it is a work whose meaning and import travels well over time and speaks to us now in ways that can still surprise us. Back in the mid-sixties, when I first encountered *Grapes* as a college student, I thought of it as a historical novel, a period piece that opened a window onto the difficulties of Depression-era America (partially familiar to me because of my family's history of economic struggle in that era) and that was all. As my understanding of and appreciation for Steinbeck grew, increased, deepened, exfoliated over the decades, especially heightened by the privilege of bringing to print *Working Days*, his *Grapes of Wrath* compositional journal, I have come to see the novel not just as a monumental literary achievement, but as a prophetic touchstone.

In our amply documented and undeniable age of extreme climate change, prolonged drought, devastating bouts of heat, unprecedented hurricane and tornado activity, extensive cataclysmic forest fires, invasive species, decline of species, and so on (the kinds of disastrous occurrences that keep a lifelong fly-fisherman like myself up at night) focusing on the broad ecological implications of *The Grapes of Wrath* seems to me to be a way of closing some interpretive gaps, so that even "woke" readers skeptical of the novel's implicit whiteness, who question the lack of racial and ethnic inclusiveness of the "We" in chapter fourteen, might find a useful path to negotiate the move from solitary individuality to collective, biomorphic, earth-centered community. A radical, prophetic statement penned around 1932 to his pal Carlton Sheffield in Steinbeck's *To a God Unknown* ledger bears directly on discussions of his holistic environmentalism: "Each figure is a population, and the stones, the trees, the muscled mountains are the world—but not the world apart from man—the world and man—the one indescribable unit man plus his environment. Why they should ever have been misunderstood as being separate I do not know" (123).

The novel can be viewed as a sustained jeremiad about a natural world "spoiled" by combined effects of unruly weather, human greed, bad husbandry practices, rapacious acquisitiveness, and environmental ignorance/arrogance. In chapter twenty-five Steinbeck says, "The decay spreads over the State, and the sweet smell is a great sorrow on the land. Men who can graft the trees and make the seed fertile and big can find no way to let the hungry people eat their produce. Men who have created new fruits in the world cannot create a system whereby their fruits may be eaten. And the failure hangs over the State like a great sorrow" (580).

This is Steinbeck "hanging his ass out there" for us, in Bruce Springsteen's colorful phrase. At least one powerful response to widespread institutionalized agricultural failure, land-managerial mistakes, or the alienating vengeance of nature gone awry (whether it is drought or flood) is abject grief and bereavement, so that *The Grapes of Wrath* can be considered a mourning book, a lament for a lost condition of naturalness. "There is a crime here that goes beyond denunciation. There is a sorrow here that weeping cannot symbolize. There is a failure here that topples all our success," Steinbeck wails (581). Lloyd Willis's assessment in *Environmental Evasion* rings true: Steinbeck, he writes, "recognized multiple forms of environmental abuse, understood its human and ecological ramifications, and recognized the problem as a cultural predilection toward irresponsible and wasteful overconsumption" (100). A decade before Willis, Eric Tamm called Steinbeck's "ecological message" among his "greatest contributions to American literature" (297).

It isn't for nothing, then, that in chapter eight Jim Casy tells of going alone into the wilderness to learn his signal lesson and earn his epiphany. For eight decades we have been in the habit of reading this action repeatedly with a markedly Christian inflection, despite Casy's insistence "I ain't sayin' I'm like Jesus" and his uncertainty about "what I mean by holy." But textual resonances travel over time, and it seems just as plausible, given our present-day growing awareness of environmentalism, climate change, and viability and sustainability of green projects, that we can imagine Casy did actually travel afield into some tract of secular wild or rural land, some liminal "wilderness" area where, through a participation "deeper down than thinking" in its myriad forms and energies (symbolized here by natural imagery of sun and stars), he came away convinced that all life is holy, all part of one big soul, sacred and interrelated: "Nighttime I'd lay on my back an' look up at the stars; morning I'd set an' watch the sun come up; midday I'd look out from a hill at the rollin' dry country; evenin' I'd foller the sun down. Sometimes I'd pray like I always done. On'y I couldn' figure what I was prayin' to or for. There was the hills, an' there was me, an' we wasn't separate no more. We was one thing. An' that one thing was holy" (295–96).

Casy's walkabout, his "errand into the wilderness," is a staple gesture of the mythic metanarrative of "American thought and American expansion," so called by Louis Owens in *The Grapes of Wrath: Trouble in the Promised Land* (51). But in Casy's lighting out for the territories, Steinbeck reverses the traditional Puritan model: instead of reinforcing separation, arrogance, dominion, genocide, and rigid authoritarianism, his journey and his felt response performs the opposite by accepting conditions as they are without artificial mediation. What might have seemed corny and mystical to readers in the 1930s now sounds prophetic as a way forward. In these deep ecological valences, the natural and the human are one elemental pairing. Interrelatedness, connection, and compassion, not discrete separation, domination, or exploitation, are the lessons to be learned and passed on. *The Grapes of Wrath* is not a closed vessel of historical periodicity, as I once thought, but a relational field, a web of interconnectedness between nature and culture, physical earth and human inhabitants. Symbolized by the double vision stereopticon in chapter ten, it isn't either ecology *or* textual structure that marks this novel's moment, but *both* aspects working together to reinscribe and to relocate the environmental imperative as an aesthetic structure, an "ecological rhetoric," in Peter Valenti's apt phrase (93).

In other words, the radical stress of *Grapes* is that to save the one w(holy) thing requires reverence and nothing less than the kind of gesture one encounters in Joseph Wayne's death in *To a God Unknown*, Casy's sacrifice, Rose of Sharon's gift of breast milk to a starving man that ends *Grapes of Wrath*, *Sea of Cortez*'s narrator extolling "all things are one thing," Kino's relinquishment of the pearl of the world in *The Pearl*, and Adam Trask's acceptance of *timshel* in *East of Eden*—that is, a gesture that dramatizes a way of being that requires humility and full commitment in the service of a realm larger than the self. (It is enticing to think that Steinbeck's true contemporaries and kin are Aldo Leopold, Rachel Carson, Loren Eisley, Edward Abbey, Peter Matthiessen, Barry Lopez, and Terry Tempest Williams rather than Ernest Hemingway, William Faulkner, F. Scott Fitzgerald, John O'Hara, and Norman Mailer.)

In that equation, Casy becomes an eco-hero, let's say, whose message of holism, fairness, equality, inclusiveness, tolerance, sustainability, and generosity planted in Tom Joad (and dispersed from Tom Joad to us) will be around everywhere if we only care to hear it, if we only continue to listen to it and act accordingly for the greater good. *The Grapes of Wrath* cannot be constrained by era, geography, or history. In its dirty, gritty realism, polemical register, and evangelical tone, it is at once a tragedy, a challenge, a prophecy, and a cautionary tale, as much for the Dust Bowl age as for our current time frame in the Anthropocene. For the interconnected biosphere of humans and animals, environmental justice, it turns out, just might become social justice if given a chance to take root and flourish.

Steinbeck understood that his signature novel was not a blueprint for nor a replacement of direct social action. Instead, in its metaphoric ramifications, it triggered powerful reformative sympathy, a phalanx-like keying "equation" based on broad audience appeal, imaginative participation, and a "commitment to others" (Marsh 138) because, as Steinbeck reminds us, "feelings do matter" (Szalay 168). Steinbeck's stated desire to make his characters the "over essence of people" (*WD* 39) suggests that he wished to make them symbolic representatives of *all* repressed, dispossessed peoples. "A story is a parable," he told a British interviewer in 1962, that puts "in terms of human action the morals—the immorals—that society needs at the time" (*CJS* 83). For Steinbeck, who over his lifetime praised John Dewey and Erich Fromm, morality was often contextual and never dissociated from lived experience. Steinbeck included the entire range of human emotion in his representation: sentimentality was part of the holistic web of common experience, part of the larger ecology of public and private affect, and so could not be eliminated from view. To do so would be to falsify the total unified field effect by which fellow feeling could be or might be achieved. In addition to whatever else can be learned from reading Steinbeck, he teaches empathy, inclusion, and embrace. In Zoe Trodd's words, he was working in a tradition "that demands active empathy rather than passive sympathy" (57). Steinbeck's unabashed compassion and avowed desire to communicate directly with people (which includes loving the earth and decrying its exploitation and diminishment) continues to be appealing, worthwhile, and necessary. After all, his "whole work drive" was "aimed at making people understand each other" (*WD* xl).

———

Lately, however, even when approached metaphorically and presented with the stark immediacy and existential dilemmas of *The Grapes of Wrath*, the qualities of sympathy, empathy, inclusion, sustainability, compassion, and understanding Steinbeck wishes us to enact are sadly in short supply. America's political and cultural landscape seems more polarized and divisive than I have ever witnessed before, worse I think than it was in the late 1960s. when the country seemed torn asunder by clashing politics and warring ideologies. That was a walk in the park compared to our current deadlocked partisan landscape. Ours is a contested home in a problematic borderland, a "monster" country both "complicated" and "paradoxical," on the one hand, and "unspeakably dear, and very beautiful" on the other, as he announced in the foreword to *America and Americans*, his final book (*AASN* 318). More to the point, few writers, Louis Owens argued in *John Steinbeck's Re-Vision of America* (1985), mounted a more "ambitious and thorough examination of the idea of America" (8). His bold claim is reinforced by Jay Parini's belief, expressed in his introduction to *Travels with Charley*, that "in the history of American literature" few writers "have thought more doggedly about the nature and fate of their own country than John Steinbeck" (vii).

In May 1939, long before he wrote the synoptic *America and Americans*, Steinbeck delved into the topic in a thirty-seven-page radio script for NBC called "This Our America," which was a fledgling attempt to give the true story behind a collective portrait of the United States. Years later, in 1953, Steinbeck suggested to critic Lewis Gannett that anyone wishing to understand the diverse, competing voices of American representation should read a metropolitan telephone book for a sense of the complicated makeup of American racial, ethnic, and social society as symbolized in names and combinations of names. Anyone who imagines only they speak for America's identity is a fool, demagogue, or liar (Letter 1). In other words, the nation as a vastly varied subject was always on Steinbeck's mind. Reason enough to pay attention and to pause, even briefly, over *The John Steinbeck Map of America*. Three-plus decades ago, a small California publishing company produced a 20" × 26" paper foldout, featuring locations of and events from fourteen of Steinbeck's books, from *The Pastures of Heaven* (1932) to *Travels with Charley* (1962). The impression created by the multicolor map is that Steinbeck's main subject was not just "Steinbeck Country" of Northern California around Salinas and the Monterey Peninsula, but America itself, not as an idealized nation-state (though he would occasionally highlight its uniqueness and exceptionalism), but as a contested home and problematic entity worth examining and inspecting, criticizing and chiding, as eminent historian David Wrobel's forthcoming book *John Steinbeck's America* will document.

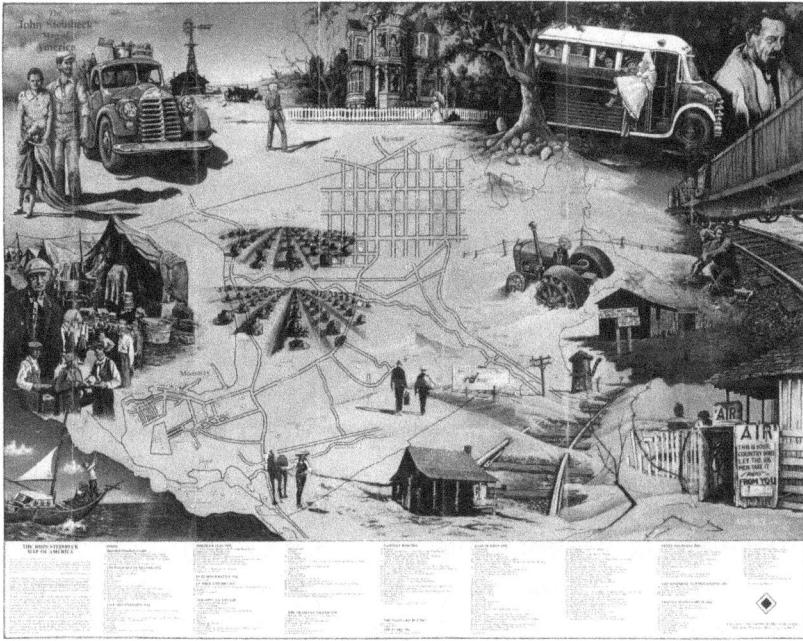

Figure 8. The John Steinbeck Map of America. Foldout, 20" × 26". Los Angeles: Aaron Blake Publishers, 1986. Used by permission of Molly Maguire and Aaron Silverman, Aaron Blake Publishers.

Now, Steinbeck's bittersweet paradoxes seem to be downright tragic and more unreconcilable and urgent than before, as the specter of former president Donald Trump clouds the body politic and continues to haunt the administration of Joseph Biden and Kamala Harris, whose 2020 election I think John Steinbeck—an avid proponent of Franklin Delano Roosevelt's New Deal and later an ardent pro–Adlai Stevenson Democrat (*AASN* 219–22)—would have applauded. In times like these, when reasonable, fair-minded ethical principles, beneficent conscience, broad-based humanistic concerns, gracious civility, and science-oriented values are more imperiled than ever by a phalanx of willful nihilists, rabid conspiracy shills, vaccine deniers, vote suppressors, book banners and burners, and inflexible authoritarian mobs, who attack every criticism of American exceptionalism with a virulent disdain and contempt for otherness, I turn again to Steinbeck's words for insight, comfort, and optimism. "'But if we ever need him again—he'll be back,'" Lazaro says in *Viva Zapata!* (1952).

I could quote a hundred different passages in Steinbeck's canon to underscore my point about his abiding relevance to our time, but I limit myself to one. This is from his courageous, impassioned essay "The Trial of Arthur Miller," which originally appeared in *Esquire* in June 1957. Steinbeck, who refused to be silent or wishy-washy, was just about the only celebrity to come to Miller's defense when the playwright was tried for contempt of Congress by Joseph McCarthy's House on Un-American Activities Committee. Steinbeck's father, the novelist wrote, "taught me rules I do not think are abrogated by our nervous and hysterical times. These laws have not been annulled," including "honor to my family, loyalty to my friends, respect for the law, love of country, and instant and open revolt against tyranny, whether it comes from the bully in the schoolyard, the foreign dictator, or the local demagogue" (*AASN* 104).

In standing up to be counted, it should come as no surprise that Steinbeck anticipated nearly all of what we have been going through recently in the arenas of politics, morality, society, and environment. The record of his rigorous dissection and inspection is in *Of Mice and Men*, *The Grapes of Wrath*, *Sea of Cortez*, *Travels with Charley*, *The Winter of Our Discontent*, and *America and Americans*, to name a few of the standouts. Steinbeck does us all a continuing service by his lifelong adherence to honoring "understanding and communication, which are the functions of literature," as he pointed out in his 1962 Nobel Prize acceptance speech (*AASN* 173). I do not think it is an exaggeration to claim that his greatest books are an antidote to—if not a blatant call to resist—the tidal wave of vain posturing, fake news, obfuscation, top-down tyranny, debasement of language, and outright lies that seem to be the stock in trade of much grievously callous and incompetent political activity and sensational discourse on both sides of the aisle. The fact that these grievances make our blood boil is a sure indication that we are not yet dead, an especially welcome sign for a geezer like me.

Simon Stow concludes his introduction to the excellent collection *A Political Companion to John Steinbeck* by aptly claiming that Steinbeck "could not be more important" and that he "remains a dangerous writer" for many needful, corrective reasons (15). More recently, in *Reclaiming John Steinbeck*, Gavin Jones concurred: "Steinbeck is a writer so difficult, but so necessary, to understand" (199). Though I wish it were otherwise, I am not naïve enough to think that, except in some unusual instances (*Uncle Tom's Cabin*, *The Jungle*, *The*

Grapes of Wrath, Silent Spring), literature any longer has the clout to effect legislative change in the political and legal sphere, but I know, even in this digital, screen-oriented, cyber-enabled social media age that moves faster than the speed of thought, without literature's power, passion, symbolism, and call to action we are far worse off than we might be otherwise. Rather than being cruelly dismissed as "the man who lived too long," as an anonymous British reviewer once claimed, Steinbeck's literary, cultural, and ethical legacy, his lifelong exercise of criticizing the collective state and body politic with an eye toward improvement, is an honorable force for good that should animate us all.

———

If this is a minority report on my part, so be it, for I write this counter-mythology not out of abject hagiography and blind partisanship, but out of critical advocacy and readerly enthusiasm where Steinbeck is concerned. "The art that matters to us," Lewis Hyde states in his marvelous book *The Gift*, "is received by us as a gift is received." And furthermore, "when we are moved by art we are grateful that the artist lived, grateful that he labored in the service of his gifts" (xii). The gift of Steinbeck's words has always provided a relief that cushions the hard places of my daily existence and gives me hope for an improved future that belongs to my grandchildren. From the Dust Bowl to Occupy Wall Street, #MeToo, and beyond into present existential anxiety and contentious debates about racial inequality, border security, immigration, voting rights, environmental degradation, or climate change/global warming, there is no gainsaying Steinbeck's writings can perform necessary cultural work in enabling connectedness, redeeming emotional benefi-cence, and historicizing social change. That, as he said in his Nobel Prize speech, is the writer's ancient commission: "dredging up to the light our dark and dan-gerous dreams for the purpose of improvement" (*AASN* 173).

John Steinbeck has been gone half a century–plus, proving once again the brutal impermanence of even the most significant corporeal existences. I am one of those people, however, who thinks fictional characters, figments of a writer's imagination, exert a real-world presence in the places we have come to. In "The Ghost of Tom Joad" (1995), Bruce Springsteen had it right: "I'm sitting down here in the campfire light / With the ghost of old Tom Joad." It's a comforting, mesmerizing thought: like Tom's ghost and the ghosts of

Ma Joad, Doc, Emiliano Zapata, Lee, and Samuel Hamilton (choose your figure), John Steinbeck remains urgent, present, and necessary. Like his pal Ed Ricketts, Steinbeck "will not die" and he "haunts" those of us who knew of him (*LSC* 700).

He is still around everywhere; his words matter as much now as they ever have, and he remains as current and timely as the most contemporary of culture heroes, icons, and disturbers, some of whom in the past twenty-five years, such as troubadour rocker Springsteen, folk singer Joan Baez, filmmakers John Sayles and Michael Moore, news analyst Rachel Maddow, civil-rights activists Ruby Bridges and Delores Huerta, environmentalist Bill McKibben, and global chef Jose Andres, among others equally deserving, have walked the righteous walk and become recipients of San Jose State University's coveted John Steinbeck Award, "in the souls of the people," for their humanitarian bravery, impact, and excellence. I am not sure we can ask anything more from the prized artists who haunt our imaginations: flaws, blemishes, frailties, inconsistences, and short-comings aside, some unalloyed core portion of themselves reaches beyond their own times and speaks knowingly and movingly to ours.

This strikes me as the true definition of classic work, whose meaning refuses to be fixed in time and place but travels over eras as conditions and audiences develop new ways of seeing, new sets of demands, and new questions to ask, and seek new solutions for the problems that go on plaguing us. It isn't that such a work exists in a static, museum-like vacuum, never to be challenged, adapted, tweaked, or reimagined, but that it responds to and speaks for—perhaps even outpaces or prophesies—our altered preoccupations and critical questions, our evolving sensibilities and perceptions, and our enhanced discursive strategies regarding fundamental existential, civic, natu-ral, and textual values. Such evolution is true no matter what we seek. We go down the road, arrive at some farther intellectual, historical, social, legal, or creative site, only to find that Steinbeck the committed artist has been there ahead of us, marked out some territory for us, and helped us think about and negotiate the new places to which we have arrived. As editors Tedlock and Wicker claimed in *Steinbeck and His Critics*, a spirited book that guided my early forays into examining the writer, "There is much still to be said about him, particularly by those willing to read him closely and patiently before attempting general statement and synthesis" (xli). Their charge continues to resonate six decades later.

Steinbeck still saves my life. There will be some factualists, obsessors of minutiae, who will find these statements and sentiments unacceptable and outmoded, hopelessly retro and backward-looking, perhaps even offensive, and will pooh-pooh them as they go through the house drawing shut the blinds, but that will be their loss. Perhaps, then, the true issue and most relevant question in this personal, over-the-shoulder, hindsight reflection is not how my travels with Steinbeck could have gone on this long, but whether we have ever needed him more than in these present moments.

Chapter 2

The Place We Have Arrived

On Writing/Reading toward Cannery Row

I. Preliminary: Broadening the Field

> The luck of the book is that we then may go back,
> to the top of the page, and begin to arrive again.
>
> —MURIEL RUKEYSER, *The Life of Poetry* (1949)

John Steinbeck was an "experimental" writer ("Mpb" 23). Six months after the publication of *The Grapes of Wrath* (1939), which had become a controversial, runaway bestseller and put Steinbeck in the public eye in unimagined and personally taxing ways, the exhausted and dismayed writer confided in his journal on October 6, 1939, that he was "battered with uncertainties" and realized he "must go to new sources and find new roots" to be "found in tide pools and on a microscope slide rather than in men" (*WD* 106). Later that month, he proclaimed to his uncle Joe Hamilton that the "field must broaden. The new work must jump to include other species besides the human. That is why my interest in biology and ecology have become so sharpened." The following month, on November 13, he confessed to his former Stanford University classmate Carlton Sheffield that he had worked the "clumsy vehicle" of the novel as far as he could. Instead, he announced his plan to explore uncharted creative horizons informed by contemporary developments in theoretical physics, among other disciplines (including marine biology, mathematics, anthropology, and psychology), which he dubbed "the form of the new" (*SLL* 194). His desire to change defined his art in the 1940–1950s era. "This experimentation is not criminal," he claimed in a 1950 *Saturday Review* essay titled "Critics, Critics, Burning Bright," but "is necessary if the writer be not moribund" (*Steinbeck and His Critics* 47).

The immediate result of Steinbeck's recuperative self-fashioning was a collaborative, 598-page volume written with marine biologist Edward F. Ricketts, *Sea of Cortez: A Leisurely Journal of Travel and Research*, published in December 1941, that consists of a 271-page narrative portion, followed by a 327-page illustrated and annotated Phyletic Catalogue of specimens obtained during the 4,000-mile collecting journey. It is an impressive book, physically imposing and intellectually weighty, that bespeaks a rare attempt at unifying literary and scientific ways of making sense of the world and serves as a prescient example of melding two distinct, often oppositional, discourses into one whole to show "how science and literature can inform each other" (Browne 59). A decade later, following Ricketts's death in 1948, the volume's narrative portion appeared as *The Log from the Sea of Cortez*, with Steinbeck listed as the sole author, augmented by a lengthy biographical introduction, "About Ed Ricketts." *The Log* wasn't the same whole thing as the original edition, but it was better than nothing at all.

Such a move on Viking Press's part in 1951 diminished Ricketts's role and cast a shadow on his already considerable professional accomplishments, especially his pioneering book (with Jack Calvin) *Between Pacific Tides* (1939), and made it seem that the narrative log portion was Steinbeck's work alone and that the biological catalogue of specimens was by Ricketts. Nothing could be further from the truth. In fact, Steinbeck and Ricketts considered the original book a true collaboration, in itself a daring, new authorial departure for Steinbeck, who was not inclined to collaborate and who had already turned away from a joint project documenting the California migrant situation with photo journalist Horace Bristol. Ricketts's travel journal and an unpublished essay on nonteleological thinking formed some of the basis for the narrative portion "shaped by John," as Ricketts stated, while Steinbeck participated in the actual collecting and preservation and cataloguing of specimens; thus, each man had a hand in the work of the other. "The structure is a collaboration," Ricketts said. Steinbeck echoed that: "This book is the product of the work and thinking of both of us and the setting down of the words is of no importance."[1] John Steinbeck thought it was the hardest writing job he had ever done, so his dismissal is somewhat disingenuous.

More to the point, *Sea of Cortez* grew out of the fertile interaction of two men's creative, philosophical, and intellectual passions that began and ended in

Figure 9. The Western Flyer,'76 purse seiner, arriving back in Monterey after Steinbeck and Rickett's six-week "leisurely journey of travel and research" to Baja California. Courtesy of Martha Heasley Cox Center for Steinbeck Studies, San Jose State University.

the seaside town of Monterey, California. But that landmark ecological book was not the final statement. Nothing of their fruitful cross-pollination was wasted. The long-range result of their broad interdisciplinary exploration appeared six years later in Steinbeck's novel *Cannery Row* (1945), dedicated to Ed Ricketts ("who knows why or should") and featuring a central character named Doc modeled on Ricketts and his Pacific Biological Laboratory in Monterey. According to Ricketts, Steinbeck's belief that "the time of pure fiction was over" and that his desire to "portray the tide pools" (*Breaking Through* 34) added immeasurably to the novel's background and substance.

What follows are some avenues of approach for understanding the place Steinbeck has brought us to/to us in his quest for the "form of the new" regarding *Cannery Row*, one of his greatest signature fictions. As with so many Steinbeckian locales, it is not only the simple nostalgic regional place we once imagined it was (and perhaps in some regards still is, as "Scrap" Lundy reminds us in his entertaining *Real Life on Cannery Row*), but it is also a rich, inflected, interstitial site, a contested space where a number of disciplinary borders and boundaries (Tatum 318; Browne 59) have been crossed, joined, and redrawn. In order to offer some speculations and approximations about the layered complexities of Steinbeck's novel, I examine a couple of underlying, often bypassed or neglected Steinbeckian tropes—"participation" and "the new"—both of which converge in *Cannery Row* and emphasize the prescient ecological belief that "everything impinges on everything else, often into radically different systems" (*LSC* 868). Examining the function and power of these overlapping ideas might rectify the belief that "no key" exists with which to unlock "the secret structural design at the center" of *Cannery Row* (Benson, "Reconsideration" 13) or ease the "difficulty" of "deciding what *Cannery Row* is precisely—a realist novel? a symbolist fantasy? a metafictional experiment?" (Jones, *Reclaiming* 195). The fact that the novel could share elements of all those categories might complicate rather than simplify its standing, but that seems to be a gambit worth taking. Steinbeck tended to eschew formulas anyway and had a habit of bending genre distinctions to his own end. If, after all is said and done, the novel still remains a puzzle to us, it will probably be for other, less easily understood reasons.

II. Participation: A Brief (Hi)story of a Word

> The law of participation.... At the moment
> it would be difficult to formulate this law in abstract terms.
>
> —LUCIEN LEVY-BRUHL, *How Natives Think* (1926)

A Monterey-area paper, the *Coast Weekly*, once ran an intriguing front-cover headline: "Who Owns Steinbeck?" Inside, the investigative story centers on the unresolvable "tug of war between commemoration and commercialization" and highlights the necessarily inconclusive "battle" between "the Monterey Peninsula and the Salinas Valley asserting their ties to the essential Steinbeck" (Duman 10). But perhaps it isn't a question of who owns Steinbeck, but how it is that he owns us, compels us to respond. To put it another way, books are metaphors as well as material products, which is to say—not to put an excessively commodificational twist to it—they can be made "use" of in any number of both routine and unexpected ways. Steinbeck understood that multiplicity better than many writers when he claimed in 1936 that reading "certain books" was "realer than experience" (*SR* xx)—in other words, the result of virtual textual seduction becomes the equivalent of an event actually happening to us.

That a Steinbeck novel happens to us is not an accident, because positing the presence of a participatory "reader" was always part of his basic storytelling project.[2] As recent commentators have realized, Steinbeck has not been adequately or widely enough credited for having an abiding, generative, ideational aesthetic (*TAJS* 231; Timmerman 3–15; Ditsky 5), though in fact he wrote from a consistent (though unpretentious) set of operative principles and a healthy dose of pragmatic optimism that his words would communicate on a variety of levels to his audience. He told George Albee in 1934 that "The Chrysanthemums" story "is designed to strike without the reader's knowledge. I mean he reads it casually and after it is finished feels that something profound has happened to him although he does not know what nor how" (*SLL* 91). In the individual space opened up by the reading experience, in the aftermath of contemplating the "what" and the "how," Steinbeck expected we would talk back, breach boundaries, and become, in short, not merely consumers of culture, but its participants.

From the start of his mature career, then, Steinbeck imagined a dynamic, interactive equation configured around a cooperative triad of Writer-Text-Reader. In the 1930s and 1940s—generally well ahead of its time—Steinbeck worked out a homemade reader-response theory, discussed frequently with Ed Ricketts, which was dubbed "participation." For instance, in *The Forgotten Village* Steinbeck and director Herbert Kline attempted to "draw" a portrait of the Indigenous Mexican culture with "something like participation." In the preface Steinbeck elaborated: "Birth and death, joy and sorrow, are constants, experiences common to the whole species. If one participates first in the constants, one is able to go from them to the variables of customs, practices, mores, taboos, and foreign social patterns. That at any rate was our theory and the pattern in which we worked" (5). No single Steinbeck text embodies all these elements in the same proportion, but they appear in sufficient regularity and concert to look like a definable pattern, embedded particularly in *The Grapes of Wrath, Cannery Row, The Pearl, East of Eden,* and *Sweet Thursday.* In much of his major writing, then, Steinbeck consciously sought to achieve a strong participatory effect by reaching a "common ground" between text and audience, a liminal site, a contact zone, where a reader can take from his book "as much" as they can "bring to it" (*JN* 11, 17).

———

It is impossible to know where Steinbeck first encountered "participation." It is reasonable to surmise that lightning-rod Ed Ricketts got the fire burning, for he employed the term frequently and it would no doubt have been part of their frequent conversations. Ricketts considered participation a profound interaction and understanding between human beings and the universe. In a note on participation he called it "the most deeply interesting thing in the world" (*Breaking Through* 28). There would also have been talks with Jungian advocate Joseph Campbell and resident Jungian psychologist Evelyn Ott aiding and abetting Steinbeck's study of Carl Jung and other influential psychologists, mythologists, and anthropologists. After all, Steinbeck wrote an entire early novel in 1930, *Murder at Full Moon* (unpublished) that turns on Jung's 1909 study *The Psychology of Dementia Praecox* (*SR* lxxii, 62–63, 156–57). The fortieth definition of "Psychological Types," which appears in chapter X, paragraph 781, of Jung's *Psychological Types*, reads in part: "Participation mystique is a term derived from Levy-Bruhl [in *How Natives Think*]. It denotes a peculiar kind of psychological connection with objects, and consists in the fact that the subject cannot clearly distinguish himself from the object but is bound to it by a direct relationship which amounts to partial identity. . . . Participation mystique is a vestige of this primitive condition" (456). Whether Steinbeck, guided by Jung's attribution, bothered to go next to Lucien Levy-Bruhl's chapter, "The Law of Participation," in his sociological study of primitive collectivism, *How Natives Think* (originally published in French in 1923, then in English in 1926), is unknown, but is highly likely.[3] In speaking without condescension of primitive subject/object perceptions, Levy-Bruhl claimed that "in various forms and degrees they all involve a 'participation' between persons or objects which form part of a collective representation. . . ." This interaction he termed "the law of participation" (76).

Steinbeck appropriated the Levy-Bruhl/Jung idea (and adopted both writers' tone of acceptance and understanding) for his own enabling ends, as he often did with inspiring sources. He transformed what was a prelogical sociological and fetishistic psychological pattern to a calculated aesthetic orientation with regard to the nature and function of mediated representation. That is, Steinbeck metaphorized the metaphor itself. He discovered in Levy-Bruhl's "multipresence" (96) and his "ensemble which depends upon the group, as the group depends upon it" (99), and in Jung's "transference relationship" (457) not an isolated primitive nor mystical condition nor an aberrant psychological quirk, but a kind of immanent palimpsest of interaction, a cognitive bridge with which to link author, text, and reader in an evolving, nonhierarchical, ecological phalanx of interpretation and perpetual (re)construction of meaning. Levy-Bruhl's investigations highlighted issues of "collective representation" (76) and affective social "communion" (90), and Jung's dealt with multiple and reciprocal attachments (456–57). Both are analogous to Steinbeck's preoccupation with phalanxes of natural and human social organization, a developing pattern of aggregate stimulus, action, and perception he had been working out since the early 1930s ("Argument of Phalanx"; "Case Study").

A great deal has been written about this "group man" theory and Ricketts's important role in it, especially regarding how when humans operate in aggregate they function in ways different than those of the individual (Astro 43–60; *TAJS* 264–70; *Mad* 134–37). Less has been said, however, about Steinbeck's writerly role in regard to the social phalanx, so it is worthwhile to focus briefly on that aspect. Steinbeck keyed into a particular kind of scriptive role as a recorder of group activity. For Steinbeck, the recording figure—the artist with a small "a"—is the egoless "spokesman" of the phalanx, "the one in whom the phalanx comes closest to the conscious." He continued to George Albee in 1933: "When a man hears great music, sees great pictures, reads great poetry, he loses his identity in that of the phalanx. I do not need to describe the emotion caused by these things, but it is invariably a feeling of oneness with one's phalanx" (Letter to George Albee 1).[4]

The spokesperson, who is capable of writing the "tremendous and terrible poetry" of the moment (3), appears when he is needed to express a group's most important or pressing needs. Thus, paradoxically, although the artist is constructed by social desire/political necessity and the conjunctive pressures of history, economics, and geography, he expresses himself not only according to the degree of felt life he brings to his work, but also according to his inventive and suasive capacities regarding theme, style, and form. "Man's art always reflects the nature and emotion of his phalanx. If it does not, it is not art, it is simply technique" (Letter to George Albee 2). The central point in this paradoxical dance of unconscious desire and conscious craft is to break through the old monolithic, totalizing conventions—the "obstacles" (Steinbeck, "Suggestion" 541)—of ignorance and oppression by building approximate living structures in language that invite audience empathy, imaginative participation, and even social action, not by mystical means, but through emotional identification and psychological investment with the mediating textual object. "Art is the phalanx knowledge of the nature of matter and life," which is to say, it is a way of expressing experience through apt form: "Art form is nature form," he concludes emphatically (Letter to George Albee 2).

———

Before treating *Cannery Row*, it will be helpful to backtrack and consider *The Grapes of Wrath*, which demonstrates a breakthrough toward participation in a variety of ways (Owens, *The Grapes of Wrath* 28), but also manifests the art form/ nature form equation that paved the way for *Cannery Row*. A special conjunction occurs in chapter twenty-three, a discursive, essay-style interchapter in which Steinbeck relates the migrant's means of creating pleasure on the road. A radical political thrust also enacts an aesthetic gambit. The group's pleasures include a storytelling round where "people gathered in the low firelight to hear the gifted ones. And they listened while the tales were told, and their participation made the stories great" (444). This is a signature gesture, an inviting way of entering the multiple levels of eco-narrativity. The whole passage (at 549 words, too long to quote here) also presents an eponymous speaker's haunting account of his reluctant but complicitous involvement in the United States Army's murderous campaign against Apache leader Geronimo from 1885 to 1886 and offers a parable of a slaughtered brave and a dead cock pheasant.

The oral performance, including the nameless recruit's confession, is at once realistically (re)presented and textually (re)flexive, because it mirrors in miniature Steinbeck's methodology regarding his writerly situation in the phalanx setting: the storyteller is positioned not above his auditors but at their level, so that they can key into his narrational experience and thereby lend it additional power and meaning. Audience participation, Steinbeck writes, "made the stories great" and allowed the man's confession to become not self-indulgent posturing, or empty technique, but a redemptive gesture applicable to the entire community of listeners both inside and outside the book. This gripping moment functions as an elaborate, poignant trope for the key social themes of *Grapes*, including tyranny of surveillance, arrogance of power, and willful destruction of peoples and resources—those unconscionable acts that cause us to "spoil" something better than ourselves, to destroy something in ourselves that can never be "fixed up."

In this transactional configuration, a radical space has been opened up for understanding and amelioration: all actions in a natural, social, and textual environment have consequences that merge, we imagine, in the audience's response and in the degree to which they—we—are implicated in issues of degradation and genocide and come away having been exposed to significant lessons of natural and ethical responsibility. In this transactional configuration, too, at its most basic level, lies part of the secret of Steinbeck's appeal and success. Hearing, reading, participating, we readers willingly transgress fixed boundaries to help create and recreate the text in front of us. Maryjane Osborne considers it a species of cinema, hypnotic but neither "exploitive" nor inviting seductive uncritical participation ("Parables" 241). Being a "gifted one" in this narratological context, then, refers to Steinbeck's mediating attention toward vocal presence and his embedded—and often unavoidably self-conflicted—role in the complex, shifting, indeterminate relationship among groups of people, events, things, words, and audience.

To put it another way, at the formal and structural level, where art form and nature form coincide, reading *Grapes* with a broadly ecological inflection, as I claimed in the previous chapter of *Steinbeck's Imaginarium*, reveals the essential stereo-like relatedness between narrative and intercalary chapters: the chapters on the Joads are text; the discursive chapters are context. Which is to say, history embeds fiction and vice versa. This congenial signature Steinbeckian pattern is evident again in *Cannery Row*'s mixing of real and fictive personalities and events. I am tempted to say that folding is done in a nonhierarchical relational manner, privilege not necessarily being granted to one mode at the expense of the other, so that working in concert they become inseparable and indivisible elements of Steinbeck's entire holistic literary project. (Expurgated, edited editions of *The Grapes of Wrath*, without the interchapters, like truncated versions of *Moby-Dick* without the cetology chapters, completely miss the point.) Just as the Joads join a larger phalanx of migrants and cross state border lines in their trek west, so we as participatory readers must actively cross boundaries between those differing realms of discourse, which require variant and flexible ways of "reading" the multiple levels of text as well as traversing its myriad spaces, especially the borderlands, the edges, the ecotonal mergings and shadings between and among chapters.

Steinbeck's work is full of small, tucked-away, encoded places, ranging from Joseph Wayne's mysterious glade in *To a God Unknown* to Ethan Allen

Hawley's secret seaside place in *The Winter of Our Discontent*. *The Red Pony*, *The Grapes of Wrath*, *Cannery Row*—they too exhibit a similar fixation for set-aside habitations of mergings and shadings. In those shadings, much of *The Grapes of Wrath* is about absences of water, money, food, dignity, sex, home, ethnicity. But as we know from reading Emily Dickinson, absences need not always be negative. The spaces where absences are most sharply desired or can begin to be recuperated are often encoded as liminal areas—a number of key scenes in *Grapes* take place in marginal zones or in "in-between" places, to apply cultural critic Homi Bhabha's term in *The Location of Culture* (29). Ranging from abandoned buildings to weed-choked ditches, myriad in-between spaces are framed by darkness, or illuminated by low light, firelight, greyness, gloom, dust, dusk, or cloudy, rain-sodden skies, for example—all of which suggest an aesthetics of indeterminate edges, an "edgesthetics" (to coin a term). Comfortably inhabited by nonhuman creatures—rats, coyotes, skunks, owls—these zones of intersection, these ecotones, function as powerful places where, because natural processes are keenly felt, life is most diverse (or divergent), which is to say, thickest with possibility, and where, as a consequence, relationships must be reinvented for the purpose of survival, continuity, and communal salvation. Animals own and even thrive in the gloaming, but humans must learn to adjust their vision to take in the larger panorama, the holistic "toto picture."

———

Steinbeck learned to adjust, too. His life changed drastically in the years following the runaway success and notoriety of *The Grapes of Wrath*. In an abstract sense, *Grapes* no longer belonged to Steinbeck at all but to an army of anonymous readers who reinvented it according to their own predilections, experiences, and desires. If this satisfied the social usefulness of proletarian literature, the theoretical destiny of phalanx art, and the power of Steinbeck's own participatory aesthetics, it did little to explain the personalism of the moment. In fact, Steinbeck resented the reductive implications of an exchange that, instead of expunging him from the public gaze, could produce a monstrous, distorted "straw man," a "fictitious so-and so . . . out there in the public eye," as he told interviewer Tom Cameron of the *Los Angeles Times* in July 1939 (*CJS* 18).

    Instead, he tried to leave behind the part of him that made *Grapes*, but it always proved difficult, primarily because his critics and reviewers expected him to write the same thing over again. But he was a relatively resilient if not always utterly centered person, and one of his responses to his own cynicism and cautionary backlash was to embark on several different kinds of writing, to reinvent himself, and to become, in effect, a man of letters, rather than, strictly speaking, a novelist only. "I have to go to new sources and find new roots" (*WD* 106). Between 1940 and 1945, besides *Lifeboat*, he brought forth a filmscript (*The Forgotten Village*, produced and directed by Herbert Kline), two works of nonfiction (*Sea of Cortez* and *Bombs Away*), a play novella (*The Moon Is Down*), a whole volume of war dispatches for the *New York Herald Tribune* (later published as *Once There Was a War*), a full-length unpublished musical drama ("The Wizard of Maine"), and, finally, a novel (*Cannery Row*). In addition, he had a hand in the first Viking Portable anthology, *The Viking Portable Library Steinbeck*, which appeared in 1943, edited and selected by Pascal Covici, Steinbeck's editor at Viking Press.

The clearest theoretical statement of the writer's participatory method appears in one of the oddest documents in the Steinbeckian archive. "Introduction by Pascal Covici" was handwritten in late September 1942 by Steinbeck himself and perhaps intended to be used or drawn upon by his Viking Press editor Covici as he arranged the publication of Viking's *Portable Library Steinbeck*.[5] Though it has never been published in its entirety, this is an especially valuable document because Steinbeck attempts to codify the affective and intuitive dimension of reading as a way of experiencing reality:

There are some books, some stories, some poems which one reads over and over again without knowing why one is drawn to them. And such stories need not have been critically appreciated—in fact many of them have not been. The critic's approach is and perhaps should be one of appraisal and evaluation. The reader if he likes a story feels largely a participation. The stories we go back to are those in which we have taken part. A man need not have a likeness of exact experience to love a story but he must have in him an emotional or intellectual tone which has keyed into the story and made him part of it. No one has ever read Treasure Island or Robinson Crusoe objectively. The chief character in both cases are merely the skin and bones of the reader. The poetical satires of Gulliver have long been forgotten but the stories go on. The message or the teaching of a story almost invariably dies first while the

participation persists. Perhaps the best balance of message and participation in all literature is the story of Jesus—for there step by step the
mind is opened by association with the man and his suffering to the
things he said. ("Introduction" [1]; *ST* 195–96)

Steinbeck's testimony—it had by this juncture of his career become a signature
rationale, even a personal manifesto, which is to say, both hopeful and resis-
tant—is a summation of a decade's preoccupation with trying to accomplish a
fundamental yet mysterious affective task: to create a "true" theory of writing
that linked nonteleological observation with an affective dimension of "religion
and emotion and poetry" (Letter to George Albee [2]; *ST* 195) in order to make
us "see a little play" in our heads, as he had once claimed in a brief 1938 essay in
Stage magazine (*AASN* 156). This is not to be confused with pejorative notions
of "escape writing and reading," for as far as Steinbeck is concerned, "all art is
escape" into a fuller dimension of reality:

> One escapes into the painter's eye, and brain in a Rembrandt, one
> escapes into the rich reality of Tolstoy out of the muddy and troubled
> reality of oneself. One escapes into the clear thinking of a physicist[,]
> into the glowing emotion of a poem. It is all escape—Next to the eating
> and reproducing urges it is probably that man's greatest quality is his
> instinct for rebellion and escape. His religion, and all his arts and all
> his sciences are simply the results of his beating against the bars of his
> world. It is natural enough that the dull coarse mind should escape into
> the super reality of the success-love story of the magazine. The hungrier
> and sharper mind may chose [*sic*] the paths of astrophysics, of poetry, or
> ethics. But the escape effort is everywhere. ("Introduction" [2])

Steinbeck's 1942 rationale not only summed up his major work to date, but also
forecast writing yet to be done in *Cannery Row*, *The Pearl*, *East of Eden*, and
Sweet Thursday. This desired end required a new way of writing that avoided
"the usual narrative method," but rather used a storytelling strategy "so natural
and unobtrusive that an audience would not even be conscious of it" (*Forgotten
Village* [6]). It is debatable how unobtrusive Steinbeck's method was, especially
in his post-1950 works, but nevertheless composing with a response theory in
mind allowed for the creation of a silent "wall of background" and a

"picture-making state," which would allow the "unexpected" to emerge, as he claimed in his *Long Valley* notebook (*TJAS* 331), or create a broadly "relational" effort that requires "living into" for its optimum effect (*LSC* 867).

———

Two years almost to the day after Steinbeck had written his ghosted "Introduction," he told Carlton Sheffield, "I finished the book called *Cannery Row*. . . . I don't know whether it is effective or not. It's written on four levels and people can take what they can receive out of it. One thing—it never mentions the war—not once" (*SLL* 273). Steinbeck did not consider those levels a "preconceived structural pattern," as Roy Simmonds rightly notes (226), but rather as fluid, interpenetrative layers that attempt to replicate life's complex holism. Steinbeck's text, then, is relational—so that classifying distinct, sharply etched referential categories is less important than seeing the interrelated pattern they create (Shillinglaw, Introduction xxiv–xxv). Indeed, *Cannery Row* is almost anti-literary; it avoids "elaborate, formal, literary structures" (Benson, "Reconsideration" 23) and builds on Steinbeck's strategy of democratically inviting us in at the outset to share the perplexing task of telling a story for which there is no preferred, favored vantage point with which to approach it, and there are no clear lines between historical reality, thinly disguised fictional creations, and utterly imagined and made-up events. Steinbeck's aesthetic conundrum becomes our shared interpretative puzzle and requires our active involvement to concretize it:

> How can the poem and the stink and the grating noise—the quality of light, the tone, the habit and the dream—be set down alive? When you collect marine animals there are certain flat worms so delicate that they are almost impossible to capture whole, for they break and tatter under the touch. You must let them ooze and crawl of their own will onto a knife blade and then lift them gently into your bottle of sea water. And perhaps that might be the way to write this book—to open the page and to let the stories crawl in by themselves. (102)

Cannery Row explicitly foregrounds both the basis of Steinbeck's real-life experience (his association with Ed Ricketts and his memories of Cannery

Row as a historical place) and the materiality of his writing (his aesthetic difficulties in achieving written representation of, or objectivity toward, oral/folk experience). The narrator's problematic position frames, or focalizes, the text. Because ideally his stance purports to be nonjudgmental, it also undercuts traditional authorial privilege, in that the narrator, like the teller in chapter twenty-three of *Grapes*, is situated at the same level as his audience and provides one perspective among many possible perspectives on the action and characters (101). He asks how the Row's intangible, evanescent qualities can "be set down alive." His response is not transcendent or imperial, but rather tentative, qualified, conditional—"perhaps that might be the way," he admits.

The image of coaxing marine worms into bottles, Jackson Benson rightly claims, "suggests to us that this will be a rather daring experiment—a non-teleological novel, a fiction as unordered as possible by previous conceptions and structures, dealing not even with a hero (the anthropocentric view of life) or with plot (concern with cause and effect), but with life as an ongoing 'is' process" ("Reconsideration" 23). If Steinbeck relied on base-level emotional power to implicate us in *Of Mice and Men* and *The Grapes of Wrath*, in this fiction he has figuratively made us accomplices, coconspirators in his eco-textual and language project, and has allowed us to enter the frame with him to witness the inherent difficulty of representing the ceaseless flow and vitality of the double signifier *Cannery Row*/Cannery Row. Contemplating these elements brings to mind Steinbeck's closing words in his "Introduction by Pascal Covici": "When reader and writer go together into a story ... pleasure is the result" ([3]).[6]

Toward that end, *Cannery Row* utilizes a few subtle, almost transparent strategies to encourage our participation: lyrical place descriptions help readers locate geographically and spatially; relatively sketchy physical descriptions of characters encourage readers to envision them in their mind's eye; emphatic dialogue creates the illusion of eavesdropping on private conversation. In addition, Steinbeck employs structural and stylistic innovations to affect our involvement. Digressive interchapters establish a rhythmic or thematic counterpoint to the main narrative, while other evocative chapters withhold disclosures and direct the reader's eye or ear toward the unsaid, perhaps even the momentously unsayable (Andy's inscrutable experience with the elderly Chinese man in chapter four, the drowned woman Doc discovers in chapter eighteen), or the egregiously unthinkable (William's suicide in chapter three, Gay's beating of his wife in chapter six). In order to arrive at a fuller-than-usual understanding of the novel, these episodes, often touching on fabular prestidigitations or magicality, require completion by an audience keyed into Steinbeck's text, readers receptive to powers of suggestion, randomness, and spatial form (*SLL* 91).

In fact, because a kind of unique heterodoxy and diversity results when barriers are broken down, and boundaries crossed, *Cannery Row* is purposely full of inviting, seductive gaps, shadows, discontinuities, and margins. As most scientists, naturalists, and ecologists know, life at these transitional sites, these ecotonal margins, is often thickest, most vital, diverse, and interesting. Steinbeck's references to hybrid microcosmic locations (Lee Chong's grocery, Palace Flophouse), physical edges and contact zones (land/sea, vacant lot/busy street, whorehouse/marine lab), and temporal boundaries between day and night, such as dusk, and especially dawn, which he names the "hour of the pearl . . . when time stops and examines itself" (155), all open up primary, originary spaces where readers can go beyond mere "skin and bones" and imagine the whole fabric of experience, the place where paradox rules: Lee Chong is a "hard man with a can of beans—a soft man with the bones of his grandfather" (108); Doc's face is "half Christ and half satyr" (117). Overseeing this aesthetics of the edge, this aforementioned "edgesthetics," Steinbeck invokes "Our Father who art in nature" (109) as a validating spirit of the paradox, hybridity, bricolage, simultaneity, and randomness necessary for survival at "the margins of society" (Shillinglaw, Introduction ix). "Monterey is lousy with this kind of paradox," Steinbeck noted in the margins of *Cannery Row*'s galley proof (*Complete Archive* [5]).

If Steinbeck's desire for his audience to share his perplexity frames one end of *Cannery Row*, then Doc's second party, a hymn to quantum unpredictability, frames the other. In order to appreciate Steinbeck's statement that "the nature of parties has been imperfectly studied" (218), we need to attend one. Every party has a "pathology" all its own, and this one is full of festivity, rowdy shenanigans, and unexpected changes; indeed, far from being innocuous, escapist fare, it reveals Steinbeck's sense of performativity and cultural spectacle. Indeed, the shindig might owe something to a legendary costume party and fundraiser gala, "A Surrealistic Night in an Enchanted Forest," Salvador Dali put on at Monterey's Hotel Del Monte in September 1941, attended by Robinson Jeffers, Ginger Rogers, Bob Hope, and Gloria Vanderbilt, and featuring animals from the San Francisco Zoo, that became the talk of the town (Arris 111–12; Briggs-Anderson). In a similar vein, Doc's party calls attention to its own "spontaneity," its sense of "play" (Meeker 10, 18)—induced by music, poetry, and

Figure 10. Ed Ricketts's Pacific Biological Laboratory, 800 Cannery Row, Monterey, California. The model for *Cannery Row's* Western Biological and the scene of outrageous parties. The building is still intact. Courtesy of Martha Heasley Cox Center for Steinbeck Studies, San Jose State University.

lots of booze, the revelers dance, eat, and even fight with abandon. This carnivalesque scene, to borrow loosely Mikhail Bakhtin's term from *Rabelais and His World*, undoes the quotidian world, unsettles the social order, undercuts authority, destroys the boundaries between hierarchies, and invites us to go beyond reading subjectively to momentarily transgressing:

> And then the party really got going. The cops came back, looked in, clicked their tongues and joined it. . . . You could hear the roar of the party from end to end of Cannery Row. The party had all the best qualities of a riot and a night on the barricades. The crew from the San Pedro tuna boat crept humbly back and joined the party. They were embraced and admired. A woman five blocks away called the police to complain about the noise and couldn't get anyone. The cops reported their own car stolen and found it later on the beach. Doc sitting cross-legged on the table smiled and tapped his fingers gently on his knee.

Mack and Phyllis Mae were doing Indian wrestling on the floor. And
the cool bay wind blew in through the broken windows. It was then
that someone lighted the twenty-five-foot string of firecrackers. (223)

This exuberant, charged scene indicates the degree to which Steinbeck, a writer
given to exploding "closed systems" (*LSC* 868) of all kinds, was continually
revising the traditional novelistic contract, the philosophical either/or proposition, the kind of gambit he would enact again in *East of Eden* (1952) and *Sweet
Thursday* (1954), the latter a fabular sequel to *Cannery Row*. It is his literary
version of the social and behavioral exchange dynamic that springs up everywhere on the Row. Furthermore, if we remember that Steinbeck told Carlton
Sheffield *Cannery Row* does "not once" mention World War II, then the novel
can be seen not only as personal therapy for (and a kind of exorcism of) nausea
brought on by his recent tour abroad writing "crap" military journalism (*SLL*
273), but also as a return to the familiar ground of localized history (Shillinglaw,
Introduction xviii–xix) and the empowering, anarchic potential of the "little"
narrative (Lyotard, 60). Indeed, *Cannery Row* anticipates what Jean Lyotard has
called the "postmodern condition" by resisting grand, totalizing narratives of
universal truth, institutional certainty, and consensual normalcy; rather, in its
satiric thrust, it functions as a critique of bourgeois pomposity, literary preten-
tiousness, social entitlement, personal arrogance, and hypocritical respectability.
In Steinbeck's turn toward subverting officially sanctioned grand narratives and
exalted literary techniques (his own included), he was making room for the
reader, who, in the new nonteleological dispensation, becomes part of the text's
conspiratorial hermeneutic process, its propulsive "anomalies . . . among the
commonest intellectual vehicles for breaking through" (*LSC* 874–75).

III. "A New World Is Growing under the Old": A Challenge/A Question

What we observe is not nature itself,
but nature exposed to our method of questioning.
—WERNER HEISENBERG, *Physics and Philosophy* (1958)

And yet there is more to Steinbeck's participatory theory than I have thus far
recounted. I turn now to another underpinning for Steinbeck's new futuristic

method in *Cannery Row*, his "escape" into the "clear thinking" of physics. On November 13, 1939, besides lamenting that the novel was an exhausted genre, Steinbeck also told Sheffield, "The real origin of the future" lies with physicists who, "puzzled with order and disorder in quantum and neutron, build gradually" a new picture of order. "I have too a conviction that a new world is growing under the old, the way a new finger nail grows under a bruised one." Steinbeck didn't know what the form of the new would be, but he knew it would be "shaped by the new thinking" (*SLL* 194). Multilayered *Cannery Row* benefited from Steinbeck's excursions into scientific realms and would exemplify Steinbeck's new form.[7] Indeed, the "new" was Steinbeck's code word for relativity theories, particle physics, and quantum mechanics, whose dizzyingly complex development in the previous forty years or so had disturbed the universe mightily and caused a severe break with classical, deterministic, Newtonian physics. Startling breakthroughs in the structure of micro-reality by the great visionary physicists Albert Einstein, Max Planck, Erwin Schrodinger, Niels Bohr, Werner Heisenberg, and other pioneers in that era (not all of whom were in agreement) had not just scientific but philosophical and cultural ramifications far beyond the rarefied world of the laboratory (Kragh 441, 449).

Steinbeck's concept of participation and fictional form as a "field" of related energy units was aided and abetted by his explorations into the literature of new physics. Stephen Katz, who has studied the relationship of the new physics and reader-response criticism, has found both to be revisionist "expressions of a movement away from the formalistic, rationalistic epistemology embodied in Newtonian" worldview, and proof of the possibility of bridging "humanistic and scientific disciplines" (4–5). Steinbeck's formulation in "Argument of Phalanx" that "Art form is nature form," which I mentioned earlier, has particular overlapping resonance here, for as Katz avers: "in New Physics and Reader Response Criticism the subjective process of reading nature and reading text seems to be similar" (42).

That Steinbeck was aware of this conceptual linkage of the "quanta" of the "whole world of fact and fancy . . . subject and object" (*LSC* 875) is evident in his correspondence. He praised the technical achievements of "Schrodinger, Planck, Bohr, Einstein, Heisenberg" and indicated that he was not only becoming familiar with their scientific projects, but considered them part of a combined effort (his own included) to ensure "destruction of boundaries."[8] Besides revolutionizing views of the material world and scientific paradigms in their own right, these discoveries had immediate philosophical and metaphorical charge (Jones, *Physics* 92). Concepts such as Bohr's so-called Theory of Complementarity (opposing, logically exclusive, seemingly incompatible entities, such as particles and waves, may be separately true at different times in a microsystem) and Heisenberg's Uncertainty Principle (also known as Principle of Indeterminacy), formulated in 1927 (the velocity and location of an electron can't be measured at the same time), became part of the new matrix of thought for many American writers who reveled in their metaphoric potential (Scholnick 14), Steinbeck among them. In the "new epistemology," so termed by British astronomer Arthur S. Eddington in his 1927 Gifford Lectures, *The Nature of the Physical World*—a touchstone text quoted in the narrative portion of *Sea of Cortez* (*LSC* 875)—subjectivity, plurality, uncertainty, interrelatedness, participation of the measurer in the measuring process (in which the act of observation affects the object observed) all became defining markers of the radical new worldview (Balaswamy 172–73). "The principle of indeterminacy is epistemological," Eddington states emphatically, and continues: "It reminds us once again that the world of physics is a world contemplated from within surveyed by appliances which are part of it and subject to its laws" (225).

In his marvelous book *The Tao of Physics*, Fritjof Capra notes, for instance, that human consciousness becomes part of the process of observation in the new physics and that observations are best understood in a context, a defining field of interrelated forces (140). The placement of *Cannery Row*'s narrator (and his readers) inside the "frame" of the narrative takes on a new significance when one considers Steinbeck's technique in light of physicist John Wheeler's statement: "Nothing is more important about the quantum principle than . . . that it destroys the concept of the world as 'sitting out there,' with the observer safely separated from it by a 20-centimeter slab of plate glass." To describe the conceptual change accurately, he continues, "one has to cross out that old word 'observer' and put in its place the new word 'participator.' In some strange sense the universe is a participatory universe" (quoted in *Tao of Physics* 141).

The implications of quantum physics on *Cannery Row* are significant and, except for direct commentary by David Farrah and Brian Railsback, and obliquely by Periaswamy Balaswamy, are nearly unremarked upon. The Great Tide Pool Steinbeck takes us to in chapter six is a major metaphor in *Cannery*

Row, a window into a remarkable ecological world of biodiversity and marine difference, but the microcosmic site can also be seen as a contextual matrix/ system of subhuman forces impinged upon by the narrative observer who cannot retain his "objectivity" (the octopus is described in freighted terms as a "creeping murderer"). Principles of indeterminacy can be seen in the many random, seemingly unplotted events that take place in the novel (Farrah 28). Characters enter and veer off in all directions, such as this moment in chapter eleven, when Steinbeck writes:

> Oh, the infinity of possibility! How could it happen that the car that picked up Gay broke down before it got into Monterey? If Gay had not been a mechanic, he would not have fixed the car. If he had not fixed it the owner wouldn't have taken him to Jimmy Brucia's for a drink. And why was it Jimmy's birthday? Out of all the possibilities in the world— the millions of them—only events occurred that lead to the Salinas jail. (143)

In a strictly naturalistic, deterministic world, or in a strictly realistic novel (if such a thing exists), these "unrelated, irrelevant details" might have no place, or might seem capricious and out of place; but in Steinbeck's quantum fictional landscape, coincidence and accident add their part to the overall "web of related discourses" (Strehle 19). In fact, it is possible to see, metaphorically anyway, complementarity operating in *Cannery Row*, not only in real-life human beings (Red Williams) interacting with fictional (Hazel, Henri) or quasi-fictional ones (Doc, Mack), but also the larger design of chapter organization, in which the causality of Doc's birthday party plot is disrupted with the equally important, though digressive and nonsequential episodes. While these elements are superficially or apparently oppositional, and perhaps even seemingly incompatible, the fact is, in Steinbeck's expanding quantum universe they complement each other in a dimensional literary structure where space (digressive chapters) and time (plot chapters) not only create a simultaneous command on our attention as readers, but for full integrative effect require our "imaginative engagement" with the text to complete the experience: "There is no such thing as an objective observer or reader in an interconnected universe, even in the fictive one of *Cannery Row*" (Farrah 23, 25).[9] Doc's emotional reaction in chapter eighteen to his startling and wholly unexpected discovery of a "pretty, pale" drowned girl in a

La Jolla tide pool, her "face burned into his picture memory" (170), is a touchstone of the kind of deep participatory quality Steinbeck sought to achieve: "Goose pimples came out on Doc's arms. He shivered and his eyes were wet the way they get in the focus of great beauty" (171). That he tears up at novel's end when he reads the ancient Kasmiri poem *Black Marigolds* should come as no surprise (228). In Keatsian fashion, life is often best felt upon the pulse.

———

In *The Cosmic Web* N. Katherine Hayles remarks that "the twentieth century has seen a profound transformation in the ground of its thought, a change catalyzed and validated by relativity theory, quantum mechanics, and particle physics." But the shift in perspective, she continues, "was by no means confined to physics; analogous developments have occurred in a number of disciplines, among them philosophy, linguistics, mathematics, and literature" (15). In *Cannery Row*, Steinbeck drew deeply from this historical moment of radical change. Steinbeck was one of the few major novelists of his era to participate in the discourse of the new sciences, to assimilate their spirit, and to employ congruent philosophical attitudes, beliefs, procedures from allied areas (Railsback, "Dreams" 278–79). Whether they came from anthropology, psychology, philosophy, ecology, marine biology, or pure science, in their metaphoric immediacy such concepts as participation, carnivalization, indeterminacy, and complimentarity all allowed Steinbeck to exceed imposed limits, to transgress and reconfigure boundaries, to bring the margins toward the center. In the long run, that achievement may have been precisely what allowed Steinbeck to "outlast" so many other modern writers (Owens, "Where Things Can Happen" 154).

Steinbeck's achievement can be understood to have been partly predicated on his ability to interrelate literature and science—two traditionally oppositional cognitive and intellectual disciplines—and to traverse the otherwise contested "permeable boundaries" between the two discourses, so as to mutually inform "their interaction" within our culture (Scholnick 3; Barthes 4; Browne 58–59). The importance and lasting effects of his involvement with Ricketts and the writing of *Sea of Cortez* cannot be overstated. Steinbeck's intertextual gambit, his discovery of "a great poetry in scientific thinking" (Fensch, *Steinbeck and Covici* 31; *SLL* 232), points up a paradox, because if Steinbeck's adoption of scientific elements in his writings puts him at risk with many established

Figure 11. Ed Ricketts (1897–1948), remarkable polymath and dedicated, innovative marine scientist who was Steinbeck's soul mate and prototype of *Cannery Row's* Doc, at the Monterey Bay coastline near Hopkins Marine Station, Pacific Grove, California. Courtesy of Martha Heasley Cox Center for Steinbeck Studies, San Jose State University.

literary critics and influential cultural tastemakers such as Edmund Wilson and Clifton Fadiman (McElrath, Crisler, Shillinglaw 183–87; 204–5; Benson, "Novelist as Scientist" 15), his "interdisciplinary habit of mind" may have been the very move, the definable "difference," that allowed Steinbeck to be "unique" by allowing him to appeal to a much wider reading public than many other fictionists of his time (Beegel, Shillinglaw, Tiffney 20; Railsback 7).

Steinbeck's admission, a kind of New Deal–inspired belief, that his "whole work drive has been aimed at making people understand each other" (*WD* xl) has relevance here once again, as do the affective dimensions of his preference for "symbol people" and "psychological sign language" (*JN* 27), as well as the far-reaching theoretical implications of considering his fiction as being essentially fabular (French and Kidd 199; Jones, *Fabulist* 10–11), which is to say, considering his texts as participatory parables that aim "to involve the reader in the story and to make the story live in the reader" (Timmerman 7). "The Word" does indeed "suck up" everything on *Cannery Row*/Cannery Row (108), including its readers, so that the place we have arrived at is not an absolute destination, but a way station in the indeterminate border country between culture and nature, writing and speech, fiction and science. Reading *Cannery Row*, then, is nothing less than an entrance into "radically different systems" (*LSC* 868).

Even those of us who have participated in the discourse on and of Steinbeck, those of us who have been complicit in constructing an evolving narrative of cultural/literary identity, can still be challenged by the places Steinbeck traveled to in his effort to uncover a nonhierarchical, related field, a place where everything is an index of everything else, and *Cannery Row*'s "poem and the stink and the grating noise—the quality of light, the tone, the habit and the dream—" can be effectively "set down alive" (102). But the real challenge now is to revise our portrait of Steinbeck the humanist, the social chronicler, the popular icon, to include Steinbeck the quantum mechanic, Steinbeck the conceptual thinker, Steinbeck the metaphorist, Steinbeck the ecologist. Fifty years ago, who would have thought it?

Chapter 3
Private Narratives/Public Texts

Steinbeck's Writing Journals

One can read a poem or a novel without coming to know its author,
look at a painting and fail to get a sense of its painter;
but one cannot read a diary and feel unacquainted with its writer.

—THOMAS MALLON, *A Book of One's Own* (1984)

It is a great deal to say of a writer that he lived for writing. Steinbeck did.

—ANTHONY BURGESS, *But Do Blondes Prefer Gentlemen?* (1986)

I

John Steinbeck was addicted to writing. It is no exaggeration to claim that, in the annals of twentieth-century American fiction, few writers have been as assiduous, obsessive, and even monomaniacal about recording the intricately related elements of their compositional practices and writerly predilections as John Steinbeck. This stems, I think, from his preference for the ritual—almost totemic—process of writing, rather than from his possessiveness about the number of books he produced.[1] He trained himself for the most part to look past the editorial, commercial, and critical reception of any given work as his preferred way to keep his eye on the day-to-day effort of inscription. Repeatedly, when a book was finished, rather than dwell on it he moved to the next project. He might be saddened for a while after the book was done, because it was a "little death" when it was over, but even in his "sadness" (*SLL* 523) he was already imagining the next one, whatever that might be. "When there isn't a book either being written or planned," he confessed to Webster Street in 1939, "I have very little life left, feel a little like a shortage of oxygen" (quoted in Shillinglaw, *Carol and John Steinbeck* 210). It was a pronounced pattern of withdrawal and engagement that he went through for decades and never out-grew. When he did start the next book he experienced the same emotional and psychological roller coaster between despair and optimism, self-doubt and confidence, sloth and energy, all over again. In large measure, the dedicated daily writing stint was his life. He told Caskie Stinnett in 1963, "Writing is a sort of nervous tic with me. I would go crazy if I didn't write" (*CJS* 85), and keeping a daily record of his writing progress was paramount to aiding and abetting his compositional endeavors.

Steinbeck wrote prodigiously in "warm up" notebooks, which he variously called "day books," "diary day books," "warm up books," or "work books," that were companion texts to his novels.[2] He explained his habit to Elaine Scott, his soon-to-be third wife, in 1949: "When I am working it is good to write a page [in a journal] before going to work. It both resolves the day things that might be distracting and warms up my pen the way a pitcher warms up. It's a matter of long practice" (*SLL* 380). These personal entries were not drafts or practice pages of the novel he was working on, but were designed as separate private accounts to record the myriad aspects of his life outside the planned book. Putting the peripheral material in his work journals allowed him—for the most part anyway—to keep the nagging, distracting day-to-day elements out of his fiction. Instead, they went into a "scapegoat book," as he called his unpublished 1946–1947 diary (101).

Steinbeck, an otherwise deeply conflicted, restless, moody, and sometimes angry and gruff—often depressed—man, was happiest when he was writing, even when he was assailing himself, often frequently, for his lack of ability. He confessed in a 1957 essay called "Rationale": "I feel good when I am doing it [writing], better than when I am not. I find joy in the texture and tone and rhythms of words and sentences, and when these happily combine in a 'thing' that has texture and tone and emotion and design and architecture, there comes a fine feeling—a satisfaction like that which follows good and shared love. If there have been difficulties and failures overcome, these may even add to the satisfaction" (*AASN* 161). As he told first-time novelist Denis Murphy, Salinas native and prodigal son of a family friend, that same year, "Your only weapon is your work. . . . After you have finished let the sons of bitches have it but while you are doing it for God's sake, keep your holy loneliness" (*Your Only Weapon* [15]).

As a way of finding a holy loneliness, Steinbeck sought "home" all his life.

Elaine Steinbeck told me on several occasions that he could only work when his writing space was just right. Susan Shillinglaw rightly claims that he needed a "skein of associations linking place, artistic creation, companionship, and security" (*Carol and John Steinbeck* 210). Beyond that, he tended to identify home as the place where "the books are kept"; that is, where he read and wrote (*SLL* 798). Writing in its most capacious sense, which is to say his pursuit of a life/identity/career in letters, was the deeply engaging residence—the intellectual habitation and creative imaginarium, the lived-in mental architecture—that Steinbeck longed for and tried to dwell in during most of his career. As one tied to the world through words (*SLL* 626), Steinbeck's writing engendered a home space of deep "association" that stemmed from "the connection between mind and being and the place inhabited,...that holy gorge where the echoes sounded, not with hollowness but rising and falling, clear and clean," as he wrote on January 9, 1946, in the first paragraph of his *Wayward Bus* journal, which he titled "My personal book"(1). Working at writing, he confessed months later, was "the only way I am ever reasonably happy" (121).

Most of the time, his journals constituted a private realm where he indulged personality, whereas his fiction created a public space where he shed personality. "Writing to me is deeply personal, even a secret function," he told fellow novelist John O'Hara in 1949, "and when the product is turned loose it is cut off from me and I have no sense of its being mine" (*SLL* 360). Both interior and exterior realms were necessary for a complete, transactional view of his art, and they provide "fertile fields for revelatory response, rather than barren ground of dead-end discourse" Cecilia Donohue claims (36). Steinbeck spoke of these working matters frequently in his voluminous correspondence and occasional publications but nowhere concentrated on them more exclusively than in his writing journals. From the early 1930s onward, beginning with *To a God Unknown* and extending through the early 1960s with *Travels with Charley*, Steinbeck kept at the very least a partial and passing record of nearly every one of his major writing projects (especially his novels), though in the case of those two works just mentioned, as well as *The Pastures of Heaven*, *Of Mice and Men*, *The Red Pony*, some of the stories of *The Long Valley*, *Sea of Cortez*, and *Travels with Charley*, he apparently lost interest in the diary portion of his ledger book and put all his energy into the primary work at hand instead.[3]

Nonetheless, at least three times in Steinbeck's life—in 1938, 1946, and 1951—as he wrote *The Grapes of Wrath* (1939), *The Wayward Bus* (1947), and *East of Eden*

(1952), respectively, Steinbeck's habitual self-reflection manifested itself in sustained composition journals, which can be considered "blueprint[s] for creativity" (Donohue 36). In fact, John Steinbeck performed something unique among writers. On at least three separate occasions, he wrote two related books at once: *The Grapes of Wrath* and *Working Days*; *East of Eden* and *The Journal of a Novel*; and *The Wayward Bus* and a 30,000-word companion text "My personal book," as yet unpublished.[4] Agatha TeMaat's claim that his "journals and ledgers . . . reveal as much about Steinbeck's practice of writing and his theory about writing as they illuminate his art" is both accurate and prophetic (7). "It seems necessary to write things down," he confessed as he launched a new day journal—"Can't stop it" (*WD* 5). E. L. Doctorow's claim about Herman Melville applies: Steinbeck, too, was nothing less than a "writing fool," a point not lost on Jay Parini, a novelist himself and a Steinbeck biographer, who claimed "Steinbeck was a writer to the bone" (xiv).

From a writerly vantage point, the importance of these journals cannot be overestimated. In the first entry, written November 24, 1946, of an unpublished 1946–1947 notebook, much of which was devoted to personal commentary about drafting a play called "The Last Joan," Steinbeck said his "interminable notebooks" serve to "warm me up and some times to cool me down. There is a rhythm to work just as there is to football or baseball and a little free throwing is good before the work starts" (1). The ledgers allowed him to prepare each day for the writing task at hand by exorcising as many destructive "nibbling" (his word) elements as possible; allowed his handwriting to settle down to a comfortable, rhythmic flow; allowed him to control the size of his script to insure a sense of concentration and intensity and discipline of thought; allowed him to plan the day's allotment of words (usually 2,000 in approximately 4 hours of writing each day) and to picture the direction of the novel's plot, including its scenic details and elements of characterization; allowed him to build up a mental toughness to combat his inveterate intellectual and creative laziness; and perhaps most importantly allowed him to enter what he called in his *Wayward Bus* journal the "creative zone," or the "work dream." This he defined as "almost an uncommon state where one feels the story all over one's body and the details come flooding in like water and the story trudges by like many children" ("Mpb" 7). In other words, he sought for a focused, perhaps even trancelike space in which he felt close to the sources of his story, his characters, their ways of talking and acting, and his own process of writing. He sought, William Souder says, to make his characters "full partners" in the imagined venture (*Mad* 308).

"In this era of self-reflection," Carol Edgarian and Tom Jenks write, "the diary—the ultimate book of self—may be more compelling than ever" (xii). So compelling that there must have been something narcotic about the feeling, for Steinbeck invoked it almost daily, year in, year out, through dozens of books. Gwyn Steinbeck, who often watched her husband as he wrote during that era, thought writing was "John's kind of drug." Once he began to work, she claimed, he was oblivious to everything "other than that pen in his hand, and he did nothing but write with incredible speed. When he finished he was like someone coming out of hypnosis" ("Closest Witness" 258).

Treating Steinbeck's journalizing as a habitual tic necessary to the technology of his novel writing, rather than as a coopted or anomalous venture, allows insights into Steinbeck's self-created authorial biography—that elusive entity approaching what scholar Leigh Gilmore has, in a different connection, handily called "autobiographics" (5). Steinbeck wasn't explicitly embarked on a project of confessional "life writing" in these journal texts, but even so in each one he manages to fashion a self-revealing and dramatic (though often piecemeal and covert) inside narrative that historicizes three different eras in his creative and personal life. Even in their occasionally purposely obscure "Pepysian shorthand" style of notation (*SLL* 380), these work diaries enable our understanding of and appreciation for his total career, his driving impulses, desires, and methods as a writer, and the content of his daily life. In *The Hidden Writer*, Alexandra Johnson says: "In the search for creative blueprints . . . writers read the diaries of those who preceded them. . . . In these diaries the link between the fabric of the life and the work is studied like a puzzle by the writers themselves and by the generations of readers and writers they've spawned" (12–13). At the very least, no matter whatever else is to be gleaned from Steinbeck's journals, attending to them nudges us toward a deeper understanding of and a fuller investment in what novelist Jane Smiley has called the linked "reading and writing life" (30).

But generally speaking, ruminating on aspects of a work in progress was intended privately for his eyes alone, or to a single imagined audience/addressee: Carlton Sheffield for his *To a God Unknown* jottings; Ed Ricketts for (and dedicatee of) *Cannery Row*; Pascal Covici for *East of Eden* and its journal; Chase Horton, then Eugene Vinaver, for his *Acts of King Arthur* letters (*SLL* 528; 590). Prewriting rituals, then, were his normal mode of procedure, his familiar way of entering into the authorial contract with himself and cozying up to his material, most of which, more than likely, he had planned out elaborately in his head, as he revealed to Robert van Gelder (*CJS* 44), or had tried to picture in a series of detailed images before actually beginning his writing labors. "And now I'm ready to go to work and I am glad to get into other lives and escape from mine for a while," he confessed on June 16, 1938, as he was starting chapter eight of *The Grapes of Wrath* (*WD* 28).

Thomas Mallon claims photographer Edward Weston's *Daybooks* "are servants of his art, never ends in themselves" (153), and in Steinbeck's case this is mostly true but needs qualification. Steinbeck's priority was the primary text, the novel of record (which is the product his publisher bought). But in order to reach the saleable text, the marketable product, he had to enter it through the regulating presence and discipline of his daily journal. "If the process follows its usual line," he wrote on January 10, 1946, in his *Wayward Bus* journal, "the writing in this book [the journal] will grow less and in the other book [the novel manuscript] it will grow more. It shouldn't take more than two or three days of doodling to get into shape" ("Mpb" 5). Doodling, a form of creative play, ludic exercise, and daydreaming, eventually led Steinbeck through the door of the anteroom and into the main house of fiction.[5]

II

Steinbeck's journal labors are indispensably linked to his novel-writing. These three sustained workbooks under consideration here reveal a totemic, even fetishistic, attitude toward writing. "Now there are the symbols for calling the power—good ink, good paper and a fine smooth pen and these I have" ("Mpb" 3). According to Gwyn, Steinbeck was a "nester" ("Closest Witness" 80), and among his lifelong quests was the need to be comfortably situated in sequestered privacy before he wrote, preferably in a small room without distracting scenic views, situated away from the main activities of the household, a site not always available to him, especially in midtown Manhattan in the mid-1940s. Steinbeck wrote each of these extended inside narratives while married to a different woman—Carol (1930–1943), Gwyn (1943–1948), and Elaine (1950–1968), respectively—as he was writing *The Grapes of Wrath*, *The Wayward Bus*, and *East of Eden*. Each novel showed the influence of his wife at the time, though in varying degrees and qualities. Steinbeck's accompanying work diaries are colored by the emotional and marital dynamic of the three different domestic households.

Every detail no matter how large or small of mental disposition and physical attitude, the kind and quality of his writing room; position of his pen's slant on the page; kind, number, and quality of writing instruments; seating arrangement; quality of paper; as well as uncontrollable effects such as weather, exterior noise, his spouse's attitude and behavior, encroachments by neighbors, degrees and kinds of interruption——all these protocols, fetishes, instigations, and disruptions are duly, obsessively noted as much to indicate the chaos and turmoil that threatened to unhinge his equilibrium, as they were to challenge those forces by writing through them, hoping to subdue them in the name of discipline or willpower, what he termed "a matter of Prussian force to break through the mind tide and submerge deep in the creative zone" in his *Wayward Bus* diary ("Mpb" 31). None of these elements can be considered trivial or frivolous insofar as they are an indisputable part of the daily reality of Steinbeck's writing life. It was a writing life he approached like a "fanatic," according to Tetsumaro Hayashi in his essay "The Art and Craft of Writing" (274, 280).

During the hours of work, Steinbeck claimed, all distractions "must disappear for a while leaving nothing but the paper and the writer and there is nothing here that discipline cannot accomplish" ("Mpb" 5). All in all, these mundane, compulsively recorded concrete details provide a "thick description," to use anthropologist Clifford Geertz's borrowed phrase (6–7) for the journals' interior drama, and the overall arc of change Steinbeck underwent in a thirteen-year period from 1938 to 1951. In fact, it is tempting to say that a completely different writer created *East of Eden* than the one who had created *The Grapes of Wrath*, and those changes, swerves, and divigations are apparent not only in the style, purpose, and texture of the novels, but in his recording journals as well.

Steinbeck's efforts in these projects have given American literature an intriguing new area in which the private and public records are not just parallel but in fact intersect. The journals are not just ancillary and incidental but can actually function as independent documents. Steinbeck created a kind of subgenre—the journal of compositional procedure, or the narrative of creative literacy—that provides a window into his complex scene of writing and indicates a tantalizing relatedness between process and product. Howard Junker's introduction to *The Writer's Notebook* puts a finger squarely on what is at stake: writers' notebooks, Junker claims, "provide necessary evidence that writing is a process, often an arduous, mysterious one. And that it is a process that can be followed along many different paths" (94).

Each of the three major journals has a different tone and mirrors the overall feel of the novel to which it is linked. *Working Days* has an embattled "headlong" air (*JN* 68). Both Steinbeck and the Joads are "battered by uncertainties" but keep plugging resolutely on, spurred by what wife Carol thought was his deep love for the migrant characters and his admiration for "the people who are so much stronger and purer and braver than I am" (*WD* 36). His *Wayward Bus* journal evidences a deep-seated psychic dislocation, emotional fragmentation, and "defeatist" tone ("Mpb" 103) that infected the novel and resulted in one of Steinbeck's least critically successful, most brittle fictions: "What is this book but a kind of treatise on the ruthlessness of nature as it is distilled through the human" ("Mpb" 61)? *Journal of a Novel*, the last in the series, has a comparatively leisurely and ruminative pace much like *East of Eden*, one of whose pronounced themes was moral and philosophical acceptance. The journals clearly indicate intentionality and authorial determination, yet also tell us that the novels' texts are not autonomous but are linked to a web of circumstances, some personal and self-willed, some worldly and imposed, some conscious, some unconscious. They signify Steinbeck's position in a negotiated middle ground between willful agency and determined construction., between individual authority and a welter of contextual "flags and tatters" (*SLL* 591).

Furthermore, each of these full-fledged composition texts was written as Steinbeck worked on novels in which a journey, literal and/or symbolic, drove each novel's plot so that the travels of his fictive characters—the Joads, for instance, in *Grapes of Wrath*, or Juan Chicoy and his pilgrims in *The Wayward Bus*—were reflected in and by the "plot" of his own creativity journey. In this analogous, dialogic sense, then, besides raising issues of power, desire, identity, and authority, both composed texts share (perhaps mirror is a better word) similar aspects of travail, hardship, reversals, and arrival, which in most cases provides a paradoxical resolution at best.

"Diaries," Alexandra Johnson claims, "also chart the underside of a writer's life" (13), and far from trafficking in naive notions of artistic genius, divine inspiration, transcendent visionary experience, more than likely they grapple with mundane issues of "work, money, family, success, rejection and exposure" (*The Hidden Writer* 7). The scene of Steinbeck's writing in all three moments took place under similar conditions in which he was writing a book, and writing a book about the writing of that book, while some furious house-building labor (either a neighbor's or his own, and sometimes both) was going on around him. This was the situation at Greenwood Road in Los Gatos when he was married to Carol and writing *The Grapes of Wrath*; at his newly purchased and renovated duplex brownstone on 175 East 78th Street in Manhattan, when he was married to Gwyn and writing *The Wayward Bus*; and in a four-story brick house at 206 East 72nd Street also in Manhattan, when he was newly hitched to Elaine and writing *East of Eden*. (The Steinbecks sold that house in 1963 and moved to the top floor of a tower apartment at 190 East 72nd street that year.)

Steinbeck's house anxiety and his need to be comfortably settled provided an additional harried backdrop to his writing and a kind of refrain that echoes through these three journals. His concerns indicate that these intratextual works can be considered cohabitational houses of fiction or textual imaginariums that, temporarily anyway, became his true mental house and home. The composition diaries themselves document the inescapable materiality of writing and emphasize the naked effects of mental endurance, hard work, sweat, and willpower Steinbeck drew upon to combat the usual and even predictable assaults of fear, anxiety, and failure, as well as the eternal yo-yo of self-confidence—though not without occasional moments of pure inspiration and, it should be noted, some prayerful beseechment thrown in: "ora pro nobis" ("Mpb" 33), he penned on May 1, 1946, as he embarked on his first day of writing *The Wayward Bus*.

III

Working Days, the posthumously published journal of the composition of *The Grapes of Wrath* and its controversial aftermath, covers the period from early 1938 through early 1941, but the center of the work is the group of 100 entries Steinbeck inscribed between late May 1938 and late October 1938, when he was doing his near-daily stint on what would turn out to be his most famous novel. Beyond what the diary tells us about the writer's large plan and artistic hope for the novel itself, *Working Days* is also the first complete, sustained daybook Steinbeck ever produced: "Here is the diary of a book and it will be interesting to see how it works out. I have tried to keep diaries before but they don't work. …In this …I shall try simply to keep a record of working days and the amount done in each and the success (as far as I can know it) of the day" (19–20).

Steinbeck "gloated" about an oversize 10" × 16" ledger book he bought at a bookstore in San Jose for a dollar and reveled in "its most wonderful paper in the world" (quoted in Shillinglaw, *On Reading* 2). The novel itself—unnamed until early September 1938, and then named by Carol—eventually took up the first 165 pages of the ledger. The novel portion of his manuscript was published recently in full-size facsimile by SP Books, a French publisher that specializes in facsimile editions of important literary texts. At the back of his "big book" Steinbeck made his near-daily entries, covering pages 361 through 372, then pages 336 through 349, and, finally, after turning back the ledger, from pages 300 through page 309. The result, John Timmerman says, is "an interior monograph, a vivisection of the author's soul" (61).

The warm-up book as a quiet, introspective, grass-growing mode of inscription quickly became something more complex and contested than simply a running record of Steinbeck's daily word count (he aimed for 2,000 a day), and in fact by the ninth entry, on June 8, 1938, Steinbeck realized: "This is the longest diary I ever kept. Not a diary of course but an attempt to map the actual working days and hours of a novel" (*WD* 23). The document, Professor Shillinglaw claims, becomes "muscular and determined," with Steinbeck going into "overdrive, his personality subsumed by the book itself" (*On Reading* 33). This exercise in private reflection on a public discourse became a model and a touchstone for Steinbeck's similar later endeavors. In fact, *Working Days* seemed to have fulfilled such a niche in his creative life as an experiment in discipline, as a contested site of writing, and as a reflection of his interior attentiveness, that he often returned to reread its hand-written manuscript as a reminder of what kind of disruptions could be endured when he was temporarily stymied by later writing, and also as a vindication of the fact that he always somehow managed to finish most of his major projects, even if he had to muddle through to reach the end zone. In this way, his diary provided a kind of uplifting cheerleading function, or a way of giving himself a good talking-to that would galvanize his efforts and spur him on.

For example, in the eighty-fifth entry, on October 4, 1938, in the middle of an embattled period when he was beginning to wrestle with the final five chapters of *Grapes*, he said:

> And now all the foolishness and the self-indulgence is over. Now there can be no lost days and no lost time. Straight through to the finish now without loss. It must be that way. And I shall do it. . . . My laziness is

Figure 12. The Grapes of Wrath journal, June 27–30, 1938. (Transcriptions of these entries appear in *Working Days*, pp. 34–37). Courtesy of The Morgan Library and Museum, MA 4684.

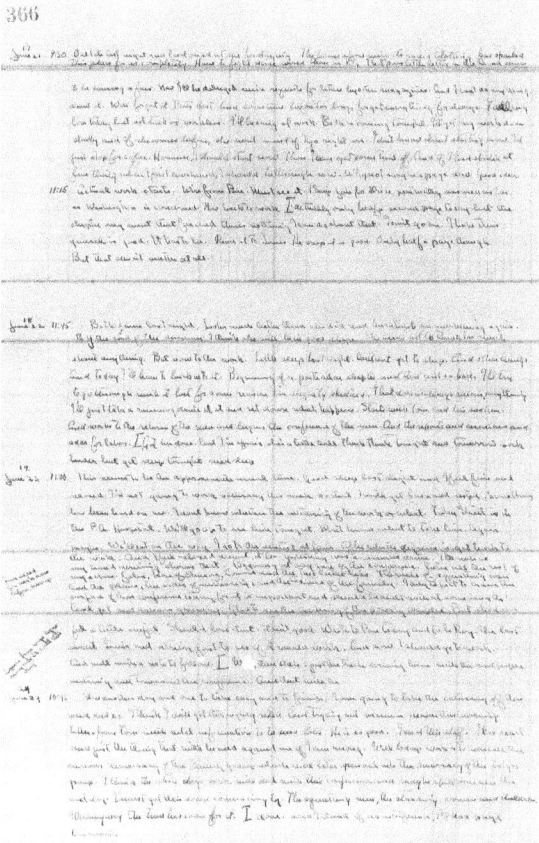

overwhelming. I must knock it over. Don't feel right about it if I don't.... And this must be a drive to the end. And now I'll read a little of the early diary and then plunge in. This time it is a GO signal and a real one. I've been looking back over this diary and, by God, the pressures were bad the whole damned time. There wasn't a bit that wasn't under pressure and now the pressure is removed and I'm still having trouble.... Now forget the end and just go gradually to work. So long, diary. (Finished). (*WD* 81–82)

If the work journal helped him clear a mental space for himself each day and gave him a focus for his own energy and a lever for engaging his all-important will (at least in the limited domain of his writing), it also allowed him to participate in the interior dimensions of his imagined world.

Working Days (and the other two journals of making) indicate that, whether he was aware of it or not, Steinbeck's own personal, emotional, and psychological states inevitably found their way into his characters, colored individual scenes and events, and even exerted pressure on the plot sequence of *The Grapes of Wrath*. Moreover, *Grapes* and its companion journal reflects and embodies Steinbeck's preferred technique, which was to alternate epic fictive narrative with more localized writerly narratives, thus creating an intratextual dance between fiction and nonfiction, novel and essay, public and private, social and psychic realms:

> Yesterday . . . I went over the whole of the book in my head—fixed on the last scene, huge and symbolic, toward which the whole story moves. And that was a good thing, for it was a reunderstanding of the dignity of the effort and the mightyness of the theme. I felt very small and inadequate and incapable but I grew again to love the story which is so much greater than I am. To love and admire the people who are so much stronger and purer and braver than I am. (*WD* 36)

Three instances among many demonstrate this generic fluidity and hybrid transportation between text and context. The first occurred on June 16, 1938, when Steinbeck wrote a full-page entry, including this:

> I dreamed a confused mess made up of Dad and his failures and me and my failures. Some way connected to the store. Poor Dad couldn't run a store, he didn't know how. And I used to eat pies at noon hour and was ashamed of selling things. No mercantile ability in either of us and the store failed and left a terrible mark on Dad. . . . And now I am ready to go to work and I am glad to get into other lives and escape from mine for awhile. Yesterday the used car lot and today Tom and Casy go home to the family. (*WD* 28)

Steinbeck didn't entirely escape his own life, but it carried into *The Grapes of Wrath* novel. Is it mere coincidence or is there something of direct import going on that this diary entry came at the moment Steinbeck was writing chapter eight, when the dream of John Ernst Steinbeck's mercantile failure found its way into his son's description of Uncle John? Uncle John Joad is powerless to prevent the death of his wife, for which he feels responsible, and because of it he remains a haunted man throughout the novel, another of its cast of male characters, like Tom Joad's father, who are diminished in embarrassing ways by circumstances in the eyes of their familial children.

The second transpersonal moment occurs in Steinbeck's desire to buy the fifty-acre Biddle Ranch on Brush Road in Los Gatos in the summer of 1938. This event may have influenced his insertion of the general chapter fourteen—the famous passage on Manself and the movement from I to We—earlier in the novel than he had originally planned. Perhaps Steinbeck hoped that by writing this section of the novel at the moment of his and Carol's greatest desire for a new home it might become a means of exorcizing his own capitalist tendencies, a timely, mindful warning to the dangers of accumulating too much personal property, even at a period when he was glad to see Carol breaking out of the poverty mentality. Then again, perhaps Steinbeck was bouncing off himself the felt needs of his characters' hunger for land of their own. In any event, it is difficult to imagine that Steinbeck failed to see the irony in writing on the same day (July 15, 1938) in one area of his ledger book: "And yesterday we saw the most beautiful [ranch] I have ever seen. I want that ranch. We'll try to get it. Carol wants it too" (*WD* 42); and this in the novel section of the same ledger book: "For the quality of owning freezes you forever into 'I,' and cuts you off forever from the 'we'" (371). One of the great silences among many in Steinbeck's journal is his lack of commentary on this striking dilemma, this paradoxical inconsistency and discontinuity between private acquisitiveness and public realms of community.

Finally, there is a remarkable epiphany very late in *The Grapes of Wrath* work journal, on the ninety-seventh day, October 20, 1938, when Steinbeck, physically and mentally weary and berating himself unmercifully that his book "isn't the great book I had hoped it would be" (*WD* 90), entered a liminal "psychic" zone where journal and novel, process and product, his life and the life of his main character, Tom Joad, intersected with each other and merged, however briefly: "'Tom! Tom! Tom!' I know. It wasn't him. Yes, I think I can go on now. In fact, I feel stronger. Funny where the energy comes from. Now to work only now it isn't work any more" (*WD* 91). Energized, Steinbeck finished his novel in three

Figure 13. John and Carol Steinbeck bought the "most beautiful" Biddle Ranch on Brush Road in Los Gatos, CA, in August 1938, built a new house on the grounds, and lived there until 1940. Photograph ca. 1939 by unknown person. Courtesy of Martha Heasley Cox Center for Steinbeck Studies, San Jose State University.

days. Later, he confessed to having "visitations so definite that I don't see how I can imagine them" (*WD* 126).

In that epiphanic, even mystical moment Steinbeck not only drew on, but actually merged text and context, married private and public realms, transgressed the boundaries of genre difference and prose distinctions, into the mutually participatory transtextuality (Genette 1). In reaching this stage of his double-voiced metanarrative, Steinbeck entered the elusive "fifth layer" of *The Grapes of Wrath* (*SLL* 178), the final, deepest strata of involvement that turns out to be the most private of dimensions, the interior space of artful consciousness where, when the looker looks, the gaze is returned. Such a pattern of generative and empathic investment might not have been possible without the deep, compulsive, almost narcissistic attentiveness Steinbeck paid to his own writerly procedures inscribed in his daybooks. Indeed, *Working Days* became a touchstone, model, and reference point on writerly conduct for the remainder of Steinbeck's artistic life.

IV

In *American Diary Literature, 1620–1799* Stephen Kagle says "the life of a diary is often born of tension, a disequilibrium in the life of its author, which needs to be resolved or held in check" (17). He might have had Steinbeck's next project in mind: *The Wayward Bus*, published by Viking Press in February 1947. To get from *The Grapes of Wrath* (1939) to *East of Eden* (1952), Steinbeck had to pass through the slough of despond. His journey through "a period of blue despair" (*TAJS* 577) is thematized in his unpublished 1946 *Wayward Bus* journal, a 9.5" × 11" bound ledger that he dubbed "My personal book."

The immediate goal of his writing, he claimed at the outset on January 9, 1946, was to recover a primal experience when he had "heard the thundering and seen the flash which must have been the universe at work. In that participation there was a glory that shadows everything else. . . . I know the way and the means and the symbol and the magical method. And what I must do is to invoke it again this year and to listen closely for the thundering. If it comes, even faintly—everything will be well. And if it doesn't come at all—if the great pictures do not form, then I will accept that but I must know whether I have the power or not" ("Mpb" 3). It was not for nothing Gwyn thought he was "a driven man" ("Closest Witness" 256).

This journal is a fairly harrowing and painful and not entirely flattering account of his life in 1946 as he struggled to write first a play-novelette called "The War and San Pedro," which he abandoned in January 1946 after ten days of writing; then, after a three-month hiatus, he turned his attention to his main project *The Wayward Bus*, which he started on May 1 and finished on September 24, 1946 (with time off from June 18 to July 10), and whose fifty-three entries (written on the recto, odd-numbered side of sixty-two different lined ledger pages) make up the bulk of his journalizing efforts. He launched his new novel by rereading his previous journal. "Yesterday I read parts of the daybook of the Grapes and it was the same thing, the worry, the insecurity, the lack of knowledge and coordination. Only then I overcame it. Remains to see whether I can again. And I think I will start the same kind of daybook. Time of starting, time of finishing, story notes and whether the daily work was completed. . . . Also the number of working days should be stressed. . . . Only by putting a kind of military conscience on myself will I be able to get into this and get it done" ("Mpb" 29).

The "My personal book" journal is extremely revealing about Steinbeck's writerly self concept and his compulsive mode of operation. We hear his usual complaints of being a fraud and a "charlatan": "My work has been taken seriously out of all proportion to its worth so that I feel I have been cheating in some ways," he confessed on January 9, 1946 ("Mpb" 1)—a verbatim sentiment recorded in *Working Days* eight years earlier. We also hear about his lack of confidence and talent—"I am not a great writer but I am a competent one" ("Mpb" 23)—as well as much more on his obsessive protocols, such as size of hand writing, fluidity of ink, sharpness of pencils, comfortableness of work station, and the like, which he admitted half humorously "are only important if they seem so and if they work" ("Mpb" 19). Biographer Jay Parini is correct in claiming that Steinbeck "had a strong attraction to the paraphernalia of writing: pencils, pads, ledgers, erasers" (304). Such items helped define him by adding an extra cushioning dimension to his writing process.

After obtaining a recording machine on January 28, 1946 (*TAJS* 584; Simmonds, "Composition" 331), he spun off a longish commentary on the advantages of dictating his work rather than writing by hand, as was his custom. Dictating, he believed, allowed him to emphasize the sound and the rhythm of spoken not literary language, Steinbeck reveals that a key part of his composition process was creating sharp pictures in his head (there are references to that visualization in *Working Days*). He goes on to say he even wants to try working in "pitch darkness" wearing a blinder because his mind pictures "should be surprisingly clear then" and "with the blackness of blindness around, there should be nothing to distract from the mind picture. These things are to be experimented with secretly and never to be told until after and then only if the method is successful. . . . This might be the first of a completely new method of composition" ("Mpb" 23–25). The mind pictures formed more quickly than he was able to write them down, causing a regrettable lag time.

Perhaps Steinbeck's critically acclaimed visual ability, however, his excellence in describing landscape, for instance, may have its source in this innate visual sensibility. Regarding dictating, however, he did not at first indulge in this unusual new method of speaking his sentences and dialogue directly into a machine, though he did record his novel manuscript after it was first written down with pen and paper. He then played the recording back to judge the proper sound and rhythm of what he had written. Corrections followed and were spoken onto a new disc for transcription at Viking. Pat Covici came to

Steinbeck's house and listened to recordings on a few occasions and liked what he heard. The resulting two dozen *Wayward Bus* recording discs, equal to about twelve hours of talk, were transcribed by a stenographer (*CJS* 45; *TAJS* 589).[6]

One thing is certain—Steinbeck never achieved the necessary comfort and succor he was used to getting from his writing totems and contrivances. Where in *Working Days* Steinbeck was often able to accommodate his shortcomings and cushion his self-doubts and anxieties, here in "My personal book" there is a constant note of edginess, uncenteredness, and despair: "Couldn't sleep last night," he wrote on January 24, 1946, "and awoke in the dark in mental unease and half despair. Then thought of the series of luck. Enough money to live beyond any imagining, respected in my profession, not much work, a beautiful wife and a beautiful child. A certain amount of fame, many friends. And still with that despair in my heart. There seems to be no connection between one's feelings and reality. Perhaps it is all glandular irregularity" ("Mpb" 17).

Again, after he abandoned "The War and San Pedro" in January, he lamented: "Now I have doodled about for four months and have arrived at nothing. Nerves shut in a state of abysmal depression. Last night a kind of psychic anesthesia and coming out of it in a depression like a post alcoholic let down . . ." ("Mpb" 29). Thinking his "jumpy" nerves and constant "stomach ache" were caused by too much caffeine, he stopped drinking coffee for two weeks and thought about taking "pills" (unspecified, but probably a downer like Dexadrine) to quiet his unease and quell discomfort. Still later, he confessed to being "shriveled up inside" ("Mpb" 35, 95). His roller-coaster emotions lent the work journal a fragmented, stop-and-start tempo, and furthermore in the various unhappy portraits of marriage and connubial existence in the novel and in his attempts at psychosomatic interpretations of his characters Steinbeck seems to have projected a distinctly bitter personal, even misogynistic coloration to that text as well.[7]

In addition, this work journal records his physical displacement and transience, a far different situation from his comparative rootedness when he was writing *The Grapes of Wrath* in Los Gatos. Here, Steinbeck tries writing at home, first on 37th Street where they were living in late 1945 and early 1946, then in an unheated bedroom at Viking Press President Harold Guinzburg's house, then in his agent Mildred Lyman's apartment at the Bedford Hotel on East 40th Street, then in several different areas of the 175 East 78th Street duplex they had bought that spring, both houses of which were being renovated. (The

Figure 14. Robert Capa recorded Steinbeck at work in one of his ledgers, ca. late 1940s. This photo appeared on the front dust jacket of Viking Press' first edition of *Working Days: The Journals of The Grapes of Wrath*. Used by permission of International Center for Photography/Magnum Photos.

Steinbecks planned to live in one half and rent out the other, with the rental income going to Gwyn.)

He liked being squirreled away in his unadorned basement work area (Parini 297), but with the remodeling going on, being settled in at home was not always a comfortable fit or an easy way to find his holy loneliness. In mid-July, after a hiatus of nearly a month when he did no writing at all, he moved at Pat Covici's urging to a quiet, vacant, and air-conditioned office at Viking Press (Simmonds, "Composition" 338), but even there the strain of lament, bordering on anger, permeates the diary, and I should add, the novel as well. In the final push to finish the novel, he worked again at home. Working in the top-floor bedroom on the day he completed *The Wayward Bus* he complained that the "fucking noise is dreadful. It is a little like working in a boiler factory. I was probably wrong in trying to work at home. Ninety thousand dollars for a place to live and still no place to work" ("Mpb" 121).

From a biographical perspective Steinbeck's personal journal tells us a great deal about his disjointed existence at the time, but it does not completely solve the puzzle of its root cause. The upshot is that that period seems almost diametrically opposed to the life recorded in much of *Working Days*. His relationship with Carol was far from perfectly rosy, as Shillinglaw has so firmly established in *Carol and John Steinbeck*, but at least in creating *Grapes*, they had a shared sense of a kind of working partnership and an end to be achieved that gave their relations solidity and elevated purpose (200–201). With his second wife Gwyn, for whom he had divorced Carol, Steinbeck lacked that sense of solidity: "No one," he lamented late in his journal, "really cares whether I finish this book but me" (101). His harsh self-critical judgment extended to his recent publications as well: "The Moon [is Down], effective as it was, was no good and before that there was the stinking Bombs Away. The [Herald] Tribune pieces [World War II dispatches] were nothing. Cannery Row was better and not really good. Now I have to have a good book—maybe this is it and maybe not" ("Mpb" 101).

Mostly he worried about Gwyn's illnesses during her pregnancy and her difficult postpartum time after John IV was born on June 12, and then sometimes directly, sometimes covertly, he reveals very dark truths about his emotional life, his too-frequent drinking and consequent hangovers, his conflicted sense of fatherhood in trying to balance his uneven feelings toward infants Thom (a "really good and handsome" son) and John (whom he refers to as the "baby," but not by name), and his startling admission that "you cannot have children and books too . . . if you cannot throw out the children while the book is being written" ("Mpb" 109). Clearly, getting rid of one for the other was impossible for the Steinbecks at this point, a live-in nurse notwithstanding, and it contributed to festering tensions, resentments, and jealousies between them. Although he was at pains to mute or even deny its causes, tension was so severe that Steinbeck repeatedly commented on his aching (and later bleeding) stomach, and he noted without irony that when Gwyn "feels good my stomach ache goes away" ("Mpb" 49).[8]

Steinbeck took to religiously rating his daily mental and physical index on an ascending scale from one to five, surely one of the most compulsive behaviors of this otherwise inordinately compulsive person.

> 1 day
> Rating 1–5
> 1 being excellent
> 5 being lousy
> May 1—
> First real
> Work day.
> Phys chart 4
> Mental [chart] 3
> 8:20 [morning starting time]
> ("Mpb" 33)

Yet the turn toward quantifiable numerical self-analysis at the start of each day's effort is indicative of the depth of his confusion: "It is odd that as the book becomes clearer, my own life grows more confused. It is becoming dream like with under current forces in it that disturb me like nightmares" ("Mpb" 73). Even in this most private of scribblings he doesn't always explicitly name the sources of unrest, yet they hover throughout the diary like a miasma. In this project he never reached that innermost fold of the bulb as he had with his epiphany in *Working Days* and would again when he discovered the liberating importance of the Cain and Abel story and *timshel to East of Eden*.

Roy Simmonds's comment that the composition of *The Wayward Bus* "was painfully achieved" is completely accurate ("Composition" 346).[9] In his work diary, for September 1, 1946, Steinbeck summed up *The Wayward Bus* by calling it "a story of insecurities, of everybody's insecurities, and of dreams and unfulfillments" ("Mpb" 97), and it is not too much to suspect that his own radical "insecurities" and "sense of fear" about his marriage, parenthood, and finances (in January he had been presented with a $45,000 income-tax bill) contributed to his belief that *The Wayward Bus* is a "morose book" ("Mpb" 115). He wondered if it were "worthless" but decided there wasn't much he could do about it, even at the end. One thing is certain—and perhaps here we catch a glimpse of the novel's root cause of disappointment—Steinbeck never seems to have loved his characters in the way he loved and admired the Joads in *The Grapes of Wrath* or would come to love the Hamiltons and Cal Trask in *East of Eden*:

> These poor damned people. What will become of them[?] I made them with all their faults and I'm sending them out on the world. I don't know what will happen to them. . . . There is nothing else to do but finish it. I am sick to my stomach with nerves. . . . Finished at 10:30—September 24, 1946 and god help it. Now it's on its own and I won't be able to do much about it . . . I wonder whether it is any good. Now I may leave this book [diary] and get another or I may continue to use it. Just have to see. ("Mpb" 123)

There were moments in the middle passage of his writing stint that he thought the work was good, but his positive opinion faded as he went on. This summary assessment is among the many chilling self-critical comments Steinbeck was capable of making regarding his own novel-writing career. *The Wayward Bus* sold by the "extravagant" truckload (*Mad* 296), but the critics were right, he admitted later: it was a "paste up job" (Simmonds, "Composition" 328). Yet even at that, it remains another testament to his writerly perseverance. It was not for nothing that Gwyn, who did not always have flattering things to say about her ex-husband, admired "the greatness of his powers of concentration" ("Closest Witness" 258). Perhaps the best that can be said is that he got his work done and moved on, as he always did.

V

For better or for worse, a career writer is always on call. Four years later, Steinbeck's next efforts at sustained journalizing led him to keep three different daybooks—the main journal of composition we now know as *Journal of a Novel: The East of Eden Letters*, plus two other unpublished bound diaries to take care of the "outside things" (*JN* 28) that inevitably crept into his field of vision: one is an oversize 10" × 16" red-leather ledger, *The Year 1951*; the other is an 8½" by 11" blank book, *The Standard Diary for 1951*. These would be repositories for the "secret writing . . . I have no wish for anyone to see" (*JN* 10). This riot of self-scrutiny was instigated during Christmas Week 1950, when he once again came across the autograph manuscript of his *Grapes of Wrath* journal. He sent it to Pascal Covici, his Viking Press editor, with a letter that said:

> Very many times I have been tempted to destroy this book. It is an account very personal and in many instances purposely obscure. But recently I reread it and only after all this time did the unconscious pattern emerge. It is true that this book is full of my own weaknesses, of complaints.... But in rereading, those became less important and the times and the little histories seemed to be more apparent. (*WD*, xlvii)

Steinbeck had two requests: that the diary not be published in his lifetime, and that it be made available to his children if they should ever want to "look behind the myth and hearsay and flattery and slander a disappeared man becomes and to know to some extent what manner of man their father was." Of course it's interesting that he didn't feel the same way about his *Wayward Bus* journal, but nevertheless, Steinbeck's paternalism and nostalgia, aroused here in response to his rereading of his *Grapes of Wrath* daybook, found its way immediately and directly into the manuscript of *East of Eden*, which (though he had been planning since at least 1948) he only actually started to write a few scant weeks later, shortly after marrying his third wife, Elaine Scott, in late December 1950 and moving with her into a renovated four-story house at 206 East 72nd Street in Manhattan.

Just at the moment he seemed at last content to settle into life as a New Yorker, in an ideal domicile with a "pretty garden" and his own workroom (*SLL* 418), his first big hot-to-trot job was to write a novel about his native California. This prayerful entry on New Year's Day 1951, in one of his secondary diaries, states unequivocally what he believed to be at stake: "A really good life is pointing out ahead of me. All I have to do is be worth it to Elaine and Way [Waverly, Elaine's daughter] and the boys [Thom and John IV].... This year I must make a new start in writing but a very good new start. I want to do the Salinas Valley book this year and I want it to be good" (*The Year 1951 Diary*). He did not want to blow his chance at a new life. From the outset, as he wrote on January 30, 1951, it was his "intention to keep two day books. One for an exact statement of things done and intended externally and this big book for things planned and thought in relation to work" (*The Year 1951 Diary*). Everything was riding on the new book, he noted on February 12, 1951, his first day of novel-writing, because

Figure 15. Selection of John Steinbeck's journal day books, including *The Grapes of Wrath* journal and three from the 1951–1952 period. Courtesy of The Morgan Library and Museum, MA 4684, 4688, 4689, 4690.

he was going to approach it as though "it were my last book" and as though "there is nothing beyond this book" (*JN* 8).

Revisiting his *Grapes of Wrath* diary was so propitious that it is no exaggeration to claim Steinbeck partly conceived of the technique of *East of Eden*, with its alteration of intimate first-person fictional narrative and personal, discursive nonfictional interchapters as a natural carryover of his journalizing method, a novelistic attempt to extend the implications of his heretofore secret writings, his private autobiographics. This radical new irrealist writing, which is to say, writing in an expressive register that was a far cry from his traditional "objective" documentary style was a project in which the private, with his full consent and knowledge, would become the public. Moreover, Steinbeck was fully aware that his work journal might itself become a publishable document: it will be "much more a public book and that is the way it has to be. Since Pat is going to get it and since what he gets will be somewhat public this little baby should carry the privacies" (*The Year 1951 Diary*). Many years later, on July 14, 1965, he told his agent Elizabeth Otis: "When I was writing East of Eden, before each day's work as a kind of warm-up I kept a work diary . . . addressed to Pat. It is perhaps as complete a record of a book as has ever been done. But I had never seen it since I sent it off in handwriting. Pat and I often discussed publishing it either in conjunction with a complete and uncut E. of E. or by itself. . . . It is a fascinating account of the making of a book" (*SLL* 824).[10]

That Steinbeck had a special public fate in mind for his novel's journal may also have been corroborated by Andre Gide's mixed-genre novel, *The Counterfeitors*, which Steinbeck had lavishly praised the year before in a special 1951 issue of *La Nouvelle Revue Francaise*: "*The Counterfeitors* is one of the greatest books I have ever read. Simply because Gide knew how to write, because his mind knew how to explore . . . because he thought what he wanted to and gave form to his curiosities" ("Un Grande" [30]; *SR* 47, 149).

Gide's *Counterfeitors* mixes modes of discourse: fiction and notebook entries exist together and interpenetrate in a kind of ongoing mutually conversational, self-generating process. Gide writes through his character Edouard: "My note-book contains, as it were, a running criticism of my novel. . . . Just think how interesting such a note-book kept by Dickens or Balzac would be; if we had the diary of *Sentimental Education* or of *The Brothers Karamazov!*—the story of the work—of its gestation! How thrilling it would be . . . more interesting than the work itself." In the sense that *Journal of a Novel* is now considered a significant Steinbeck text, Gide's wish became reality. Jackson Benson suggests that *East of Eden*'s "unconscious companion" may be a "greater" book than the novel (691), but I disagree that the journal is an "unconscious companion"—rather, it reflects a high degree of literary self-consciousness that is prophetically postmodern in its portrayal of geographic place, the unpredictable effects of memory, and the slipperiness of authorial agency and fictive representation constructed through language:

> It is so strange what one writes down. And curious what one remembers. I suppose one remembers just what one wants to remember for his own safety and his own good. And if this is so, why should I not say it in a book? And I should and I will. Because a book—at least the kind of book I am writing—should contain everything that seems to me to be

true. There are few enough true things in the world. It would be a kind of sin to conceal any of them or to hide their little heads in technique as the squeamishness of not appearing in one's own book. For many years I did not occur in my writing. But this was only apparently true—I was in them every minute. But in this book I am in it and I don't for a moment pretend not to be. (*JN* 24)

In his original and far more spacious first-draft version, *East of Eden* was addressed directly to his young sons Thom and John IV, then seven and five years old. As with *The Grapes of Wrath* texts, this linked manuscript was written in another of Steinbeck's preferred blue-ruled oversize ledger books—11" × 14" in size—in which he composed almost daily from January 29, 1951, to November 1, 1951. Like *The Grapes of Wrath* ledger book, this too was another "double-entry" affair: on the left-hand page of the oversize ledger Steinbeck wrote his daily warm-up "letters" (each one addressed specifically to Pat Covici), and on the right-hand page of the ledger he wrote the day's fiction stint, variously titled "Cain Sign," "The Salinas Valley," "MY VALLEY," and finally *East of Eden*. Eventually the novel pages were cut out of the ledger and sent regularly, on a weekly basis, to Covici at Viking Press so a secretary could begin creating an easier-to-read typescript for him and for his agent Elizabeth Otis. The journal portion was later typed by Covici's wife, Dorothy (Brittain 176).

Unlike the often cryptic and arcane *Working Days*, which needed lots of editorial elaboration and biographical/historical explanation (ditto regarding *Wayward Bus* journal, should it ever be published), the letters addressed to Covici on the verso side of the ledger were published almost verbatim by Viking Press in 1969 as a stand-alone book with hardly any editorial or historical contextualizing, which gives some idea of how drastically this effort departed from Steinbeck's previous two examples. After editorial surgery the novel Viking Press brought out in September 1952 was a truncated version of the original text, and as such it eliminated Steinbeck's running commentaries to his boys, as in this sample snippet:

You are little boys now, when I am writing this. . . . The kind of life you lead is very different from the life your father led and your grandfather and your great grandfather. All of us came from a place called the

Salinas Valley. We were molded and formed by this place, and I suppose to a certain extent you were also since no strong influence ever dies. . . . And it has changed very much in the nearly fifty years that I have known it. Now I think I will tell you a book about that Valley so that you will come in time to know what your father was like and how he lived and what your grandfather and great grandfather were like and how they lived. If I do not tell you you will never know, and may be that is not very important but it seems so to me. (*East of Eden* ms 1)

Besides presenting the history of the Hamilton family line through the subjective conducting medium of their own father, Steinbeck wanted his sons to learn the greatest story in all literature—"the story of good and evil" (*JN* 4). In telling the story of his country and the story of himself Steinbeck was slowly, elaborately, self-consciously (and somewhat laboriously) building the book he thought would be his greatest achievement, the capstone book he had rehearsed all his life to write: "The craft or art of writing is the clumsy attempt to find symbols for the wordlessness. In utter loneliness a writer tries to explain the inexplicable. . . . A good writer always works at the impossible," he says in the opening entry of *Journal of a Novel*, and immediately one feels a distinct qualitative difference from his other diaries, for here he is more reflective, philosophical, self-assured, and speculative than ever before regarding existential, aesthetic, moral, and personal issues (4). Nowhere is this more pertinent than in his discursive framing of the characters' discussion of the saga of Cain and Abel that precedes the naming of Adam Trask's boys, which occupies section four of chapter twenty-two of *East of Eden*:

> And my discovery of yesterday [June 11, 1951] is still burning in me. I have finally found a key to the story. The only one that has ever satisfied me. I think I know about the story after all this time. It is a fascinating story and my analysis which is going in today should interest you. It should interest scholars and it should interest psychiatrists. Anyway at the risk of being boring I'm going to put it all in today. And it will only be boring to people who want to get on with the plot. The reader I want will find the whole book illuminated by the discussion: just as I am. . . . It is using the Biblical story as a measure of ourselves. (*JN* 104–05)

As this declarative passage suggests, the result is a much more measured, confident, upbeat style than in the other daybooks.

Indeed, even as the epic book project dragged on into the eighth month and Steinbeck, exhausted, jotted increasingly elliptical journal entries, one rarely finds him bitterly castigating himself or bemoaning his lack of talent. "The time seems endless and yet I can't see what I can leave out without there being holes. But it seems endless to me. I wish I were finished and at the same time I am afraid to be finished. I wonder whether you know how that could be. . . . I'm trying to keep some kind of discipline together—as much as I can anyway," he said a couple of days before finishing (*JN* 175). Some entries were penned when there was renovation work going on at the Steinbeck's house, but his attitude here is far different, far calmer, than it was years earlier, as this entry on February 19, 1951, indicates:

> Today the house is full of pounding. I remember in the Grapes of
> Wrath book how I complained about the pounding. And this does not
> bother me at all. For some reason, it does not seem important to me.
> . . . I think I will buy a meerschaum pipe and see whether I can age
> it a delicate lovely brown while I am working on this book. They are
> very beautiful when they are well handled. And I am going to be here
> at this desk for a very long time. I can think of no pleasanter way to
> spend the rest of my life than in this house, with these people and at
> this drafting board. . . . (*JN* 13–14)

Fantasy of cozy habitation or not, the slow, pleasurable mellowing of a meerschaum pipe seems a fit symbol for Steinbeck's new, more deliberate creative process as "self-reflexive" and "confessional" (Zane 2)—and another in a long line of totemic contrivances and quasi-sacred protocols he was never able to abandon at the scene of writing.[11]

But if it seems naive to believe in magic to aid and abet a task as basic and even mechanical as writing, it is also a charming, endearing part of Steinbeck's self-portrait as author. And furthermore, who is to say that the mystically endowed objects—the pipe, the oversize ledger book, the endless supply of perfectly sharpened pencils, the box crafted by hand to hold the manuscript—aren't so much empty fetishes as they are physical counterparts to *timshel*, which is the esoteric linguistic touchstone that moves the entire moral weight of the tale? Here we pay our money and make our choice.

And while Steinbeck eventually lost control of *East of Eden*'s original design, the book remains, I think, one of those magnificent "preposterous" (*JN* 168) compulsions (like *Moby-Dick* or *The Counterfeiters*) that places it in a special category of reference in Steinbeck's canon, a point vigorously advanced by Henry Veggian in his energetic reevaluation of *East of Eden*'s biomorphic narrative qualities (89–93). In building a new textual architecture, an elaborately creative hybrid domicile, which melded journal, memoir, history, and fiction, Steinbeck found yet another way to inhabit its interior spaces, in a way reminiscent of but different (less mystical, more deliberate) from the Tom Joad visitation late in *Working Days*.

In a startlingly forward-looking, avant-garde strategy, Steinbeck situated himself as an actor in the fictive world he was making: fictional Adam Trask visits the young real-life John Steinbeck at his parents' home on 130 Central Avenue in Salinas. In a move worthy of contemporary fictionist Paul Auster's *New York Trilogy*, the reclusive authorial John Steinbeck leaves the sequestered private space of his compositional narrative to enter the public space of his historical fiction. In this seemingly bizarre, boundary-crossing, self-mirroring gesture he becomes "John Steinbeck," another version of his historical self, though—depending on whether we are talking about fiction or autobiography—which version is the "real" John Steinbeck can never be known for sure. I suspect that conundrum is the point to be grasped; here again we pay our money and make our choice. Writing the *East of Eden* multi-text Steinbeck rewrote himself, gave form to his curiosities, and invented himself anew as a force for performative creativity. No wonder, then, that the narrators of the journal and of the novel place such a premium on presence. Steinbeck's claim that he is "in this book . . . and I don't for a moment pretend not to be" (*JN* 24) dovetails with his belief in the "one creative instrument, the individual mind and spirit of man" (*East of Eden* 446). For the later Steinbeck, both skeins make up his cognitive signature. The journal text and the novel text flow toward each other and enhance and complete each other.

Daniel Halpern says, "To observe and note with care the unrolling of [a] life is also to provide insurance against the gradual and possibly inevitable collapse of our human memory" (6). In forging an intratextual autobiographics, John Steinbeck never took the linkage between his private and public texts for granted; in taking himself and his art seriously he preserved for all of us a valuable cultural heritage of scriblomania. The story, Barbara Johnson claims, "of the role and nature of writing in Western culture is still in the process of being written. And the future of that story may be quite unforeseeable, as we pass from the age of the book to the age of the byte" (48–49). Given the intense scrutiny and intellectual theorizing in the past forty years of the oft-contested ideology, politics, and poetics of "writing" and authorship, Steinbeck's forays in this contested domain point up an intriguing room in his house of language, and one yet to be fully explored if we are to understand the true dimensions of his career, his true place in the annals of twentieth-century letters.

Chapter 4

Of Fish and Men

On John Steinbeck, Fly-Fishing, and Me

> O Sir, doubt not but that Angling is an art;
> is it not an art to deceive a Trout with an artificial fly?
>
> —IZAAK WALTON, *The Compleat Angler* (1653)

> Any man who pits his intelligence against a fish and loses has it coming.
>
> —JOHN STEINBECK, "ON FISHING" (1954)[1]

I. Reading the Water[2]

John Steinbeck loved to fish. The Nobel Prize–winning novelist did not habit-ually employ traditional fly-fishing methods, and so there is nothing compre-hensive to be said about that subject, in the extensive way, for example, that historian Hal Wert recently revealed the heretofore secret depths of President Herbert Hoover's fly-fishing fanaticism in *Hoover the Fishing President*—a fanaticism, by the way, not fully discernable by reading Hoover's somewhat whimsical, offhand musings in *Fishing for Fun and to Wash Your Soul*. Neverthe-less, Steinbeck was an avid though somewhat quirky amateur angler, who was cognizant of some fly-fishing elements even though he often favored the means more than the ends of fishing, but he was just predatory enough to enjoy his catch as table fare. While he cast flies on occasion, he preferred bait and hard lures. And he was certainly not above criticizing or satirizing fishing. The wealthy sport-fishing clients of Guaymas, Mexico were "outfitted with equip-ment to startle the fish into submission" and "mentally on tiptoe to out-think the fish" (*LSC* 946), as if such a thing might be possible.

Steinbeck fished, according to his youngest son, John Steinbeck IV, in his memoir *The Other Side of Eden*, because "this alliance between fish and fisherman, even the so-called thrill of the chase, was not really the reason or point of . . . his almost daily endeavor. Basically it was . . . a fine and elaborately feudal style of daydreaming" (22). In his contribution to *John Steinbeck: Centennial Reflections by American Writers*, Thom Steinbeck corroborated his younger brother's memory: "my father had little interest in catching fish. . . . Instead, he considered a line in the water as a perfect cover for reading or daydreaming. I have known him on many occasions to ignore baiting his hook altogether, because a strike . . . would distract his train of thought" (89). Around the same time, in an interview for the Arts and Entertainment television network, Thom recalled that if his father went fishing after a morning's stint of writing, he "put the line in the water with this ugly homemade lure, maybe asked a couple dumb questions of my brother and myself, and sat there and played and wrote in his head" ("My Father" 6). Recovering from surgery in Manhattan in 1968, Steinbeck confessed to Carlton Sheffield he would soon be going out to Sag Harbor "to maybe take my boat out and to do a little fishing with no interest in catching anything. I like that. And if I go alone, I don't even have to talk" (*SLL* 851).[3]

Though Steinbeck once opined that no political candidate "would think of running for public office without first catching and being photographed with a fish" ("On Fishing" 133), ironically his attitude resembled President Hoover's, who believed that "fishing is not so much getting fish as it is a state of mind and a lure for the human soul into refreshment" (30). Steinbeck enjoyed catching (and eating) game fish—from freshwater trout during the 1920s when he was living at Lake Tahoe, to hard-fighting bonito and sierras caught on trolling gear in the Gulf of California in the 1940s, to saltwater bluefish and striped bass during the late 1950s and 1960s when he summered on eastern Long Island. He was also utterly content to eschew the role of angling expert, so much so, in fact, that John IV considered it "great stuff" when he "learned how little [his father] cared about being a good" fisherman (21).

Rather, Steinbeck seemed comfortable with the paradoxes and complications of the angling life, and he considered fishing variously on a continuum from food-gathering, to existential play, to private therapy, to quasi-sacred calling. In 1927 and 1928 when he lived at Lake Tahoe in the California Sierras, he often landed trout by necessity for dinner (by what method he does not say): "I caught a nine pound trout last night. The fish commissioner doesn't mind if we who live here catch them for food. . . . Lord what a fight he put up. Pulled me clear into the lake once. He will last a week."[4]

Figure 16. John Steinbeck with son John Steinbeck IV on leave after basic training, getting ready to fish, or just having come in from fishing, Sag Harbor, New York, May 1, 1966. Unidentified photographer but possibly Elaine Steinbeck. Courtesy of Martha Heasley Cox Center for Steinbeck Studies.

He does not say what kind of trout he caught, though Lake Tahoe is known for rainbow trout (*Oncorhynchus mykiss*) and imported brown trout (*Salmo trutta*), as well as very large Mackinaw or lake trout (*Salvelinus namaycush*), which is actually a member of the char family and can routinely reach weights of twenty to thirty pounds. My hunch is it was an obstinate laker that provided his dinner. Forty years later, in *America and Americans*, Steinbeck recalled working at the California state fish hatchery at Tahoe City in the late 1920s as a kind of obstetrical fish midwife: "Our job was to trap big lake trout when they ran into a stream to spawn, to strip the eggs from the females and the milt from the males to fertilize the eggs, raise the little fish, and bring them up in tanks until they were ready to be transplanted" (327). A decade later, according to Thom, his eldest son, Steinbeck, ever whimsical and like most anglers perhaps given to

Figure 17. Lake Tahoe fish hatchery where Steinbeck worked in the late 1920s. Photo courtesy of Martha Heasley Cox Center for Steinbeck Studies, San Jose State University.

embroidering fish stories, placed a large piece of broken mirror in a mountain stream near Los Gatos so that the stream's single resident—a small trout—on seeing its own image would not feel lonely (Interview).

In his next-to-last book *Travels with Charley*, Steinbeck records an unsuccessful Michigan fishing outing, which includes a pointed barb at Melville's *Moby-Dick* (1851) and/or Hemingway's *The Old Man and the Sea* (1952). Armed with his spinning rod and "some fancy jigs and poppers I'd bought at Abercrombie and Fitch," Steinbeck and his companion "walked and cast and did everything we knew to interest bass and pike. My friend kept saying, 'They're right down there if we can just get the message through.' But we never did. If they were down there, they still are. A remarkable amount of fishing is like that, but I like it just the same. My wants are simple. I have no desire to latch onto a monster symbol of fate and prove my manhood in titanic piscine war, but sometimes I do like a couple of cooperative fish of frying size" (842–43). This from a man who was an integral part of the Sag Harbor Old Whalers' Festival in the mid-1960s (*TAJS* 953).

Plainly, Steinbeck is in good company among American writers—novelists and poets in particular—who have not only been dedicated fisherpersons but who have written tellingly about the sport in and out of their art. Steinbeck is in the company of obvious figures such as Washington Irving, Henry David Thoreau, John Burroughs, Zane Grey, and Ernest Hemingway, but also less widely canonized contemporaries such as the late Richard Brautigan, Ray Carver, Russell Chatham, John Engels, Jim Harrison, John Hersey, Richard Hugo, William Humphrey, Norman Maclean, Howard Mosher, Louis Owens, and Robert Traver (aka John D. Voelker), plus these other author-anglers still alive and casting: Bill Barich, Rick Bass, Kevin Canty, Todd Davis, Anthony Doerr, Guy de la Valdene, Chris Dombrowski, David James Duncan, Ian Frazier, John Gierach, Carl Hiassen, Pam Houston, Greg Keeler, John Maclean, Thomas McGuane, John McPhee, John Nichols, Craig Nova, Annie Proulx, Scott Sadil, Frank Soos, Callan Wink, W. D. Wetherell, and others. All of them have given us impressive examples of fishing's marriage with excellent writing and the realization that, as the late Jim Harrison said between casts on one of our annual fly-fishing trips on Montana's Yellowstone River, " it's as hard to write well about fishing as it is about anything else." "Writing and fishing," Mark Kingwell claims in his nifty little treatise *Catch and Release*, "share this transcendental ability to heal the breach between thought and deed, to bridge the world of imagination and the so-called 'real' one" (81). In his otherwise useful book *The Unreasonable Virtue of Fly Fishing*, Mark Kurlansky misses the point when he claims "Steinbeck . . . judged fishing harshly" (2). Not so. For Steinbeck, as with so many other literary types, fishing and writing were twin aspects of a similarly attentive calling and an immersion in an utterly satisfying process.

Anglers have a phrase—"reading the water"—that is our version of the land traveler's desire to discern "the lay of the land." It means observing carefully the subtleties and nuances of current and flow in rivers, streams, lakes, estuaries, and so forth to figure out what predator/prey action is occurring and where the fish—all of whom are finely honed opportunistic feeders—are most likely to be waiting for their next meal, which of course you hope will be the fly, lure, or bait you have on the end of your line that particular day. Reading the water is learning the language of rivers: "River reading is creative reading," Mark Browning claims in *Haunted by Waters* (148). In a sense, then, all water is a "text" to be interpreted, and fishermen are critical interpreters who participate in an ongoing indeterminate hermeneutic process; or better yet, all critics and writers are fishers, or fishing guides, trying to puzzle out methods of hooking experience that will produce the best results, though the process of puzzling things out is often satisfying enough because, as anglers, when do we ever receive the tangible rewards we expect?

I have long been a proponent of Steinbeck's occasional pieces (*ST* 234–64). His out-of-the-way texts provide interesting, unique, neglected, and fruitful (and sometimes unguarded) approaches to his literary preoccupations at given times in his life, and they reveal facets of his writing life often unremarked by most critics and readers. To put it another way: I like angling in the waters of Steinbeck's offbeat texts. In that vein, I approach this somewhat fanciful and admittedly elliptical and digressive topic on "Of Fish and Men" by focusing not on Steinbeck's obvious mainstream works, but on some less prominent side channels in his art and life in which angling pursuits play a strong role: a relatively neglected scene from *East of Eden*; a biographical anecdote recorded by Graham Watson (1913–2002), Steinbeck's British literary agent; and a couple of tongue-in-cheek nonfiction essays by Steinbeck called "On Fishing" (1954) and "Then My Arm Glassed Up" (1965). I utilize some of the common and more or less nontechnical elements and lingo of fly-fishing to provide explanatory context for a few of Steinbeck's short, unheralded fishing texts. This essay, then, may be considered a kind of fishing expedition, perhaps best thought of as a "meandering" one at that, to steal a crucial metaphor from Ted Leeson's *Jerusalem Creek*, one of the finest fly-fishing memoirs.

II. Some Fish to Remember, Some Fish to Forget
(With Apologies to the Eagles)

John Steinbeck was a fisherman. I mean that in the most honorable as well as the most capacious sense of the word. According to biographer Jackson Benson, Steinbeck developed from childhood a "particular affinity for the seashore" (*TAJS* 8), and while you don't necessarily have to be a fisherman to love water, it does help. Later, Benson claims, Steinbeck "spent a lot of time plotting against fish," and he "considered himself an experienced sailor and fisherman" (841). Which is to say that Steinbeck not only loved all manner of fresh and saltwater bodies of water, including swamps, springs, streams, creeks, brooks, rivers, lakes, sloughs, tide pools, estuaries, and oceans, but he also prized the myriad live finny things that inhabited the depths of what he once called "life water." Steinbeck, who was well versed in Jungian psychology (*SR* 62–63, 156–57), understood the implications of water's primal archetypal relationship to the human unconscious—a mythic, elemental, and symbolic relatedness evident throughout his fictive work, from *Cup of Gold* in 1929 to *The Winter of Our Discontent* in 1961. But he also understood water's commodity value and the dangers faced by commercial working fishermen who harvest the fish we need for our insatiable appetites.

More than that, John Steinbeck understood the ecological importance of bodies of water in the vast web of planetary biodiversity and how humans are but a small part of an endless linked chain of species. His work with marine biologist Edward F. Ricketts on *Sea of Cortez*—the book he confessed he was "proudest" to have written (Waldmeier 220)—is a monumental love song to piscatorial interspecies relatedness that has proven brilliantly prophetic in its deep ecological message. The conjoined narrative and phyletic catalogue portions of *Sea of Cortez* make up a text in which life water and its countless aquatic creatures are main characters, highlighted by a prescient ecological vision whose "synonym . . . is 'ALL'" (*LSC* 820). I have often believed that the current ethical and philosophical attitude toward fly-fishing in this century owes a great deal to Steinbeck's and Ricketts's holistic approach of seeing the whole fabric of life in and around a tide pool or a similar body of water. It is no longer only a focus on catching as many fish as possible in a trout stream, for example, but on the encompassing experience of immersing oneself in the whole web of riverine existence, where, it is written in chapter fourteen, "the whole is necessarily everything" and everything is an index of something else, so that all things are intimately related, all "parts of a larger whole," whose nature can be felt, "but not its size" (*LSC* 875).

Read any current issue of the Anglers' Club of New York *Bulletin*, *Fly Fisherman*, *FlyFusion*, *Flylords*, *Hatch*, *MidCurrent*, or *Trout* (the journal of national cold-water conservation group Trout Unlimited), or log onto any one of hundreds of fly-fishing blogsites, and there is plenty of the same emphasis on the intertwined totality of the angling experience. "Fly fishing," Paul Guernsey says in *Beyond Catch and Release*, "is one of the most fulfilling ways of experiencing nature" and "one of the few activities that allows us to interact with the natural world as a participant rather than as a mere tourist" (11). It should have come as no surprise that during the 2020–2021 COVID-19 pandemic, getting outdoors alone, one of the chief attractions of angling, caused the sale of fishing licenses in the United States to skyrocket.

Steinbeck certainly understood that in angling it is more than fish we seek. We fish for a hundred different reasons too, and my guess is that, among them, Steinbeck loved the intimate process of fishing, the simple rituals and preparations associated with the act, the tactile and physical feel of the equipment, the freedom and challenge of being on or near the water, the rush and sense of well-being that came from doing something for himself outside his workaday routine, and now and then a fresh fish dinner. Recreational fishing or boating, for instance, was a form of therapy for Steinbeck, who spoke of Gardiner's Bay off his Bluff Point summer home in Sag Harbor, New York ("my little fishing place"), at the eastern end of Long Island, as "healing waters." In a 1955 letter to Ritch and Tal Lovejoy, longtime California pals, he apologized for being "remiss about writing" because, he claimed, "I have been doing a lot of fishing and not much work and I find that sloth begets sloth and I also find that I love it." Beyond that, water-gazing and its manifold concomitant activities created a respite from daily obligations, imposed deadlines and duties, and created a masculine sphere of retreat and introspection in which he recharged himself, as he noted in "Then My Arm Glassed Up":

> I love a certain kind of fishing above all other so-called sports. It is almost the last remaining way for a man to be alone, without being suspected of some secret sin. By fishing without bait it is even possible to avoid being disturbed by fish. I am surprised that the dour brotherhood of psychoanalysts has not attacked fishing, since it seems to me it is in competition. Two hours with a fishing rod is worth ten hours on the couch. (*AASN* 127–28)

In Steinbeck, as in Melville's Ishmael, water and meditation seemed truly wedded together. Which is to say that, in an analogous sense, fishing was akin to writing, both of which for Steinbeck required no other justification than being downright pleasurable. Freudian implications aside, besides the fact that both pursuits require a long, hard instrument—pen/pencil or fishing rod—they also require imagination, discipline, observation, problem-solving, patience, and contemplation. Moreover, fishing, like writing, thrives on memory, because as soon as a writer records their fishing experiences (or any experiences for that matter) they are always already past, always already part of mythic angling memory, and therefore given to selection, enlargement, exaggeration, embroidery, distortion, and even fantasy—all of the elements that complicate representation. "We do well to remember," Odell Shepard writes in *Thy Rod and Thy Creel*, "how memory and imagination work together in adding ounces and inches . . . to the fish of yesteryear" (77).

These elements come together in a moving lyrical scene in chapter twenty-three of *East of Eden* that treats Steinbeck's reminiscence of a fishing excursion in his youth with his Uncle Thomas Hamilton, his mother's brother. (Steinbeck does not say how old a child he was, but since Thomas Hamilton died in 1912, John would have to have been a very impressionable eight years old or younger.) This was the first chapter Steinbeck wrote in June 1951, soon after he and his third wife, Elaine, had removed from Manhattan (where he had written the previous twenty-two chapters) to a vacation rental house on a windswept coastal bluff in Siasconset, next to Sankaty Lighthouse, on the island of Nantucket where, as he said in his posthumous companion text, *Journal of a Novel*, their daily routine included "fishing"(105).[5]

It strikes me as more than coincidental that, as soon as Steinbeck entered a water-bound environment, one of his first compositional acts was to write about fishing. "What I know about," Steinbeck recalls early in chapter twenty-three of *East of Eden*, "will be the result of memory plus what I know to be true plus conjecture built on the combination. Who knows whether it will be correct?" (602). Indeed, this statement works on both small and large levels to encapsulate one of the main themes of his most personal and epic novel of remembering. In addition, it is also a commentary on the slippery nature of elegiac prose. Where does truth reside? The child's experience is immediate, but he lacks the language to define it fully; the adult has the language capacity and sophistication to reconstruct the past, but in doing so—no matter how movingly—the experience inevitably owes more to language than to unmediated reality.

In other words, this experiential dilemma is also the fisherman's domain: the liminal space where personal memory, factual experience, alleged falsehood, and language skills mix and mingle, and the combination—the result of Steinbeck's angle on reality—leads us to a storied truth, which in this case is the ineluctable truth of narrative. To put it another way, the river that runs through it—à la Norman Maclean—is language and memory as much as it is water and fish. In *Rivers of the Heart*, Steve Raymond claims "words define the essence of the sport" (167). As water-gazing writer and angler, Steinbeck understood this indivisible linkage very well, for which this neglected scene in *East of Eden* is a touchstone.

"Sometimes Tom took me fishing," Steinbeck declares.

> We started before the sun came up and drove in the rig straight toward Fremont's Peak, and as we neared the mountains the stars would pale out and the light would rise to blacken the mountains. . . . I don't remember that Tom talked. Now that I think of it, I can't remember the sound of his voice or the kind of words he used. I can remember both about my grandfather, but when I think of Tom it is a memory of a kind of warm silence. Maybe he didn't talk at all. *Tom had beautiful tackle and made his own flies. But he didn't seem to care whether we caught trout or not. He needed not to triumph over animals.* (606; my emphasis)

Steinbeck continues:

> I remember the five-fingered ferns growing under the little waterfalls, bobbing their green fingers as the droplets struck them. And I remember the smells of the hills, wild azaleas and a very distant skunk and the sweet cloy of lupin and horse sweat on harness. I remember the sweeping lovely dance of high buzzards against the sky and Tom looking long up at them, but I can't remember that he ever said anything about them. . . . I remember the smell of crushed ferns in the creel and the delicate sweet odor of fresh damp rainbow trout lying so prettily on the green bed. (606)

This patently nostalgic scene is an elegy for a long-lost person, place, and way of life, and as such—potentially fuzzy sentiments aside—it functions as a private origin myth (which is what most fly-fishing memoirs are). It is a generative moment, frozen in time, born out of a certain kind of reflective silence, a fisherman's silence, the kind of idyllic pastoral repose Izaak Walton claimed 369 years ago in *The Compleat Angler* that complemented "contemplation and quietness" (37), two of the angler's most desired states.

Thus this scene in chapter twenty-three of *East of Eden* is a small yet sharply etched portrait of the beginnings of Steinbeck's lifelong involvement with fishing (not exclusively fly-fishing) as a physical and philosophical adventure, his incipient fascination with its material allure and thingness, and by extension his long-buried relatedness (and perhaps indebtedness) to his favorite uncle, Tom Hamilton, one of the least visible of the Hamilton clan, who was a skilled fisherman and adept at fly-tying (a nonmechanized, throwback craft that requires observation, precision, dexterity, attention to minute details, and a correspondingly steady hand).[6] We learn later in chapter twenty-three of *East of Eden* Thomas Hamilton was also a "secret" poet (607), which is to say, he was an angler of words.

The writing fisherman, the fishing writer: Uncle Tom's "artistic" influence and example may have been far greater on his famous nephew's habits of being than has yet been calculated. And though the scene ends with a basket of dead rainbow trout (perhaps foreshadowing Tom's suicide ten chapters later), their bodies seem less to be tangible trophies of the outing than accidental byproducts, which is to say that they are but a tiny part of the overall "catch." The passage is lyrical and painterly as much as fly-fishing writing tends to be: it is noteworthy for its textured density and the way Steinbeck, like our best fishing memoirists such as Christopher Camuto, Jerry Dennis, Lorian Hemingway, Ted Leeson, Nick Lyons, Harry Middleton, Howell Raines, and Paul Schullery, just to name a few, embeds the angling moment in a contextual surround, a thickly descriptive swirl of sights, odors, objects, physical gestures and processes, shaded interplay of light and dark, and sharp, discriminating insights, all of which occur in a striking geographic setting that at once triggers and frames the experience.

Political correctness and cancel culture aside, the dead rainbow trout in *East of Eden*, like the trout Nick Adams lands in Ernest Hemingway's "Big Two-Hearted River," seems the least important part of the equation, and to miss that is to miss the way Steinbeck is honoring the gift of trout as a kind of blessing. Novelist Craig Nova, in his lucid memoir *Brook Trout and the Writing Life*, speaks for many anglers when he says of his own experience, "These fish are forever associated in my mind with the depths of thankfulness for good fortune, just as they always reminded me of beauty and a sense of what may be possible after all" (111).

In Steinbeck's case, the momentary spot of time was made possible as much by Thomas Hamilton's generosity, noncompetitive nature, and warm silence as it was by the unequivocally painful knowledge that those attributes could not save him from himself, from his own depression and self-destruction. In the wake of Tom's literal and metaphorical silences (they too are part of the surrounding emotional experience), authorial and readerly interpretation flourishes and leads to a sense of redemption and a sense of being in the world that Steinbeck never abandoned. Steinbeck's talismanic fly-fishing story—a twist on the old tale of "the one that got away"—keeps his uncle alive. In constituting Thomas Hamilton's subjecthood via his fly-fishing passion, Steinbeck was creating part of himself as well, and creating a legacy for his own sons, Thom and John IV, for whom the novel was originally intended.

III. Steinbeck and I Shop at Hardy Brothers

In his wonderfully diverting memoir *Book Society* (1980), Graham Watson recalled that, at their first meeting in 1952, while their wives shopped in Bond Street, Graham and John "repaired to Hardy's—*always his most important call in London*" (my emphasis), where Steinbeck "bought a rather ridiculous fishing hat covered in salmon flies" (108). Hardy's, founded in 1872 by two brothers—William and John James—and headquartered in Alnwick, England, is the premier fishing-tackle manufacturer in the British Isles.

Along with America's Vermont-based Orvis Company (founded in 1856), the Hardy Brothers firm (known after 1985 as the House of Hardy) is considered one of the best—and most venerable—makers of fine rods, reels, and equipment in the world. Hardy's understated shop at No. 61 Pall Mall (rebuilt after being bombed out in World War II) is a required stop for fly-fishing and outdoor aficionados and sporting enthusiasts from around the world, and Steinbeck was not only a frequent visitor to the store but also conversant with the sporting tradition it embodied. Edward Weeks, essayist and longtime editor of *Atlantic Monthly*, notes in *Fresh Waters*, his genteel book of fishing essays, "Hardy's is the cornucopia of English angling; the shop is run with a quiet air of authority and it has everything . . . from . . . big Salmon flies . . . [to] . . . the latest word in fishing hats and waterproofs" (87). More to the point, British angler Arthur Ransome claimed in *Rod and Line*, "it is as mistaken to think that we go to tackle-shops only because we need tackle as to think that we go fishing only because we want to eat fish" (15). For an angler, a fishing store is a cornucopia of alluring delights, a little sanctum of seductive materiality. A visitor's first thought is often, "what can I not live without?"

England is the birthplace of modern fly-fishing, a tradition of artful skill that has been written about in English continuously for more than 500 years, from the 1496 *Treatise of Fishing with an Angle* (attributed—rightly or wrongly—to a nun, Dame Juliana Berners, and included in *The Book of St. Albans*), through Isaak Walton's *The Compleat Angler*, especially the fifth edition of 1676 (which includes a fly-fishing section penned by Charles Cotton), and then on to the pioneering writings of Frederic Halford, G. E. M. Skues, and others in the late nineteenth and early twentieth centuries, and extending on from there via Frank Sawyer and others into our own time.[7] The Brits cornered the market in expounding their country's glories and traditions as a fishable nation. In fact, the "British style" of fly-fishing for trout (as it can be loosely called) is essentially an upper-class, genteel tradition because it is not only elitist (the only proper quarry are trout and salmon; other species are considered "coarse" or "rough"), but it is also highly structured, code-regulated, and protocol-driven.

This was especially true in fly-fishing as it was promulgated around the turn of the last century on the privately owned, gin-clear limestone chalk streams of southern England's Hampshire County—for instance, the highly groomed and manicured Rivers Test and Itchen—by purists such as Frederic Halford and his fellow members and cronies who belonged to the exclusive Houghton Club (limited to twenty-two members) and to the legendary Flyfishers' Club of London, founded in 1884 (and still going strong). Halford codified in *Floating Flies and How to Dress Them* the practice of casting a floating imitative dry fly (constructed of some combination of fur, feather, and yarn) upstream to rising trout that were dining on the tiny duns, or adults, of hatching winged insects that floated a short distance on the river's surface before taking flight. This came to be considered the only thoroughly sporting and ethical way of presenting an artificial fly, and soon—for a brief span of a couple decades anyway—the method became fly-fishing's version of High Church gospel truth.[8]

In *Vermont River*, the first of his trilogy of nonfiction fly-fishing books, novelist W. D. Wetherell calls Hardy's shop in Pall Mall "the snobbiest fishing store in the world" (99). Having visited it a couple of times myself I can testify that to walk into Hardy's, with its hushed air of understated luxury and its somewhat condescending but very informed sales staff, is to glimpse, as if from the outside looking in, the world of what Howell Raines calls the "Tweedy Gent" in *Fly Fishing Through the Midlife Crisis* (98). This is the sphere of privileged British rural sporting life (displayed, for instance, in the pages of *The Field*, a venerable

Figure 18. The Hardy retail store and sporting emporium, 61 Pall Mall, St James, London. Photograph courtesy of Dr. Andrew Herd.

magazine in continuous publication since 1853) that the Hardy firm simultane-
ously caters to and characterizes, though it also supports and markets various
other forms of angling styles and equipment, including spin-casting and
bait-casting gear. For many fly-angling enthusiasts, The Hardy bothers' reputation in fly-fishing seems to override all else, however. Steinbeck encountered
this exalted aspect of Hardy's as well and came away chastened. "Do you
remember the day when we went to Hardy's," he wrote Graham Watson in
1966, "and I asked about an automatic reel? The sneer in the reply was so sharp
that it cut the clark's lips to ribbons."[9]

In other words, Hardy's exudes an aura of gentility, upper-class insularity,
earnest leisureliness and confident, even condescending knowingness, but even
at that it has not succumbed to the gonzo level of professional specialization
fostered in such American magazines as the defunct *Wild on the Fly* and the
now current *The Drake*, as well as in the rapidly proliferating do-it-yourself,
over-the-top electronic magazine sites and personal blogs that cater to
globe-trotting fly-rod extremists—the sport's "new paradigms," as novelist
Thomas McGuane (himself a world-class angler) calls them in his acclaimed
collection *The Longest Silence*—"the bum, the addict, and the maniac" (ix), who
like to rip lips, take no prisoners, and otherwise put a hurt on the fishy population. Rather, Hardy's more subdued, slow-handed image was symbolized by an
advertising campaign, dubbed "A Tradition of Innovation," that was all the rage
a decade-plus ago, in that it featured the mysterious, fetching, redhaired, fresh-
faced "Hardy Girl" (decked out in angling regalia,) as she has come to be known
in the British and American sporting press.[10]

Sexy pinup/wet-dream fantasy of Miss Hardy Girl aside, few of us have the
social standing or financial resources to feel at ease in such an intimidating
environment or to acquire its accoutrement with guiltless abandon. Indeed,
class does matter: decades ago I recall being cowed by the prices of Hardy's rods
and reels, and I left their Pall Mall store (which took me half a day to find)
feeling deflated because, on my junior faculty's salary, I was only able in good
conscience to afford an insignia baseball cap, a few neoprene leader pool ten-
ders, a small six-compartment plastic fly box emblazoned with the Hardy logo,
and a few bucks worth of flies, including a wet fly pattern called Coch-Y-
Bonddu, one of Hemingway's go-to flies when he fished the Clark's Fork of the
Yellowstone River at Lawrence Nordquist's L-T Ranch in Wyoming in the
1930s (I confess to having never tried them), and some dry flies called Tups

Indispensibles, a pattern that was originated around 1900 by a British tobacconist, R. S. Austin, but was named and made famous, according to Gordon Wickstrom's delightful *Notes from an Old Fly Book*, by one of fly-fishing's undisputed heroes, G. E. M. Skues (18), who also pioneered fishing subsurface flies and made significant inroads into the Halfordian dry fly–only congregation.[11]

Anyway, to carry this willful digression from the sublime all the way to the ridiculous, into a little byway of history I can't help thinking Steinbeck would have relished had he known about it, the Tups Indispensible was traditionally tied with urine-stained wool from a ram's genitals, not exactly an easy ingredient for commoners to lay hands on nowadays. My modernized versions turned out to be effective on western cutthroat trout, which took them for *epeorus albertae*, a pinkish-hued mayfly insect (sometimes called Pink Lady or Pink Albert by anglers), so I suppose my pilgrimage to Hardy's, like Steinbeck's many years earlier (which I will shortly get to), paid unforeseen, though not nearly so comic or incisive, dividends after all.

Before attacking Steinbeck for "going Hardy" and selling out, however, we should remember that, like many anglers who love the myriad gizmos of fly-fishing and who enter what Jan Zita Grover calls "the Cult of Stuff" in *Northern Waters*, her book on becoming a fly-fisher, it is helpful to recall that our old left-wing proletarian novelist was actually a gear head who loved "hardware stores" (*CJS* 53) and working with his hands. Shirley Fisher, his longtime friend and agent at McIntosh and Otis, summed it up in a lively 1978 *New York Times* reminiscence: "John loved tools" (20).

Indeed, besides his fishing tackle, some of which he purchased at renowned original (and now defunct) sporting purveyor Abercrombie and Fitch in Manhattan (*SLL* 424), Steinbeck possessed and coveted all kinds of tools, sporting traps, and mechanical contraptions (typewriters, Dictaphones, pencil sharpeners), machines (outboard motors), gadgets (knives, Abercrombie and Fitch marine cannon), firearms (lever action .30–.30 carbine, Remington bolt action .222 with telescopic sight, Smith and Wesson 9 mm pistol), and nifty British vehicles (Land Rover, Jaguar), to name a few prominent examples. He enjoyed boats, too, about which he could be both lyrical and emotional (*LSC* 762), and vain, as in this July 5, 1955, letter to Webster Street, where he gushes about his newly purchased Boston Whaler:

This afternoon, we are taking our boat off Montauk Point to fish for blues. They are fine fighting fish and wonderful to eat and they are said to be running well right now. It is about a forty-five minute run in our boat which will do thirty-four miles an hour if it has to. It is a sea skiff, lapstrake, twenty feet long and eight feet of beam and a hundred horse power Grey marine engine. I could cross the Atlantic in her if I could carry the gasoline. . . . Also it only draws eighteen inches so we can take it into little coves and very near the shore if only we watch the charts for rocks and depth. This is fabulous boating country and fishing country too. (*SLL* 505)

When Steinbeck could not indulge in his favorite outdoor pleasures—gardening, boating, fishing—life was a "bloody bore" (*TAJS* 1028).

Graham Watson recalled that Steinbeck, who "loved fishing," "was an intensely physical man. He loved the sound of a line stripping off a reel, the feel of a newly honed knife, the smell of beeswaxed leather, the texture of a well-oiled rifle stock" (109). He also reveled in suitable raiment. Watson remembered that Steinbeck "loved acquiring sports clothes and no London visit would pass without his buying a new yachting cap or a pair of shooting boots or a heavy macintosh" (109), whether he actually used those items on a regular basis. Witness again the fishing hat covered in salmon flies. A check of both the 1951 and 1952 editions of *Hardy's Anglers' Guide*, at 260 pages in length probably the most comprehensive fishing tackle instruction manuals and sales catalogues of that postwar era, lists besides utterly serviceable and "Thoroughly Reliable Well-Made" clothing (including "Double-Texture Waterproof Wading Coat," "Fishing Coat," and "Boating Trousers") only a single entry for a Deerstalker-style "Sou'-Wester" waterproof hat that can be "rolled up and carried in the coat pocket" and one entry for a "sateen lined" Oilskin Sou'-Wester hat (Hardy 231, 235). Harwood, Herd, and Stanley's *Gear & Gadgets: An Irresistible Collection of Hardy Fishing Tackle* came up empty as well, though it does note that Hardy occasionally offered "salmon fly brooches and hat pins" (114). No mention, however, in those resources of Steinbeck's gleeful purchase, which of course makes it even more serendipitous and noteworthy. Whether the lures in question on his oddball, one-of-a-kind discovery were real flies dangling from the brim or one-dimensional artistic representations, both modes of artifact signaled the novelist's fascination with a rarefied element of angling history.

Salmon flies of the mid-nineteenth century and well into the twentieth century were often extremely colorful and extravagantly dressed, and they looked like miniature hand-painted, overly busy Victorian works of art. In Andrew Herd's *The Fly*, his exhaustively researched history of fly-fishing, he calls these fanatically appointed, over-the-top feather creations "gaudy" flies (262).[12] These brilliantly colored creations, often dependent on the bright fathers of rare or exotic fowl, are more attractive to the fisherman than they are to the fish, but then that is the point, as fishing tackle manufacturers discovered long ago. (Spawning Atlantic salmon don't feed when they return to their natal freshwater rivers to breed, so why they strike a fly is a mystery, but of course they do so just often enough to keep anglers fishing.) And with names such as Silver Doctor, Stoat's Tail, Thunder and Lightning, Greenwell's Glory, General Practitioner, and Jock Scott, the onomastic Steinbeck would have found them catchy in other ways as well. (The latter pattern, conceived in 1845 by John Scott, an expert Tweedside gillie and skillful fly-tier, is often considered the most representative emblem of the fully dressed salmon fly.) Nevertheless, even if Steinbeck's cache of salmon flies were of the plainer, less flashy, easier and quicker to tie, hair-bodied style typical of the mid-twentieth century and beyond, it isn't hard to see why the novelist might have been so fascinated by their intricate designs and their provenance and history.

It would be misleading, however, to argue that Steinbeck's adherence to a dyed-in-the-wool British sporting tradition marked his total capitulation to elite capitalism. While fly-fishing for trout and salmon is often a pricey matter,

Figure 19. Alberto Calzoleri's fully dressed contemporary version of Jock Scott salmon fly, originated 1845 by Scottish tier John Scott and based on a tying recipe that appears in George M. Kelson's *The Salmon Fly: How to Dress It and How to Use It* (1895). The vibrant yellows, reds, and blues made this pattern so distinctive and eye-catching. Photograph courtesy of Dr. Andrew Herd and American Museum of Fly Fishing, Manchester, Vermont.

Steinbeck's view of the fishing life is too varied and complex for such a reductive assessment. On one level, Steinbeck's purchase of the salmon fly–adorned hat may be considered an homage to careful artisanship and certainly connects thematically with the scene in chapter twenty-three of *East of Eden* I spoke of above, and with the spirit of his long-dead Uncle Thomas Hamilton who as a fly tier and slow-handed angler valued authentic, one-of-a-kind items.

Or to put it another way: the old adage that you get what you pay for is true. I received a Hardy LRH Lightweight single-action fly reel as a Christmas gift in 1968, and I have used it continuously for more than five decades without it ever needing repair or factory service. The LRH's throwback simplicity and bulldog reliability, which defy obsolescence, remain its chief attractions, although no mention of its appeal would be complete without noting the delightful ratcheting noise the reel makes when you crank the handle to turn the spool and retrieve the line. Some of the more advanced, costlier, high-end fly reels are silent, though I prefer my LRH's click-and-pawl drag system and its reassuring onstream racket that always gives me the impression of being linked one-to-one to something real (pardon the pun) and immediate, especially in the unforgettable moments when the clatter is set in motion by a fast fish making a strong run.

In fact, thinking about my well-traveled fly reel, I have come to realize that no matter what other motives Steinbeck may have had for his frequent priority visits to Hardy's, he certainly understood and appreciated the quality of their manual, made-to-hand trademark gear, as did Ernest Hemingway, who owned a substantial amount of Hardy equipment until most of it was lost in transit to Sun Valley, Idaho, in 1940.[13] As for Steinbeck's salmon fly–festooned hat, he told Watson in 1956, "I am wearing the hat with great success. Men, prone to take it lightly as a piece of solid British frippery, are thrown into a paroxysm of admiration at the beautiful salmon flies" (*SLL* 498).

IV. The Outdoor-Indoor Sport: Watching Other People Fish

Far from being an example of untroubled materialism, I suggest that the Hardy's episode has a deeper import, for in the middle of one of the world's largest, densest urban areas, far from the nearest wild salmon river (whether in London or in New York), the flies' eventual use—other than their obvious ornamental, aesthetic, and ceremonial value—led Steinbeck indirectly to a kind of reductio ad *absurdam*, a cultural satire of sorts, the kind of broadly comic (and occasionally self-deprecating) angle toward popular sporting and athletic pursuits he later struck in his 1965 *Sports Illustrated* piece "Then My Arm Glassed Up," when he quipped: "I have studied fish both zoologically and ecologically, and once long ago [1928] I worked for the California Fish and Game Commission, where I helped at the birth and raising of a good many millions of trout. At that time I learned to admire them but not greatly to respect their intelligence. And it has seemed to me that a man who can outthink fish may have a great future, but it will be limited to fish. His acquired knowledge will do him little good at a Sunday-school picnic or a board meeting" (*AASN* 128).

While Steinbeck wrote about fishing, metaphorically anyway, in all his books (he was, after all, a fisher of men and women who has managed to hook a worldwide audience), he also penned savvy and humorous nonfiction pieces in which fishing is prominent. In "On Fishing" Steinbeck boasts that he is "one of the world's foremost observers of other people's fishing," and he continues: "I believe that certain national characteristics emerge in fishing and attitudes toward fishing. With this in view I have for many years studied the relationship of fisherman to fish" (*AASN* 132).

"On Fishing" is an intriguing and resonant essay that anatomizes in a very broad and playful way American, British, and French attitudes toward fishing. I'll start with Steinbeck's waggish take on the British, which I think puts a different spin on his Anglophilia and the House of Hardy episode. In short, like Twain in the lighter moments of *A Connecticut Yankee in King Arthur's Court*, Steinbeck beards the lion (or rather the trout), goofs with an elite tradition, and signifies on what he called the "English passion for private property," which "rises to its greatest glory in the ownership and negotiability of exclusive fishing rights in rivers and streams" (*AASN* 133).

The Yank democrat then spins his version of "the ideal British fishing story," based on a set of "gentlemanly rules of conduct set up between trout and Englishmen," in which "the fisherman rereads Izaak Walton to brush up on his philosophic background, smokes many pipes, reduces all language to a series of grunts and finally sets out of an evening to have a go at Old George," an ancient and brilliant trout that has resided many years in a nearby meadow stream. Steinbeck writes:

He creeps near to the sunken log and drops his badly tied dry fly

upstream of the log so that it will float practically into Old George's
mouth. This has been happening to Old George every evening for ten
or fifteen years. But one evening perhaps Old George is sleeping with
his mouth open or maybe he is bored. The hook gets entangled in his
mouth. Then the fisherman, with tears streaming from his eyes, pulls
Old George out on the grassy bank. There with full military honors and
a deep sense of sorrow from the whole community, Old George flops to
his death. The fisherman eats George boiled with brussels sprouts, sews
a black band on his arm and gains the power of speech sufficiently to
bore the hell out of the local pub for years to come. (*AASN* 134)

This fanciful little tale is a savvy send-up on one aspect of the storied and
hoity-toity British tradition of blood sports and fly-fishing, which the Hardy
firm represents, and which Steinbeck suggests has already, by the middle of the
twentieth century, entered the nether universe of cultural stereotype.

But it isn't just the British that come in for a hooking; the Americans, too,
get their comeuppance, and in fact Steinbeck is especially hard on his fellow
countrymen, perhaps because he recognizes elements of himself in the gener-
alized portrait of the well-dressed, excessively outfitted angler.

The American conceives of fishing as more than a sport: it is his personal contest against nature. He buys mountains of equipment: reels,
lines, rods, lures, all vastly expensive. Indeed, the manufacture and sale
of fishing equipment is one of America's very large businesses. But
equipment does not finish it. The fisherman must clothe himself for the
fish with special and again expensive costumes. Then, if he can afford
it, he buys or charters a boat as specialized for fishing as an operating
theater is for surgery. He is now ready to challenge the forces of nature
in their fishy manifestations. (*AASN* 132)

American fishermen "enter a kind of piscatorial religion all for the purpose of
demonstrating his superiority over fish," a national attitude of acquisitiveness
and conquest that Steinbeck finds ruthless and unsavory, and which reaches its
zenith in a view of fishing as a testosterone-fueled battle:

He prefers the huge and powerful denizens of the sea which have great

nuisance and little food value. Once fastened to his enemy, the fisherman subjects himself to physical torture while strapped into a chrome
barber's chair, and resists for hours having his arms torn off. But he has
proved that he is better than the fish. . . . The fisherman endows the fish
with great intelligence and fabulous strength to the end that in defeat-
ing it he is even more intelligent and powerful. (*AASN* 133)

It is not too difficult to sense the shadow of Hemingway as writer and iconic
sporting celebrity in Steinbeck's dissection of the big-game fishing craze. In an
era before catch-and-release fishing became a fairly standard practice among
fresh- and saltwater sport fishers, trophy fishing held no interest for Steinbeck.
Photographs of Hemingway posing with his catch of astonishingly big ocean
fish—blue marlin, mako shark, sailfish, tarpon, barracuda, or tuna—are legion.
Photos add a powerful visual dimension to such books as Kip Farrington's *Fishing with Hemingway and Glassell* and Nick Lyons's edition of *Hemingway on
Fishing* and remind us dramatically of a way Steinbeck never cared to be. In fact,
one looks in vain for photos of Steinbeck and his fish. As far as I know, there
are none, which I believe proves a point made by Jackson Benson, in a 1985 essay
originally called "Hemingway the Hunter and Steinbeck the Farmer," that
"where Hemingway was drawn toward the action to participate, Steinbeck was
drawn toward it to observe" (*Looking for Steinbeck's Ghost* 220).

Steinbeck's implicit criticism of the performative Hemingway is in some
sense an ethical one, for he descried the waste of such great creatures. In fact, a
decade later, in "Then My Arm Glassed Up," Steinbeck was especially critical
of "the shark hunter," who, though not named in his essay, was very probably
Montauk charter captain Frank Mundus (the alleged model for Peter Bench-
ley's character Quint in *Jaws*). Mundus was already making a publicized name
for himself in eastern Long Island Sound waters for having successfully har-
pooned a 4,500-pound Great White in June, 1964 and was gaining a reputation
as one of the only captains regularly targeting sharks as rod-and-reel quarry.
Steinbeck's response is telling: "He kills these great and interesting animals not
only with glee but with a sense of administering justice to a cruel and hated
enemy. The carcasses are usually thrown away after photographing. There is
utterly no understanding that sharks may well be factors in an intricate ecological balance" (*ASSN* 128).

Anyone who has watched Discovery Channel's popular "Shark Week" or a now canceled reality show from 2013, NBC Sports Channel's Montauk-based *Shark Hunters* (which seems directly descended from Frank Mundus's kill-them-all project), or current National Geographic TV's "SharkFest" (extended to six weeks in 2021) will recognize immediately not only the prophetic import of Steinbeck's statement, but also the way his criticism carries forward his life-long ecological concerns. "We in the United States have done so much to destroy our own resources, our timber, our land, our fishes, that we should be taken as a horrible example and our methods avoided by any government and people enlightened enough to envision a continuing economy" (*LSC* 956). In fact, Lloyd Willis claims Steinbeck is "unique among U.S. authors because he may have recognized the scope, scale, and implications of twentieth-century environmental destruction better than any other 'major' American author before Edward Abbey" (91).

So what was Steinbeck's ideal fishing scenario? Not surprisingly, in an article that appeared on commission in a French paper, Steinbeck reserves his highest praise for the version of fishing he encounters "on the banks of the lovely Oise on a summer Sunday afternoon."[14] The French method appeals because it is sedentary, simple, playful, and both nonhierarchical and nonteleological, which is to say, in a material sense, it is useless (I am inclined to say "un-American"). Instead, the French method (if I may crib from venerable Izaak Walton's *The Compleat Angler*) is "like virtue," an end and "reward" in itself (25). Steinbeck sums up this avocation:

> Here is no sentiment, no contest, no grandeur, no economics. Now and then a silly baby fish may be caught but most of the time there seems to be a courteous understanding by which fish and fisherman let each other strictly alone. Apparently there is also a rule about conversation. The fisherman's eyes get a dreaming look and he turns inward on his own thoughts, inspecting himself and his world in quiet. Because he is fishing, he is safe from interruption. He can rest detached from the stresses and pressures of his life. . . . From the sanctity of this occupation, a man may emerge refreshed and in control of his own soul. He is not idle. He is fishing. (*AASN* 134–35)

This passage proves a point about cultural difference that Paul Schullery makes in "Civilized Fishing": "The codes of behavior by which we define what is acceptable in fishing in fact require a great deal of flexibility of us. Fishing is what we make of it and what we decide, in each location, is best" (*Royal Coachman* 165).

In his *Le Figaro* passage, Steinbeck is writing with the ghost of his uncle Thomas Hamilton in mind, and he has cast his line back to chapter twenty-three of *East of Eden*, where he had extolled a similar kind of pastoral, ruminative silence and a civilized noncompetitive deportment that allowed his elder not to care whether fish were caught or not: "He needed not to triumph over animals." I don't know whether it is as simple as saying "like uncle, like nephew," or that "blood (or perhaps ink) is thicker than water," but in an age when the real contextual determinants of fly-fishing for trout in the United States are increased angling pressure, viral whirling disease, prolonged drought following global warming, invasive New Zealand mud snails, drastically reduced insect populations, habitat degradation, acid rain, hatchery-reared fish, and increasingly embattled public-access rights, the river-gazing persona's serene attitude toward angling that emerges in "On Fishing" is worth serious consideration. In fact, Steinbeck's postmodern take on fishing, which sanely emphasizes process over product as the true register of success, is a precursor of a trending activity taking hold on some American rivers, in which dry flies are dressed on a hook that has no bend or barb. The goal of this "bite and relinquish" effort (my term) is to fool the trout to rise and take a fly without the inevitable stress and traumatic mishandling caused by hooking and playing fish. The tug of the rise and take are everything, not the hook set and catching. If this hookless technique makes fly-fishing more of a dilettantish aesthetic exercise than ever before, it also has the concrete value of extending renewability of the world's already beleaguered trout population (Bodo 34).[15]

V. A Fish by Any Other Name

Besides John Steinbeck, how many other American novelists can be said to have had a new species of sea creature named after them? I don't have any hard facts and provable data about this, but my guess is none. According to Eric Tamm's *Beyond the Outer Shores*, in 1939 ichthyologist Dr. Rolf Bolin, of Stanford University's Hopkins Marine Station, named the longfin lampfish, *Lampanyctus steinbecki* (277), and a year later, in 1940, Ricketts identified a new species of sea anemone, *Phailoba steinbecki* (25).[16] These are honors that, were they more widely known, might rival—even eventually surpass—the prestige of Steinbeck's Nobel Prize among us fishy types. It proves a point made years ago by the redoubtable Sparse Grey Hackle (aka Alfred W. Miller) to the effect that the best fishing is not always in water but in print. Think of the possibilities: from his early days as Lake Tahoe "Piscatorial Obstetrician" overseeing the propagation of millions of trout for the California Fish and Game Commission, to participant on a landmark marine-collecting trip to Gulf of California, to self-proclaimed expert observer of other people's fishing, to internationally acclaimed author of such classics as *The Fish of Wrath*, *Fishery Row*, *The Wayward Fish*, *The Fish of Our Discontent*, and *The Acts of King Arthur and His Noble Fish*, John Steinbeck was truly one with the fishes.

Indeed, he is all aroun' in the dark water; wherever there's a fish being hooked, he'll be there; wherever there's a poacher beatin' up a fish, he'll be there. Why, he'll be there in the way kids laugh when it's time to go fishing, and, since his ashes were committed to the ocean off Point Lobos, we can say, in Sicilian fashion, Steinbeck still sleeps with the fishes. Whenever we remember Lennie stroking a dead fish in his pocket or asking George to let him please tend the fishes, whenever we dress our flies, bait our hooks, or wet our lines, whenever we sit down to baked salmon or grilled trout at a trendy bistro or over a campfire (as I often did back in the day), whenever we are tempted to be haunted by waters, we should remember John Steinbeck's words from "On Fishing": "It has always been my private conviction that any man who pits his intelligence against a fish and loses has it coming" (*AASN* 133).[17]

NOTES

Chapter 2

1. Comments about the nature of the two men's collaboration are in Astro's *John Steinbeck and Edward F Ricketts* (12–14). Anyone wishing to read the original Ricketts sources Steinbeck drew upon, especially "Essay on Non-Teleological Thinking" and "Verbatim Transcript of Notes of Gulf of California Trip, March–April 1940," should consult Katherine Rodger's indispensable edition of Ricketts's writings, *Breaking Through* (119–201). While we attribute *Sea of Cortez*'s words to Steinbeck as a matter of convenience, it might be better to think of them as coming from a composite narrator, Ed/John, or John/Ed. The speaking voice in the narrative portion is "we," not "I." Ricketts himself said the book was a "true compilation." I still own the copy of *The Log* I bought in college in 1964 when I was working on my senior thesis at Assumption. It is the paperback Viking Press/Compass Books edition, and it is still intact after fifty-plus years of spine-bending, ink-stained markings, and underlinings. The current commercial paperback is Richard Astro's Penguin Books edition of *The Log from the Sea of Cortez* (1995) with his excellent introduction. Readers with deep pockets might want to acquire the Arion Press's limited, hand-set, letterpress edition (250 copies) of *Sea of Cortez*, which, in one of its extreme manifestations, is presented in a handmade box incorporating Douglas fir planks from the *Western Flyer* itself. It is a stunning product of the bookmaker's art, but at 250 exceptionally expensive copies, it is not exactly designed to give the Steinbeck and Ricketts classic a wide broadcast. When I refer to the narrative log portion of *Sea of Cortez* throughout this chapter, it is to the Library of America version, which includes a selection of explanatory notes and annotations. For a timely study regarding the background of Ricketts's and Jack Calvin's groundbreaking study *Between Pacific Tides* (1939), and the profound importance of a holistic habitat approach to marine classification, consult Astro and Kohrs, *A Tidal Odyssey*.

2. "Reader" is a term I use here loosely as a hybrid amalgam of actual, hypothetical, implied readers and "narratees" to whom I have attributed a cheerful, rather than hypercritical or hypersceptical attitude. I am not concerned with the ideological particularities or hair-splitting distinctions of and among different methods of audience-oriented interpretative strategies, but rather I am interested in reading back on Steinbeck the general, symbolic implications of reader-centered criticism's cumulative effect: "all reader-response criticism has shared in shifting attention from the inherent, objective characteristics of the text to the engagement of the reader

with the text, and the production of textual meaning by the reader" (Childers and Hentzi 253). Participatory reading, Randall Roorda claims, is an act of "surpassing, superceding or transcending" routine reading (78).

3. Passages on cause-and-effect reasoning and naive acceptance of the *post hoc, ergo propter hoc* fallacy (after that, therefore because of that) in the exploration of non-teleology that appear in the "Easter Sunday" chapter of *Sea of Cortez* (866–67) bear a striking resemblance with Levy-Bruhl's prominent statements on that same reasoning fallacy and on related naive causal relations. Especially pertinent is Levy-Bruhl's tone throughout—he is never condescending toward primitive worldviews but posits the need to understand difference and otherness as a primary effect; certainly this dimension is apparent throughout Steinbeck's works. In his chapter "The Form of the New': Pragmatist Ecology and *Sea of Cortez*," Neil Browne makes a compelling argument for the presence of American philosopher John Dewey's ideas on participation in the Ricketts/Steinbeck cosmos. Steinbeck, he claims, "would have felt quite at home in pragmatism's insistence on the all-important interrelationships of science, philosophy, and literature" (61). Katherine Rodger makes a strong argument for Ricketts as the main proponent of participation (Introduction 28–29).

4. Steinbeck's 1933 letter to George Albee, which is three and a quarter typed pages long, appears in edited form in *Steinbeck: A Life in Letters* (79–82). The published version excludes a number of Steinbeck's statements on, among other things, the phalanx artist's role, and for that reason I refer to the original text of the letter from here on. In her stellar biography *Carol and John Steinbeck*, Susan Shillinglaw devotes several pages to an excellent discussion of the artist's role in the phalanx (129–31).

5. Written in Steinbeck's hand, "Introduction by Pascal Covici" is two and a half pages long and is accompanied by a twenty-six-line handwritten letter from Steinbeck, composed in September 1942, from Sherman Oaks, California, where Steinbeck and his soon-to-be second wife, Gwyn, were living. "I have a little time today," Steinbeck wrote Covici, and "will take a crack at this introduction you asked me to do. Don't know how it will be but I'll give it a try. . . . There I finished it and I hope it is what you want."

6. Although it has not been my angle here, an alternate and less overtly pleasurable analysis of *Cannery Row* is possible for the resisting reader who approaches Steinbeck's text from perspectives of ethnicity, race, and/or gender. See the revelatory studies by Carol McKibben and Mimi Reisel Gladstein.

7. The letters, sources, and texts scholars such as Richard Astro and Brian Railsback have employed to demonstrate Steinbeck's immersion in evolutionary biology indicate that, in constructing his phalanx thesis, Steinbeck also boned up on other branches of scientific discourse, including mathematics, especially the work of Paul Dirac, and that he was dipping into literature about contemporary physics as early as 1929 when, after reading Edward U. Condon and Philip M. Morse's theoretically detailed and equation-heavy *Quantum Mechanics*, Steinbeck told Robert Cathcart, "I have been having a good bit of fun," though he admitted to not understanding the theories even in their "primer for the man in the street stage" (quoted in *SR* 28). Steinbeck's claim

that "the only true poets are found among the physicists, mathematicians and bio-
chemists," which was quoted by Stanley Brodwin as an epigram to his excellent essay
on *Sea of Cortez* (142), again reveals a wider interest on Steinbeck's part in branches of
science than has been acknowledged. In the decade following his admission to Cathcart, Steinbeck seems to have remedied his deficiencies not so much in the realm of
hard, practical science, but in the philosophical and metaphoric implications of the
new physics. Nuclear chemist Peter Englert argues that in *Sea of Cortez* Steinbeck
and Ricketts's "use of terms borrowed from quantum mechanics, relativity theory, and
field theory is doubtful in many respects" (186), but he also finds value in the authors'
approach: "one can cross boundaries of traditionally separate subject areas with an ease
that facilitates innovative discussion. Such openness can lead to speculation as well
as to simplified statement, but the risk is worthwhile" (192). In *The Epistemic Music of
Rhetoric*, Katz considers crossing boundaries between literature and science as a kind
of "imperative," which "underlie[s] the nature and pursuit of knowledge across disciplines and constitute[s] cultural ways of knowing" (20).

    8. Steinbeck wrote this letter to Carlton Sheffield on June 30, 1933, but unfortu-
nately the section I quote was excised in the published version (*SLL* 78). The original
is in Stanford University's Department of Special Collections (Riggs 80).

    9. The fullest explanation of Steinbeck's ordering of plot and digressive chapters in
the manuscript, typescript, and published text of *Cannery Row* (they differ) occurs in
Simmonds (321–22). Given the novel's elastic episodic form, in which all chapters (each
its own quanta of energy) are supposed to fit equally into the overall (though ultimately incomplete) design of the novel, one puzzle remains, and that is why Steinbeck
took out a chapter (Simmonds calls it a "self-contained short story") later published
independently in *'47 Magazine of the Year* called "The Day the Wolves Ate the Vice
Principal." It was originally labeled as Chapter VI in both the manuscript and the
typescript. Editor Shillinglaw states that thematically the interchapter fits the novel
"seamlessly" ("Fiftieth Anniversary" 1). She proposes several reasons why Steinbeck
might have omitted the chapter, including the fact that the "violence of the plot" may
have been offensive, but ultimately why it was excised remains conjectural. A page of
the holograph manuscript of *Cannery Row*, later excised by Steinbeck, which describes
a character named Cameron (apparently based on Steinbeck himself), can be viewed
in William McPheron's *John Steinbeck: From Salinas to Stockholm* (46) and in Luchen
Li's *John Steinbeck: A Documentary Volume* (148).

Chapter 3

    1. Although this essay focuses on the artistic and literary implications and inter-
connectedness of Steinbeck's allied writing processes—the twinning of private jour-
nals/public novels—it should be noted that Steinbeck understood that writing was
a business and that his financial success and economic well-being depended on his
continued production of a marketable product. Steinbeck supported himself and his

wives and children by his pen. After the failure of Covici Friede in the summer of
1938 (Steinbeck's publisher from *Tortilla Flat* through *Of Mice and Men*), Viking Press
bought his contract and paid him $5,615.71 and Pascal Covici $9,384.29, according to
a letter from Viking Press President Harold Guinzburg to McIntosh and Otis, dated
August 9, 1938. "Now a new era," Steinbeck quipped on that same day. "Now cleared
in N.Y. Viking Press brought contract. New one made" (*WD* 53). Steinbeck's new
contract with Viking Press, dated September 12, 1938, for his short-story collection,
The Long Valley, reveals that he was expected to produce four additional optioned
books. The incentive and the payoff was considerable, as Steinbeck, whose works sold
prolifically, earned a royalty of 17½% "up to and including 3000 copies; 20 percent on
all copies sold over 3,000 and up to 5,000; 25 percent on all copies sold thereafter"
("Memorandum of Agreement" Part One). Seven years later, on April 10, 1945, Steinbeck's value to Viking had skyrocketed, and his publisher's contract for "a work as yet
untitled" that would become *The Wayward Bus* stipulated a flat royalty fee of 25 percent
("Memorandum of Agreement" Part One). Although the journals demystify to some
degree his compositional practices, revealing instead the nuts and bolts of protracted
isolated labor, they also rarely mention Steinbeck's legally binding contractual commit-
ments. For a writer who delegated all financial and legal arrangements and activities
to his agents, McIntosh and Otis, this silence may have been less a matter of willful
avoidance than a matter of self-preservation. No matter what other function the journals served, they were certainly a way for Steinbeck to keep commerce in the background, to distance himself from the less savory elements of commodification, and to
maintain an image—perhaps even an illusion—of independent authorial control. The
construction of Steinbeck, Inc.—his iconic literary/cultural reputation—is probably
due as much to market-driven economic factors as it is to myriad cultural and historical values and to single-minded writerly perseverance. (Contractual documents courtesy of Eugene Winick and McIntosh and Otis.)

2. The term "journal" has for better or worse gained currency as a catchall term,
though in fact Steinbeck also called these personal writings "diaries," "diary day books,"
and "day books," and so the best estimate is that he used the terms interchangeably
throughout his career to refer to a private mode of writing distinct from his social and
professional correspondence and his contracted work.

3. Steinbeck's *Long Valley* ledger book, entered primarily in 1934, shows several
stop-and-start entries as he labored over a series of new short stories, some of which
would become signature pieces, such as "The Chrysanthemums," "The White Quail,"
and "The Harness," and others such as "The Cow," "The Sisters," and "Case History"
(an early attempt to fictionalize his evolving phalanx theory) that would never be
completed: "What's the matter with me. I'm not written out. I can't pull any stories
out of the darkness out of the half real. Thinking and throwing out and building and
throwing out. I'm wasting time" (126). Later, on the third day of composing *Sea of
Cortez* (January 30, 1941), his entry ends summarily: "The clock is running down, my
clock. . . . I think I'll leave this book now" (*WD* 128). Steinbeck started to keep a work

journal/daybook for *Travels with Charley* after he had already written fifty-one pages of the narrative. Between February 3, 1961, in New York and March 3, 1961, when he and Elaine were closing out their three-week vacation in Barbados, he made eighteen entries on the left-hand pages of his ledger, then quit abruptly when a sense of despair deepened and he got "too wound up" in "dismal repetitiveness" (94).

4. In a 1961 interview with Steinbeck Hal Boyle said that the "ledgers in which he writes would be a gold mine to future literary scholars—if Steinbeck kept them. But he says he throws them away. 'They don't seem awfully damn important to me'" (*CJS* 76–77). The facts belie Steinbeck's willful misrepresentation. The handwritten manuscript of Steinbeck's *Grapes of Wrath* journal, the basis for *Working Days*, is at the Morgan Library and Museum, New York, as is "My personal book," his *Wayward Bus* journal. The Morgan Library, a rich trove of primary Steinbeck materials, also has several other notebooks, including 1951 and 1952 daily planners and two lengthy unpublished journals, one from 1948 and one from 1950 (both are restricted). His *East of Eden* letter/journal, which became *Journal of a Novel*, is at the Harry Ransom Center at University of Texas, Austin. A handwritten journal he kept from November 1946, to June 1947—much of it devoted to an abandoned play, "The Last Joan"—is in the private collection of SJ Neighbors, who kindly shared it with me. The posthumous publication in 1969 of *Journal of a Novel: The East of Eden Letters* and in 1989 of *Working Days: The Journals of The Grapes of Wrath* signaled moments when the "private" became public and went from being sequestered in the Steinbeck Archive to occupying shelf space in libraries and bookstores—when, in other words, Steinbeck's secret writing was outed, so to speak, actions over which Steinbeck, being dead, obviously had no control (though about which he'd had prophetic opinions). Motives for the belated publication of those texts, therefore, can be regarded as a mixture of commercial attempts to capitalize on his reputation and fame, a way of plugging into the ubiquitous phenomenon of contemporary interest in tell-all expression, and as a significant service to readers and scholars of twentieth-century American letters who want to know more about writers' inner lives and the creative background of their books.

5. Steinbeck can be considered a practitioner of what Louise DeSalvo has dubbed "slow writing." DeSalvo, who refers to *Working Days* and *Journal of a Novel* frequently in her study, considers slow writing a "meditative act" that acknowledges that all writers are "beginners." "Slow writing," she claims in *The Art of Slow Writing*, "is a way to resist the dehumanization inherent in a world that values speed." It returns us to "our authentic selves" (xxv). Writing with pen or pencil as Steinbeck habitually did seemed to aid and abet the slow-handed, crafted nature of his writing. See also Hayashi's edition *John Steinbeck on Writing* (23–27), and Sarah Stodola in *Process: The Writing Lives of the Great Authors*, who calls such care "the quality of perseverance" (xix).

6. Steinbeck employed dictation on a Thomas Edison–developed machine called an Ediphone when he worked on *Bombs Away* in 1942. He does not mention the brand of machine he received January 28, 1946, though in *Odd Type Writers* Celia Johnson assumes it was a Dictaphone (138).

7. Shortly after being a featured guest at one of the very first John Steinbeck conferences, "Steinbeck Country: A Conference and Film Festival," organized by Martha Heasley Cox, James Clark, and Robert Woodward and held at San Jose State College in February 1971, Gwyn Steinbeck, the writer's second ex-wife, hired Douglas Brown to help her record her memories of her nine-year relationship with John (1943–1948 as his wife). The interviews, conducted from March 30, 1971, to May 28, 1971, were never fully completed because Gwyn fired Brown and relieved him of his duties, and thus the projected memoir she envisioned writing was abandoned. After her death at fifty-eight in 1975, her sons, Thom and John IV, sold the original recordings to Jenkins Rare Book Company of Austin, Texas. The eleven oral tapes were later transcribed, adapted, and edited by Jenkins's literature manager Terry Halladay and became the basis for "The Closest Witness," his 1979 master's thesis at Stephen F. Austin University in Texas. The thesis has only been available in rare instances in xerox form on demand. Halladay explained his rationale for editing and creating a logical chronology and readable first-person narrative, making every attempt to "stay true to her voice" and reduce Brown's often irrelevant questions and comments ("Closest Witness" 16). In 2018, another version of Gwyn's interviews appeared in *My Life with John Steinbeck*, prominently announced "as told to Douglas Brown," which is the version farthest removed from the original tapes. *My Life* shows further editorial smoothing and narrative intervention, so that it is difficult to tell if it is Gwyn speaking or Douglas Brown. In Halladay's version, she says: "I think John Steinbeck was miserable most of his life. He sacrificed a great deal of happiness to his work, and when he was not working, he was miserable too. Work may have been John's kind of drug" ("Closest Witness" 258). Here is Brown's version: "While alive, he had the courage for many things, and the greatest of these was his urge to write. The relentless drive of the man was unique. Here was a man who sacrificed everything for the sake of his work. To him, the writing was a miracle drug" (*My Life* 182). As William Souder suggests, Gwyn's reminiscences have to be used with care and sparingly and are often "hard to evaluate" because "telling the truth was never [her] strong suit" (*Mad* 301). Where applicable I have referred to Halladay's version in my essay. Having met and talked with Gwyn at that 1971 San Jose conference mentioned above, I feel his version is closer to her voice. Gwyn's observations in her autobiography corroborate Steinbeck's tense, conflicted view of their marriage.

8. Steinbeck's private writings in the period from the mid- to late 1940s, notably unpublished daybook/journals written in 1946, 1947, 1948, and 1950 reveal a restless, tortured soul who exhibited extreme degrees of morbidity, moroseness, and hypercritical self-awareness. Reading those journals is an exercise in unrelenting pessimism, a descent into a voyeuristic rabbit hole. Something was amiss, but it is never clear what caused Steinbeck's disaffection, though he wondered whether it was "glandular irregularity." Sometimes even the raw documents of the archive are no help. In *Looking for Steinbeck's Ghost*, Jackson Benson says Steinbeck's discovery that Gwyn had cheated on him was a trigger to an emotional free fall (171–72). Even Gwyn was silent on that

period. After she recorded her tell-all memoir, she destroyed the audiotapes covering March 1945 to December 1946, which would have covered *The Wayward Bus* period ("The Closest Witness" 196), for what reason we cannot know for certain. Alcohol, uppers and downers, massive hits of vitamins, shots of testosterone administered by the neurosurgeon Juan Negrin, his physician, all failed to ease Steinbeck's internal trauma and his fears that he was "cracking up." Recently, biographer William Souder shed strong light on the period when he speculated that "the nervousness, nightmares, and insomnia that plagued" Steinbeck during those years may be traceable to the debilitating and recurring aftereffects of a "brain-changing" concussion he suffered during his combat reporting in 1943 (*Mad* 283). "This might explain many things about his later life—from his depressions to his mercurial behavior with his sons, to the difficulties he had with his writing long before his vital working life should have been over" (305). Dark and tortured as the period was, one admirable takeaway from this era is that Steinbeck soldiered on despite obstacles and further that the composition journals are constant reminders of his daily application of willpower and perseverance to stay on his writerly tasks. When Viking sent an advance reader's copy of *Working Days* to Elaine Steinbeck, she wrote me a lovely congratulatory note, but added: "At first I hated John's own entries—all that moaning! Then I realized he really never changed much. How often I heard it all, and probably Gwyn too if she was listening. Of course by the time I knew him he had more self-assurance and was a bit more used to success. He loved to write, but oh, how he pitied himself. Always his 'stomach was going to pieces.' I wish I could hear him say it right now, bless him."

9. In a May 20, 1996, letter to Roy Simmonds, Julie Fallowfield at McIntosh and Otis, Steinbeck's agents, speaking for the Steinbeck Estate, disapproved of his attempts to publish Steinbeck's *Wayward Bus* journal. Simmonds eventually became disillusioned by the depressing nature of the journal and questioned whether it should ever be published. In a letter to me written on March 11, 1997, from his home in England, Roy said, "Everything that you have said about him [Steinbeck] in . . . *Working Days* . . . cannot be said about the writer and man that is revealed in this journal." In their biographies, Benson (574–85), Parini (294–303), Wagner-Martin (99–106), and Souder (292–96) have all treated the *Wayward Bus* period with varying degrees of attention, but the most meticulously researched and detailed account is Roy Simmonds's "The Composition, Publication, and Reception of John Steinbeck's *The Wayward Bus*, with Biographical Background." Based on an unpublished 1997 typescript, "The Bus That Failed," it was serially published in *Steinbeck Review* in seven sections over a period of three years. A compressed but utterly workable version of Roy's study is his "The Composition of Steinbeck's *The Wayward Bus*" in *John Steinbeck: A Centennial Tribute*.

10. John Ditsky was among the first critics to suggest that "*Journal of a Novel* and *East of Eden* . . . constitute a single work, exactly as written" (3).

11. According to an entry on Tuesday, February 20, 1951, in his *Standard Diary for 1951*, Steinbeck owned eight pipes and he planned to smoke "each one twice a day," but

he planned to smoke the Merschaum "every other time if it is cool enough." Four of his pipes are at the National Steinbeck Center in Salinas, California.

Chapter 4

1. Steinbeck's article (written in English then translated into French by Jean-François Rozan) originally appeared as "Sur les bords de l'Oise" ("On the banks of the Oise") in the French journal *Le Figaro Littéraire* on July 10, 1954, and was collected with a number of his *Figaro* pieces as the eighth chapter in a little-known, limited-edition paperback volume, *Un Américain à New York et à Paris* (Paris: Rene Julliard, 1956). Between August 1954 and January 1955 the article was reprinted in English under different titles in *Punch* ("Fishing in Paris"); *Sports Illustrated* ("Of Fish and Fishermen"); and American, British, and Canadian editions of *Reader's Digest* ("How to Fish in French"); and elsewhere, and most recently it turned up as "On Fishing" in *America and Americans and Selected Nonfiction*, ed. Shillinglaw and Benson, which is the source I employ throughout this essay. Benson quotes a June 1953 letter by Steinbeck regarding his newly completed fishing essay. Steinbeck told Pascal Covici, his editor at Viking Press: "I enclose . . . the newest article for Figaro. An essay on fishing. I think it is true and hope you find it amusing. The boys [sons Thom and John IV] have poles now and are ready to do some fishing in the Seine. And about time too. Catbird [family nickname for John IV] would rather fish than do anything in the world. It is the only thing that can hold his attention indefinitely" (*TAJS* 760).

2. This essay is dedicated to Jackson Benson, biographer and scholar extraordinaire, old friend, valued colleague, and fly-fishing gentleman, who made a day of trout angling on Utah's Green River especially enjoyable while we were playing hooky from a Western Literature Society conference. Fishing was so-so, but the day was brilliant in every other way. Fly-fishing—fishing in general—is often about serendipitous discoveries. So is scholarship. In the early 1980s, when Jack and I were in the final stages of preparation on *Steinbeck's Reading* and *The True Adventures of John Steinbeck*, we exchanged research information that found its way into each other's books. Or most of it anyway. As I was preparing this essay for its reappearance, I found a list of book titles Jack had copied down from the shelves in Joyous Garde, Steinbeck's writing studio in Sag Harbor. The two-page list apparently had separated from another six-page list Jack had sent (some of which I had been able to use in *Steinbeck's Reading*) and had fallen out of sight in the back of a file cabinet where it had been hiding for more decades than I care to count. I found among the lost list of titles: *The Fireside Book of Fishing: A Selection from the Great Literature of Angling*, ed. Raymond R. Camp, illus. William K. Plummer (New York: Simon and Schuster, 1959); one volume of an unspecified edition of Jonathan Couch's *A History of the Fishes of the British Islands*, which was originally published in London in four volumes (1862–1865) but then frequently reprinted; and *How to Catch Salt Water Fish*, a bibliographic maverick I have not been able to locate. Were the first two back-entered into *Steinbeck's Reading*, they

would become numbers 154a and 206a, respectively. More recently, I discovered that a copy of Henry Van Dyke's *Fisherman's Luck and Some Other Uncertain Things* (New York: Charles Scribner's, 1899), a popular and often reprinted text on the spiritual qualities of fishing by an eminent polymath writer, scholar, educator, minister, and statesman, was part of a Steinbeck-Hamilton family library that is now held at the National Steinbeck Center in Salinas. The volume belonged to Steinbeck's older sister, Elizabeth, who acquired it in May 1912 (Josephs 1). How familiar Steinbeck was with this volume is not known, but he certainly shared one of its main tenets: "It seems as if almost all the men who could write well had a friendly feeling for the contemplative sport" (147–48).

3. Steinbeck was not alone in his preference for uninterrupted angling solitude. In his *Simple Beauty of the Unexpected*, Dartmouth physics and astronomy professor Marcello Gleiser writes: "fly fishing is a form of meditation, of letting the self go, a way of approaching an emptiness of being that is its fullest expression. By doing you don't do, by acting you don't act. With a shudder, I realized that catching a fish, the end result of the act, was an interruption. . . . Catching the fish spoiled my experience of fishing, my search for timelessness" (165).

4. John Steinbeck, personal correspondence with parents, April 1927. Over the next eight months or so Steinbeck mentioned fishing to his family half a dozen different times. Ever the epicurean, Steinbeck always showed enthusiasm for eating the occasional quarry. "We spent the last long weekend at the [Elia] Kazan's in Connecticut," he told his sister. "Chris Kazan, who is fourteen, and I did a lot of Pickeral [*sic*] fishing and got a lot of Pickeral—I'm going to smoke them in my new barbecue. . . . I love smoked fish" (John Steinbeck, letter to Esther Steinbeck Rodgers, June 7, 1953). Two years later he told Webster Street that in Sag Harbor, "we bring [fish] home alive and cook them while they are still kicking and are they delicious. My fear if starvation disappears when I am near the ocean. I figure I can always catch my dinner" (*SLL* 505–6). There is a delicious scene in *Travels with Charley* where he recounts an experience at a spring-fed trout pond at a host's ranch in Texas. He picked up a trout rod already rigged with a tiny "black gnat" fly and started casting and landed four trout on as many casts. He brought his cleaned catch to the ranch cook, who "dipped my fish in cornmeal and fried them crisp in bacon fat." It had been a long time, he said, "since I had eaten trout like that, five minutes from water to pan. You take him up in your fingers delicately by head and tail and nibble him from off his backbone, and finally you eat the tail, crisp as a potato chip" (924–25). For background information on and illustrations of the black-gnat fly that Steinbeck used, see Ian Whitelaw's *The History of Fly-Fishing in Fifty Flies*, which features a gnat pattern developed by chalk-stream pioneer Frederic Halford in 1885 (66–71). For a partial view of the trout pond at the Hagy Ranch in Clarendon, Texas, where John and Elaine spent a Thanksgiving holiday (the ranch was owned by Elaine's former brother-in-law), see Bill Steigerwald's *Dogging Steinbeck* (209–11).

5. Steinbeck's sons remembered their father's predilections well. During Steinbeck's

working summer on Nantucket, fishing was sometimes an excuse for daydreaming about his novel project. On July 13, 1951, Steinbeck told Covici, "I took Thursday off and went fishing. . . . The fishing trip got no fish and I got a painful sunburn but out of it I got a whole new extension of the book. I guess I never really do stop working" (*SLL* 424). Regarding the family's stay in Nantucket, Elaine Steinbeck recalled that her husband "spent as much time as possible on the sea, in the sea, and studying that particular bit of sea" (xi). Angling for fish and/or words, often at the same time, was never far from his mind.

6. Susan Stewart's brilliant treatise on nostalgia, *On Longing*, has suggestive implications for the fly-fishing community that prizes the small, scaled-down (and often hand-tied) objects of our sport, such as flies: "the miniature object represents an antithetical mode of production: production by the hand, a production that is unique and authentic . . . [and is] . . . located at a place of origin (the childhood of the self)" (68).

7. This is a ridiculously truncated chronology. For the fuller story, consult books by Arnold Gingrich, Andrew Herd, and Glen Law, listed in the bibliography of this book. Also see Justin Hanisch's *A Contemplative Angler*, a bounteously illustrated showcasing of Bruce P. Dancik's historical angling book collection. Consult Andrew Herd and Jon Ward-Allen's informative and lively online site (www.fishinhgmuseum.org.uk), as well. The history of European fly-fishing keeps being interrupted by remarkable new discoveries that push back its origins. The most recent find I was able to examine in person (at Yale's Beinecke Library) is a medieval Austrian/Latin text, *The Breviary of Leonardus Haslinger*, a handwritten devotional text bound in beech boards circa 1440–1460, decades before the *Treatyse*. A tract at the end includes instructions on "how one should bind hooks" (i.e., create artificial flies) and includes the earliest known collection of fly-tying patterns known to exist, as well as additional comments on fly-fishing. Given Steinbeck's interest in both fishing and the Middle Ages, I think he would have relished this rarity. For the shorter-lived development of US fly-fishing, the story is available in Paul Schullery's definitive study, as well as in William Black's entertaining account.

8. Two decades ago, I fished the River Test in two locations and wrote about it in "Marryat's Fly Box," a chapter of *Angling Days* (108–13). I was fascinated to find that as late as the turn of this century, some of the same strict ethical procedural protocols and regulations are still in effect: you are expected to cast only to visible, feeding fish, and you are not supposed to leave the bank and wade into the water. Break these rules and you risk being chided as a loutish Yank, as Texas novelist William Humphrey, in his entertaining chapter about British chalk-stream fishing "Bill Breaks His Duck," characterized this way: "down on the river there awaited us a fishing catechism as strict as any church's. It was to be a series of Thou Shalt Nots" (176).

9. Automatic fly reels, pioneered by an American firm, Martin, and still being manufactured, never caught on in elite fly-fishing circles because they were considered ungainly contraptions due to "excessive weight, over complexity, and tendency to break down" (Brown 62). They retrieved line rapidly by means of a spring-loaded lever

rather than by the usual, slower method of turning the reel spool by hand. In some angling situations they proved useful and efficient but for purists they were frowned upon as excessively gimmicky. Undeterred by the Hardy clerk's dismissal, Steinbeck later bought an automatic fly reel as an "experiment" at the fishing department of Abercrombie and Fitch in Manhattan. "I took the reel to Sag Harbor, mounted it on a trembling, sensitive bit of bamboo whimsy [fly rod] I have there." As a gag, he planned to send the reel to his British agent Graham Watson to use at his private angling club's stretch of the River Itchen, where, Steinbeck said, "this ghastly contrivance might well cost you your membership." He continued, "I do hate to give in to authority. I detest having to say that they are right. The thing is no damn good, and beyond that, it is actually evil and besides that, I hate it, and I wouldn't think of sending it to you" (Letter, March 29, 1966). Steinbeck hoped Abercrombie and Fitch would take the reel back, but there is no proof they did so.

10. See the anonymous pieces, "Fly Fishing's Mystery Woman," and "Hardy Girl Update," in *Fly Rod & Reel* (2005). For an informative account of the Hardy manufacturing firm, see James Leighton Hardy, *The House the Hardy Brothers Built*, and the documentary film by Andy Heathcote and Heike Bacheller, *The Lost World of Mr. Hardy*. The company, which had purchased rival tackle-maker Grey's in 2004, was purchased by a South Carolina conglomerate, Pure Fishing, in 2013 but still retains its signature identity.

11. For more on the background of the Tups Indispensibles, see Ian Whitelaw's *History* (84–87). Except for an offbeat parable by Skues, "Mr. Theodore Castwell," which appears in *The Fireside Book of Fishing* Steinbeck owned (mentioned above), I have never been able to determine absolutely if Steinbeck ever heard of Skues, much less read his mainstream angling writings. My hunch is that Graham Watson, whose angling club had a private beat (stretch) on the Itchen, where the legendary Skues fished most of his life, would certainly have been familiar with his name and reputation and perhaps passed on that knowledge to Steinbeck. I always found it tantalizing and perhaps even a bit curious that the names of two chief characters in *East of Eden*—brothers Adam and Charles Trask—mirror the names of Skues's London publisher, Adam and Charles Black.

12. In his authoritative *The History of Fly Fishing, Volume I*, Andrew Herd has significantly expanded his earlier study, *The Fly*. There are numerous books devoted to the exquisite art of the salmon fly, or rather, the salmon fly as art, which was the province of an especially sumptuous and glossy contemporary magazine (2001–2006) edited by renowned collector, tier, and bibliophile Paul Schmookler and by Ingrid Sils called *Art of Angling Journal* that regularly featured stunning color photo spreads of fully dressed, hand-tied, gaudy flies. The magazine, however, which was itself exorbitantly priced (and later went bankrupt), carried the materiality of fishing to a level of fetishism, perhaps—given the dimensions and vagaries of our cultural discourse these days—to a level of near-pornography. Consult Woit's lavishly illustrated *Fly Fishing Treasures* (68–87) for an overview of Schmookler's achievements. For a lyrical treatment of

classic salmon-fly production, see *Kiss the Water*, Eric Steel's award-winning documentary film on legendary UK salmon-fly dresser Megan Boyd (who apparently had no intertest in fishing herself). Since her death in 2001, Boyd's exquisite flies have become eagerly sought collector's items. A recent authoritative history is Herd and Frandsen's *The Story of the Salmon Fly*. For a superb view of Hardy's involvement in salmon-fly dressing, consult Lanigan-O'Keeffe's profusely illustrated *Hardy's Salmon Flies* and Keith Harwood's *The Hardy Book of the Salmon Fly*.

13. One of Hemingway's personal favorites—a split bamboo Hardy "Fairy" fly rod—is on permanent display at the American Museum of Fly Fishing in Manchester, Vermont.

14. The Oise enters the Seine northwest of Paris. In an earlier *Figaro* piece, "J'aime cette Ile de la Cite" ("I Love This Isle of the City"), which appears as "One American in Paris (fourth piece)" in *America and Americans and Selected Nonfiction*, ed. Shillinglaw and Benson, Steinbeck wrote evocatively of watching the Seine River fishermen with his young sons, Thom and John IV, who "wait patiently for some of the many fishermen to catch a fish and when some tiny thing is hooked we run to examine and to congratulate. This minnow is a trump beyond which the big game fisherman cannot rise" (247).

15. A 2020 issue of *Flylords* newsletter featured a report on a Colorado trout angler who has fished with a hookless fly for more than two decades and finds the practice completely satisfying. For a critique of *piscatorus interruptus*, and a sarcastic view of the "new generation of humane fly fishers," see Quigley, *In the Company of Rivers* (203–5). Steinbeck, I think, would have been on Bodo's side. I am guessing, too, that Steinbeck might have embraced the ancient Japanese reel-less angling method called Tenkara, because it is similar to the French method he praised. Tenkara requires only a long, light rod of eleven to fourteen feet and a corresponding length of line and leader to which is attached a lightly dressed barbless hook fly. The method, which reduces fishing to its simplest elements, is becoming increasingly popular with American anglers interested in low-impact, minimalist techniques (Chouinard, Mathews, and Mazzo).

16. See Tamm, *Beyond the Outer Shores* (25, 277), for illustrations of the creatures in question. In 1987 a Pacific coast nudibranch (sea slug) was named *Eubranchus steinbecki* by David Behrens. Dr. Rolf Ling Bolin (1901–1973), ichthyologist and oceanographer, was the assistant director of Stanford's Hopkins Marine Station in Pacific Grove, California. In *Sea of Cortez* Steinbeck and Ricketts praise Bolin because "he loves true things" (*LSC* 775). Steinbeck noted on June 17, 1938, "Doc Bolin here yesterday. Fine people. He is going on a collecting trip to the south seas and is very excited about it." Deep in the writing of *The Grapes of Wrath*, Steinbeck noted ruefully, "I'd like to go but won't or can't or something" (*WD* 29).

17. Steinbeck's presence among contemporary fly-fishers has odd ways of making itself felt. James Babb, in *Crosscurrents*, quotes from *Sea of Cortez* as an epigraph for his chapter, "Cabo Wabo" (155). In his last interview, the late fly-angling pioneer and innovator Gary La Fontaine told Craig Oberg he considered Steinbeck's *Cannery Row*

and *Sweet Thursday* "perfect books. That's what I tried to pattern *Fly Fishing the Mountain Lakes* after. They had just the right number of words to get across the effect of the story, and they had the perfect amount of information" (11). Rick Wollum, host of thirteen episodes of ESPN's nationally broadcast *Fly Fishing America* in 1999, revealed that the format of his peripatetic series was indebted to Steinbeck's *Travels with Charley* (Interview). David O'Hara and Matthew Dickerson launched *Downstream* by quoting Steinbeck's *Log from the Sea of Cortez*. Mark Kurlansky riffs on Steinbeck as well in his latest book.

Author's Publications on John Steinbeck

BOOKS

DeMott, Robert. *Steinbeck's Reading: A Catalogue of Books Owned and Borrowed*. New York: Garland Publishing, 1984. 239 pp. [Available digitally with new Preface (2012) from Martha Heasley Cox Center for Steinbeck Studies at San Jose State University.]

———, ed. John Steinbeck, *Working Days: The Journals of The Grapes of Wrath, 1938–1941*. New York: Viking Press, 1989. 180 pp. [Penguin Books paperback, 1990. Translated into Japanese by Yukio Nakata, published as Volume 17 of *The Complete Works of John Steinbeck* (Osaka: Osaka Kyoiku Tosho, 1999).]

———, ed, and Elaine A. Steinbeck, Special Consultant. John Steinbeck, *Novels and Stories 1932–1937*. New York: Library of America, 1994. 909 pp. [Includes *To a God Unknown*, *The Pastures of Heaven*, *Tortilla Flat*, *In Dubious Battle*, *Of Mice and Men*. Vol. 72 in Library of America series.]

———, Donald V. Coers, and Paul D. Ruffin, eds. *After The Grapes of Wrath: Essays on John Steinbeck in Honor of Tetsumaro Hayashi*. Athens: Ohio University Press, 1995. 303 pp.

———. *Steinbeck's Typewriter: Essays on His Art*. Troy, NY: Whitston Publishing Company, 1996. 353 pp. [2nd printing, 1997. Reprinted with new Preface, Bloomington, IN: iUniverse, 2012.]

———, ed., and Elaine A. Steinbeck, Special Consultant. John Steinbeck, *The Grapes of Wrath and Other Writings 1936–1941*. New York: The Library of America, 1996. 1,067 pp. [Includes *The Long Valley*, *The Grapes of Wrath*, *Log from the Sea of Cortez*, "The Harvest Gypsies." Corrected text of *The Grapes of Wrath* prepared by Gila Bercovitch based on collation of manuscript, typescript, and galleys. Volume 86 in the Library of America series.]

———, ed. John Steinbeck, *Novels 1942–1952*. New York: The Library of America, 2001. 983 pp. [Includes *The Moon is Down*, *Cannery Row*, *The Pearl*, and *East of Eden*. Volume 132 in the Library of America series.]

———, ed., with Brian Railsback. John Steinbeck, *Travels with Charley and Later Novels 1947–1962*. New York: The Library of America, 2007. 1008 pp. [Includes *The Wayward Bus*, *Burning Bright*, *Sweet Thursday*, *The Winter of Our Discontent*, and *Travels with Charley in Search of America*. Volume 170 in the Library of America series.]

LIMITED-EDITION CHAPBOOKS

———, ed. *Your Only Weapon is Your Work: A Letter by John Steinbeck to Dennis Murphy.*
San Jose, CA: Steinbeck Research Center, 1985. 20 pp. [500 copies. Reprinted.
in Luchen Li, ed., *John Steinbeck: A Documentary Volume* (Detroit: Gale, 2005),
243–47.]
———*John Steinbeck: A Checklist of Books by and About.* Bradenton, FL: Opuscula Press,
1987. 32 pp. [200 copies.]
———. *"A Play to be Played": John Steinbeck on Stage and Screen, 1935–1960.* New York:
Columbia University Rare Book and Manuscript Library, 2002. 10 pp. [600
copies. Reprinted in Luchen Li, ed., *John Steinbeck: A Documentary Volume*
(Detroit: Gale, 2005), pp. 347–51.]

INTRODUCTIONS, PREFACES, FOREWORDS

———. "New Directions in Steinbeck Studies." *Steinbeck Quarterly* 10 (Summer–Fall,
1977), 68–70.
———. "Mapping *East of Eden*." *Steinbeck Quarterly* 14 (Winter–Spring, 1981), 4–5.
———. "Introduction." In *A New Steinbeck Bibliography. Supplement I: 1978–1981*, 1–4.
By Tetsumaro Hayashi. Metuchen, NJ: Scarecrow Press, 1983
———. "Foreword." The Steinbeck Research Center at San Jose State University: A
Descriptive Catalogue. By Robert Woodward. San Jose, CA: *San Jose Studies* 11
(Winter 1985), 5–7. [Also published as limited-edition casebound book.]
———. "What Goes Around, Comes Around." Introduction to Donald Siefker, Tetsu-
maro Hayashi, and Thomas Moore, eds., *The Steinbeck Quarterly: A Cumulative
Index to Volumes XI–XX* (1978–87), Steinbeck Bibliography Series No. 2, 1989,
6–9.
———. "Introduction." *The Grapes of Wrath*. By John Steinbeck. New York: Penguin
Books, 1992, vi–lv. [Twentieth-Century Classics Series edition.]
———. "Introduction." *To a God Unknown.* By John Steinbeck. New York: Penguin
Books, 1995, vii–xl. [Twentieth-Century Classics Series edition.]
———. "Contemporary Steinbeck." *The Steinbeck Newsletter* 12 (Spring, 1999): 9.
———. "Introduction." *The Grapes of Wrath*. By John Steinbeck. New York: Penguin
Books, 2006, ix–lviii. [Revised version for redesigned Penguin Classics Series
edition.]
———. "Introduction." *Sweet Thursday*. By John Steinbeck. New York: Penguin Books,
2008, ix-xxxii. [Penguin Classics Series edition.]
———. "About this Volume." In *Critical Insights: Of Mice and Men.* Ed. Barbara Heavi-
lin. Amenia, NY: Gray House Publishing/Salem Press, 2017, vii–xxi.

CHAPTERS IN BOOKS

———. "Steinbeck and the Creative Process. First Manifesto to End the Bringdown

Against *Sweet Thursday.*" In S*teinbeck: The Man and His Work.* Ed. Richard Astro and Tetsumaro Hayashi. Corvallis, OR: Oregon State University Press, 1971, 157–78.

———. "Steinbeck's *To a God Unknown.*" In *A Study Guide to Steinbeck: A Handbook of His Major Works.* Ed. Tetsumaro Hayashi. Metuchen, NJ: Scarecrow Press, 1973, 187–213. [Translated into Japanese by Kiyohiku Tsoboi for a selected edition of *A Study Guide to Steinbeck* (Tokyo: Eihusha Publishing Company, 1978), 23–49.]

———. "'Voltaire Didn't Like Anything': A 1939 Interview with John Steinbeck." In *Conversations with John Steinbeck.* Ed. Thomas Fensch. Jackson: University Press of Mississippi, 1988, 21–27.

———. "Creative Reading/Creative Writing: The Presence of *Dr. Gunn's New Family Physician* in Steinbeck's *East of Eden.*" In *Rediscovering Steinbeck: Revisionist Views of His Art, Politics and Intellect.* Ed. Cliff Lewis and Carroll Britch. Lewiston, New York: Edwin Mellen Press, 1989, 35–57.

———. "After *The Grapes of Wrath*: A Speculative Essay on Steinbeck's Suite of Love Poems." In *John Steinbeck: The Years of Greatness.* Ed. Tetsumaro Hayashi. Tuscaloosa: University of Alabama Press, 1993, 20–45.

———. "*Sweet Thursday* Revisited: An Excursion in Suggestiveness." In *After The Grapes of Wrath: Essays on John Steinbeck in Honor of Tetsumaro Hayashi.* Ed. Donald V. Coers, Paul D. Ruffin, and Robert J. DeMott. Athens: Ohio University Press, 1995, 172–196. [Reprinted in Don Noble, ed., *Critical Insights: John Steinbeck* (Pasadena and Hackensack: Salem Press, 2011), 320–51; and in Lawrence Trudeau, ed., *Short Story Criticism: The Novellas of John Steinbeck* (Columbia, SC: Layman Poupard Publishing, 2018).]

———. "'A Truly American Book': Pressing *The Grapes of Wrath.*" In *Biographies of Books: The Compositional Histories of Notable American Writings.* Ed. James Barbour and Tom Quirk. Columbia: University of Missouri Press, 1995, 187–225. [Reprinted in Keith Newlin, ed, *Critical Insights: The Grapes of Wrath* (Pasadena and Hackensack: Salem Press, 2011), pp. 267–311.]

———. "Steinbeck's *East of Eden.*" In *Steinbeck on Stage and Film.* Ed. Joel A. Smith. Louisville: Actor's Theatre of Louisville, 1996, 56–58.

———. "[The Success of *Of Mice and Men*]." In *Readings on John Steinbeck.* Ed. Claire Swisher. San Diego, CA: Greenhaven Press, 1996, 133.

———. "'Working at the Impossible': *Moby-Dick's* Presence in *East of Eden.*" In *Steinbeck and the Environment: Interdisciplinary Approaches.* Ed. Susan Beegel, Wes Tiffney, and Susan Shillinglaw. Foreword by Elaine Steinbeck. Tuscaloosa: University of Alabama Press, 1997, 211–228. [Reprinted in Harold Bloom, ed., *John Steinbeck.* New Edition (New York: Infobase Publishing, 2008), 77–104.]

———. "The Writing of *The Grapes of Wrath.*" In *Readings on The Grapes of Wrath.* Ed. Gary Wiener. San Diego: Greenhaven Press, 1999), 32–39.

———. "Robert DeMott on California." In *John Steinbeck* (Bloom's Major Novelists). Ed. Harold Bloom. Broomall, PA: Chelsea House, 2000, 49–51.

——. "The Place We Have Arrived: On Writing/Reading Toward *Cannery Row*." In *Beyond Boundaries: Rereading John Steinbeck*. Ed. Susan Shillinglaw and Kevin Hearle. Tuscaloosa: University of Alabama Press, 2002, 295–313.

——. "'Of Ink and Heart's Blood': Episodes in Reading Steinbeck's *East of Eden*." In *John Steinbeck: A Centennial Tribute*. Ed. Stephen K. George. Westport, CT: Praeger Publishers, 2002, 121–31.

——. Entry on *East of Eden*. In *A John Steinbeck Encyclopedia*. Ed. Brian Railsback and Michael Meyer. (Westport, CT: Greenwood Press, 2006), 87–93.

——, with Brian Railsback. "Prospects for the Study of John Steinbeck." *Resources for American Literary Study*, Volume 32. Ed. Jackson Bryer and Richard Kopley. Brooklyn, NY: AMS Press, 2009, 9–47.

PERIODICALS AND JOURNALS

——. "Toward a Redefinition of *To a God Unknown*." *University of Windsor Review*, VIII (Spring 1973): 34–53.

——. "The Interior Distances of John Steinbeck." *Steinbeck Quarterly* 12 (Summer–Fall 1979): 86–99.

——. "'Culling All Books': Steinbeck's Reading and *East of Eden*." *Steinbeck Quarterly* 14 (Winter–Spring 1981): 40–51. [Reprinted in *Twentieth Century Literary Criticism: East of Eden*, By John Steinbeck. Ed. Lawrence Trudeau. Columbia, SC: Layman Poupard Publishing, 2018.]

——. "Cathy Ames and Lady Godiva: A Contribution to *East of Eden*'s Background." *Steinbeck Quarterly* 14 (Summer–Fall 1981): 72–83.

——. "'A Great Black Book': *East of Eden* and *Gunn's New Family Physician*." *American Studies* 22 (Fall 1981): 41–57. [Reprinted in *John Steinbeck's East of Eden*. Ed. Harold Bloom. Bloom's Modern Critical Interpretations Series. New York: Chelsea House/Infobase, 2015, 150–95.]

——. "Steinbeck's Reading: First Supplement." *Steinbeck Quarterly*, 17 (Summer-Fall, 1984): 97–103.

——. "Steinbeck's *East of Eden* and *Gunn's New Family Physician*." *The Book Club of California Quarterly Newsletter* 51 (Spring 1986): 31–48.

——. "The Steinbeck Research Center: A Checklist of Autographed First Editions." *The Steinbeck Newsletter* 1 (Fall 1987): 1, 3–4.

——. "Vintage Steinbeck." *TWA Ambassador Magazine* (April 1989): 33–34.

——. "Steinbeck's Reading: Second Supplement." *Steinbeck Quarterly* 22 (Winter/ Spring 1989): 4–8.

——. "'Working Days and Hours': Steinbeck's Writing of *The Grapes of Wrath*," *Studies in American Fiction* 18 (Spring 1990): 3–15. [Reprinted. in John Steinbeck, *The Viking Critical The Grapes of Wrath: Text and Criticism*. Ed. Peter Lisca and Kevin Hearle (New York: Penguin Books, 1997), and in *Readings on The Grapes of Wrath*. Ed. Gary Wiener (San Diego, CA: Greenhaven Press, 1999.)]

———. "The Best-Brewed Plans of Malt and Hop: Steinbeck's Minimalist Elegy for Ballantine Ale." *The Steinbeck Newsletter* 3 (Winter 1990): 6–7.

———. "Special Message for the Twenty-Fifth Anniversary of the Steinbeck Society." *Steinbeck Quarterly*, XXIV (Winter–Spring, 1991): 17–18.

———. "Legacies." *Steinbeck Quarterly* XXIV (Summer–Fall 1991): 81–83.

———. "Of Ink and Heart's Blood: Adventures in Reading *East of Eden.*" *Connecticut Review* 14 (Spring 1992): 9–21.

———. "Steinbeck on the Novel: A 1954 Interview." *The Steinbeck Newsletter* 5 (Spring 1992): 6–7.

———. "Steinbeck's Other Family: New Light on *East of Eden.*" *The Steinbeck Newsletter* 7 (1994): 1–4.

———. "The Status of *The Grapes of Wrath.*" *The Steinbeck Newsletter* 12 (Spring 1999): 22.

———. "Remembering Roy Simmonds." *The Steinbeck Newsletter* 14 (Fall 2002): 49–50.

———. "Remembering Louis Owens." *Southwestern American Literature* 28 (Spring 2003): 29–31.

———. "Remembering Elaine Steinbeck." *Steinbeck Studies* 15 (Spring 2004): 179–80

———. "*Grapes of Wrath*, a classic for today?" BBC.com, April 14, 2009. [Reprinted in John Steinbeck, *The Grapes of Wrath*. Ed. Rudolph F. Rau. (Braunschweig, Germany: Diesterweg, 2016), 423–24.]

———. "A New Preface to *Steinbeck's Reading.*" *Steinbeck Review* 7 (Spring 2010): 30–34.

———. "Remembering Warren French (1922–2009)." *Steinbeck Review* 9 (Fall 2012): 54–56

———. "Of Fish and Men." *Steinbeck Review* 11 (Fall 2014): 113–37.

———. "Viva Thom Steinbeck!" *Steinbeck Review* 13, no. 2 (2016): viii–x.

———. "Private Narratives/Public Texts: Steinbeck's Journals." *Steinbeck Review* 13, no. 2 (2016): 123–50.

———. "Fifty Years Gone." *Steinbeck Review* 15, no. 2 (2018): 116–21.

REVIEWS

———. Rev. of *The Thirties: Fiction, Poetry, Drama*. Ed. by Warren French. *Kyushu American Literature* XI (December 1968): 91–94.

———. Rev. of *John Steinbeck: An Introduction and Interpretation*, by Joseph Fontenrose. *Steinbeck Newsletter* I (December 1968): 1–6.

———. Rev. of *John Steinbeck: The Errant Knight* by Nelson Valjean. *San Jose Studies* I (November 1975): 136–39.

———. Rev. of *The Novels of John Steinbeck*, by Howard Levant and *Theodore Dreiser*, by H. R. Mookerjee. *Modern Fiction Studies* 21 (Winter 1976): 651–53.

———. "Looking East from California's Shore: Steinbeck in Japan." Rev. of *John Steinbeck: East and West*. Ed. Tetsumaro Hayashi, et al. *San Jose Studies* 6 (February 1980): 54–58.

———. Rev. of *The Intricate Music: A Biography of John Steinbeck*, by Thomas Kiernan and *Steinbeck and Covici: The Story of a Friendship* by Thomas Fensch. *Journal of Modern Literature* 8 (1980–1981): 617–19.

———. Rev. of *A Study Guide to Steinbeck, Part II.* Ed. Tetsumaro Hayashi. *Steinbeck Quarterly* 15 (Winter–Spring 1982): 51–56.

———. Rev. of *Steinbeck Bibliographies: An Annotated Guide* by Robert B. Harmon. *Bulletin of Bibliography* 44 (December 1987): 294–97.

———. Rev. of *John Steinbeck's Re-Vision of America*, by Louis Owens. *Journal of English and Germanic Philology* 87 (Summer 1988): 464–67.

———. Rev. of *The Collectible John Steinbeck: A Practical Guide* by Robert B. Harmon. *The Steinbeck Newsletter* 2 (Fall 1988): 10–11.

———. Rev. of *The Grapes of Wrath: Trouble in the Promised Land* by Louis Owens. *Western American Literature* 25 (Spring 1990): 91–92.

———. Rev. of *The Short Novels of John Steinbeck: Critical Essays with a Checklist to Steinbeck Criticism* by Jackson J. Benson. *Southern Humanities Review* XXVI (Summer 1992): 295–97.

———. Rev. of *FDR'S Moviemaker: Memoirs and Scripts* by Pare Lorentz. *The Steinbeck Newsletter* 5 (Spring 1992): 13.

———. Rev. of *Steinbeck's Literary Dimension: A Guide to Comparative Studies, Series II*, by Tetsumaro Hayashi. *Western American Literature* 27 (November 1992): 237–38.

———. Rev. of *The Steinbeck Question: New Essays in Criticism.* Ed. by Donald R. Noble. *South Atlantic Review* 60 (September 1995): 131–34.

———. Rev. of *John Steinbeck: The Contemporary Reviews.* Ed. by Joseph McElrath, Jesse Crisler, and Susan Shillinglaw. *Resources for American Literary Study* 25 (1999): 126–29.

———. Rev. of *The Betrayal of Brotherhood in the Work of John Steinbeck: Cain Sign.* Ed. Michael J. Meyer. *Steinbeck Studies* 13 (Winter 2001): 16–17.

———. Rev of *Steinbeck, the Good Companion* by Carlton A. Sheffield. *Steinbeck Studies* 15 (Spring 2004): 99–102.

———. Rev. of *Renaissance Man of Cannery Row: The Life and Letters of Edward F. Ricketts*, by Katharine A. Rodger. *Steinbeck Studies* 15 (Fall 2004): 141–47.

———. Rev. of *Leopold's Shack and Ricketts's Lab: The Emergence of Environmentalism*, by Michael J. Lannoo. *Steinbeck Review* 11 (Spring 2014): 93–98.

———. Rev. of *The Song of the Pearl: An Essay about Steinbeck's Short Novel, The Pearl.* By Wesley Stillwagon. *Steinbeck Review* 17 (Spring 2020): 94–96.

———. Rev. of *Chasing Steinbeck's Ghost: The Definitive Timeline for John Steinbeck's "Travels with Charley" Road Trip from the Author of "Dogging Steinbeck."* By Bill Steigerwald. *Steinbeck Review* 18 (Fall 2021): 204–6.

Bibliography

Algee-Hewitt, Mark, and Mark McGurl. "Between Canon and Corpus: Six Perspectives on 20th-Century Novels." *Stanford University Literary Lab Pamphlet* 8 (January 2015): 1–27.

Altick, Richard D. *The Scholar Adventurers.* New York: Macmillan, 1950.

Anon. "Fly Fishing's Mystery Woman." *Fly Rod & Reel,* 27 (July/October 2005): 14.

Anon. "Hardy Girl Update." *Fly Rod & Reel,* 27 (November/December 2005): 10.

Anon. *The John Steinbeck Map of America.* Los Angeles: Aaron Blake, 1986.

Arris, Bruce. *Inside Cannery Row: Sketches from The Steinbeck Era.* San Francisco: Lexicos, 1988.

Astro, Richard. *John Steinbeck and Edward F. Ricketts: The Shaping of a Novelist.* Minneapolis: University of Minnesota Press, 1973.

———. Introduction, *The Log from the Sea of Cortez.* By John Steinbeck. New York: Penguin, 1995, vii–xxvi.

———, and Donald Kohrs. *A Tidal Odyssey: Ed Ricketts and the Making of Between Pacific Tides.* Corvallis: Oregon State University Press, 2021.

Babb, James R. *Crosscurrents: A Fly Fisher's Progress.* New York: Lyons Press, 1999.

Bachelard, Gaston. *The Poetics of Space.* Translated by Maria Jolas. Foreword by Etienne Gilson. New York: Orion Press, 1964.

Bailey, Kevin. *The Western Flyer: Steinbeck's Boat, the Sea of Cortez, and the Saga of Pacific Fisheries.* Chicago: University of Chicago Press, 2015.

Bakhtin Mikhail. *Rabelais and His World.* Trans. Helene Iswolsky. Cambridge, MA: MIT Press, 1968.

Balaswamy, Periaswamy. "From Shimmering Planktons to Spinning Planets: Steinbeck's Expanding Quantum Universe and Brahmandanirmana." Kyoko Ariki, Luchen Li, and Scott Pugh, eds. *Steinbeck's Global Dimensions.* Lanham, MD: Scarecrow Press 2008, 167–81.

Barden, Thomas E. Preface. *Steinbeck in Vietnam: Dispatches from the War.* Ed. Thomas E. Barden. Charlottesville: University of Virginia Press, 2012, vii–ix.

Barthes, Roland. *The Rustle of Language.* Trans. Richard Howard. Berkeley: University of California Press, 1989.

Beegel, Susan F., Susan Shillinglaw, and Wesley N. Tiffney, Jr, eds. "Introduction." *Steinbeck and the Environment: Interdisciplinary Approaches.* Tuscaloosa: University of Alabama Press, 1997, 1–23.

Benson, Jackson. "John Steinbeck's *Cannery Row*: A Reconsideration." *Western American Literature* 12 (1977): 11–40

———. "The Novelist as Scientist." *Novel: A Forum on Fiction* 10 (1977): 248–264.

———. *The True Adventures of John Steinbeck, Writer.* New York: Viking Press, 1984.

———. *Looking for Steinbeck's Ghost*. Norman: University of Oklahoma Press, 1988.

Bhabha, Homi. *The Location of Culture*. New York: Routledge, 1994.

Black, William C. *Gentlemen Preferred Dry Flies: The Dry Fly and the Nymph, Evolution and Conflict*. Albuquerque: University of New Mexico Press, 2010.

Bodo, Peter. "Hookless Fly-Fishing Is a Humane Advance." *New York Times*, November 7, 1999, 34.

Brittain, Craig. "Steinbeck's Use of Ledgers in the Writing of *East of Eden* and *Journal of a Novel*." *Script & Print* 31 (2007): 172–79.

Brodwin, Stanley. "'The Poetry of Scientific Thinking': Steinbeck's Log from the Sea of Cortez and Scientific Travel Narrative." Susan F. Beegel, Susan Shillinglaw, and Wesley N. Tiffney, Jr, eds. *Steinbeck and the Environment: Interdisciplinary Approaches*. Tuscaloosa: University of Alabama Press, 1997, 142–160.

Brooks-Anderson, Barbara. *Salvador Dali's "A Surreal Night in an Enchanted Forest."* NP: Xlibris, 2012.

Brown, Jim. *A Treasury of Reels: The Fishing Reel Collection of the American Museum of Fly Fishing*. Photographs by Bob O'Shaughnessy. Manchester, VT: American Museum of Fly Fishing, 1990.

Browne, Neil W. *The World in Which We Occur: John Dewey, Pragmatist Ecology, and American Ecological Writing in the Twentieth Century*. Tuscaloosa: University of Alabama Press, 2007.

Browning, Mark. *Haunted by Waters: Fly Fishing in North American Literature*. Athens: Ohio University Press, 1998.

Buell, Lawrence. *The Dream of the Great American Novel*. Cambridge: Belknap/Harvard University Press, 2014.

Burgess, Anthony. *But Do Blondes Prefer Gentlemen?* New York: McGraw Hill, 1986.

Capra Fritjof. *The Tao of Physics: An Exploration of the Parallels Between Modern Physics and Eastern Mysticism*. Berkeley, CA: Shambala, 1975.

Childers, Joseph, and Gary Hentzel, eds. *The Columbia Dictionary of Modern Literary and Cultural Criticism*. New York: Columbia University Press, 1995.

Chouinard, Yvon, Craig Mathews, and Mauro Mazzo. Illus. James Prosek. *Simple Fly Fishing: Techniques for Tenkara and Rod & Reel Book*. Ventura: Patagonia Books, 2014.

Condon, Edward, and Phillip Morse. *Quantum Mechanics*. New York: McGraw Hill, 1929.

Cox, Martha Heasley. "In Search of John Steinbeck: His People and His Land." *San Jose Studies* 1 (November 1975): 41–60.

DeMott, Robert. "Steinbeck and the Creative Process: First Manifesto to End the Bringdown Against *Sweet Thursday*." *Steinbeck: The Man and His Work*. Ed. Richard Astro and Tetsumaro Hayashi. Corvallis: Oregon State University Press, 1971, 157–78.

———. *Angling Days: A Fly Fisher's Journals*. New York: Skyhorse Publishing, 2019.

———. *Steinbeck's Reading: A Catalogue of Books Owned and Borrowed*. New York: Garland, 1984.

————. *Steinbeck's Typewriter: Essays on His Art*. 1996. Reprinted with new preface, Bloomington, IN: iUniverse, 2012.

————. "Toward a Redefinition of *To a God Unknown*." *University of Windsor Review* VIII (Spring 1973): 34–53.

————. "The Interior Distances of John Steinbeck." S*teinbeck Quarterly* 12 (Summer–Fall 1979): 86–99.

————. "The Status of *The Grapes of Wrath*." *The Steinbeck Newsletter* 12 (Spring 1999): 22

————. with Brian Railsback. "Prospects for the Study of John Steinbeck." *Resources for American Literary Study*, Volume 32. Ed. Jackson Bryer and Richard Kopley. Brooklyn, NY: AMS Press, 2009, 9–47.

Dennis, Jerry. *The River Home: An Angler's Explorations*. New York: St Martin's, 1998.

Ditsky, John. *John Steinbeck and the Critics*. Rochester, NY: Camden House, 2000.

————. *Essays on East of Eden*. Steinbeck Monograph Series 7. Muncie, IN: Steinbeck Society/Ball State University, 1977.

Donohue, Cecilia. "'The teller would be opinionated'... and so will the reader: Opportunities for Response to John Steinbeck's *Journal of a Novel* and *East of Eden*." *Steinbeck Review* 9 (Fall 2012): 26–38.

Duman, Jill. "Searching for Steinbeck." *Coast Weekly* 4 (August 1994): 10, 12–13, 15.

Edgarian, Carol, and Tom Jenks, eds. "Introduction: The Diarist's Art." In *The Writer's Life: Intimate Thoughts on Work, Love, Inspiration, and Fame from the Diaries of the World's Great Writers*. NP: Narrative Library, 2011, xi–xix.

Englert, Peter A. J. "Education of Environmental Scientists: Should We Listen to Steinbeck and Ricketts' Comments?" Susan F. Beegel, Susan Shillinglaw, and Wesley N. Tiffney, Jr, eds. *Steinbeck and the Environment: Interdisciplinary Approaches*. Tuscaloosa: University of Alabama Press, 1997, 176–193.

Eddington, Arthur S. *The Nature of the Physical World*. New York: Macmillan, 1929.

Fallowfield, Julie. Correspondence from McIntosh and Otis to Roy S. Simmonds. May 20, 1996.

Farrah, David. "'The Form of the New' in Steinbeck's *Cannery Row*." *Shoin Literary Review* 25 (1992): 21–30.

Farrington, S. Kip. *Fishing with Hemingway and Glassell*. New York: David McKay, 1971.

Fensch, Thomas, ed. *Conversations with John Steinbeck*. Jackson: University Press of Mississippi, 1988.

Fiedler, Leslie. "Looking Back After 50 Years," *San Jose Studies* 16 (Winter 1990): 54–64.

Fisher, Shirley. "Steinbeck's Days in Sag Harbor." *New York Times*, December 3, 1978, Long Island Section 20.

French, Warren. "John Steinbeck." *Sixteen Modern American Authors: A Survey of Research and Criticism*. Ed. Jackson R. Bryer. New York Norton, 1973, 499–527.

————. *John Steinbeck*. 2nd ed. Revised. Boston: Twayne, 1975.

————, and Walter Kidd, eds. *American Winners of the Nobel Prize*. Norman: University of Oklahoma Press, 1968.

Geertz, Clifford. *The Interpretation of Cultures: Selected Essays*. New York: Basic, 1973.

Gennete, Gerard. *Palimpsests: Literature in the Second Degree*. Translated by Channa Newman and Claude Dubinsky. Foreword by Gerald Prince. Lincoln: University of Nebraska Press, 1997.

George, Stephen. "Crossing the Oceans: The Future of Steinbeck Studies in America, Japan, and Beyond." *John Steinbeck's Global Dimensions*. Ed. Kyoko Ariki, Luchen Li, and Scott Pugh. Lanham, MD: Scarecrow Press, 2008, 193–201.

Gide, Andre. *The Counterfeitors*. Translated by Dorothy Bussy. With Journal of *The Counterfeitors*. Translated by Justin O'Brien. New York: Random House, 1927.

Gilmore, Leigh. *Autobiographics: A Feminist Theory of Women's Self Representation*. Ithaca: Cornell University Press, 1994.

Gingrich, Arnold. *The Fishing in Print: A Guided Tour Through Five Centuries of Angling Literature*. New York: Winchester Press, 1974.

Gladstein, Mimi R. "Masculine Sexuality and the Objectification of Women: Steinbeck's Perspective." *Steinbeck Review* I (Spring 2004): 109–23.

Gleiser, Marcello. *Simple Beauty of the Unexpected: A Natural Philosopher's Quest for Trout and the Meaning of Everything*. Lebanon, NH: University Press of New England/Foredge, 2016.

Grover, Jan Zita. *Northern Waters*. St Paul: Graywolf Press, 1999.

Guernsey, Paul. *Beyond Catch and Release: Exploring the Future of Fly Fishing*. New York: Skyhorse Publishing, 2011.

Guinzburg, Harold. Correspondence with McIntosh and Otis. August 9, 1938.

Hackle, Sparse Grey. [Alfred W. Miller]. *Fishless Days, Angling Nights*. New York: Nick Lyons Books, 1971.

Halford, Frederic. *Floating Flies and How to Dress Them*. (1886). Rpt. Winchester, England: Barry Shurlock, 1974.

Halpern, Daniel. Preface. *Our Private Lives: Journals, Notebooks, and Diaries*. New York: Vintage Books, 1990, 5–6.

Hanish, Justin. *A Contemplative Angler: Selections from the Bruce P. Dancik Collection of Angling Books*. Edmonton: University of Alberta Press, 2018.

Hardy, John James. *Hardy's Anglers' Guide*. 58th and 59th editions. Alnwick, England: Hardy Brothers, 1951 and 1952.

Hardy, James Leighton. *The House the Hardy Brothers Built*. 2nd ed. Ellesmere, England: Medlar Press, 2006.

Harrison, Jim. Conversation with author. Livingston, MT. August, 2002.

Harwood, Keith. *The Hardy Book of the Salmon Fly*. Ellesmere, England: Medlar Press, 2006.

——, Andrew Herd, and David Stanley. *Gear and Gadgets: An Irresistible Collection of Hardy Fishing Tackle*. Ellesmere, England: Medlar Press, 2012.

Hayashi, Testumaro. "John Steinbeck: The Art and Craft of Writing." *A New Study Guide to Steinbeck's Major Works, with Critical Explications*. Ed. Tetsumaro Hayashi. Metuchen, NJ: Scarecrow Press, 1993, 274–84.

Hayles, N. Katherine. *The Cosmic Web: Scientific Field Models and Literary Strategies in the 20th Century*. Ithaca, NY: Cornell University Press, 1984.

Hearle, Kevin. "'The Boat Shaped Mind': Steinbeck's Sense of Language as Discourse in *Cannery Row* and *Sea of Cortez*." *After The Grapes of Wrath: Essays on John Steinbeck in Honor of Tetsumaro Hayashi*. Donald Coers, Paul D. Ruffin and Robert J. DeMott, eds. Athens: Ohio University Press, 1995, 101–12.

Heathcote, Andy, and Heike Bacheller. *The Lost World of Mr. Hardy*. London: Trufflepig Films, 2008. Video.

Heisenberg, Werner. *Physics and Philosophy: The Revolution in Modern Science*. New York: Harper, 1958.

Hemp, Michael. *Cannery Row: The History of John Steinbeck's Old Ocean View Avenue and Its Connections to the Pacific Northwest*. 4th ed. Monterey, CA: The History Company, 2019.

Herd, Andrew. *The Fly*. Ellesmere, England: Medlar Press, 2003.

———. *The History of Fly Fishing, Volume I*. Ellesmere, England: Medlar Press, 2019.

———, and Bob Frandsen. *The Story of the Salmon Fly, 1496–1884*. Ellesmere, England: Medlar Press, 2021.

Hemingway, Ernest. "Big Two-Hearted River." *Hemingway on Fishing*. Ed. Nick Lyons. Foreword by Jack Hemingway. New York: Lyons Press, 2000, 3–24.

———. [Portfolio of 32 Fishing Photographs]. *Hemingway on Fishing*, ff. 114.

Hemingway, Lorian. *Walk on Water*. New York: Simon & Schuster, 1998.

Hoover, Herbert. *Fishing for Fun and to Wash Your Soul*. Ed. William Nichols. New York: Random House, 1963.

Howe, Susan. *Spontaneous Particulars: The Telepathy of Archives*. New York: New Directions/Christine Burgin, 2014.

Humphrey, William. "Bill Breaks His Duck." In *Open Season: Sporting Adventures*. New York: Dell, 1989, 173–203.

Hyde, Lewis. *The Gift: Imagination and the Erotic Life of Property*. New York: Random House, 1979.

Johnson, Alexandra. *The Hidden Writer: Diaries and the Creative Life*. New York: Doubleday, 1997.

Johnson, Barbara. "Writing." In *Critical Terms for Literary Study*. Ed. Frank Lenthricchia and Thomas McLaughlin. 2nd edition. Chicago: University of Chicago Press, 1995, 39–49.

Johnson, Celia Blue. *Odd Type Writers: From Joyce and Dickens to Wharton and Welty, the Obsessive Habits and Quirky Techniques of Great Authors*. New York: Perigree, 2013.

Jones, Gavin. *Reclaiming John Steinbeck: Writing for the Future of Humanity*. New York: Cambridge University Press, 2021.

Jones, Lawrence William. *John Steinbeck as Fabulist*. Ed. Marston La France. Steinbeck Monograph Series, No. 3. Muncie, IN: Ball State University/John Steinbeck Society of America, 1973.

Jones, Roger S. *Physics as Metaphor*. Minneapolis: University of Minnesota Press, 1982.

Josephs, Lisa C. Email to Author. June 23, 2021.

Jung, Carl. *Psychological Types: The Psychology of Individuation.* Trans. H. G. Barnes. New York: Harcourt, Brace, 1923. [*Psychological Types. A Revision* by R. F. C. Hull of the Trans. H. G. Baynes. Bollingen Series XX. Princeton: Princeton University Press, 1971.]

Junker, Howard, ed. "Introduction." In *The Writer's Notebook.* San Francisco: Harper-Collins West, 1995, 1–4.

Kagle, Stephen. *American Diary Literature, 1620–1799.* Boston: Twayne, 1979.

Katakis, Michael, ed. *Ernest Hemingway: Artifacts from a Life.* Foreword by Patrick Hemingway. Afterword by Sean Hemingway. New York: Scribner, 2018.

Katz, Stephen B. *The Epistemic Music of Rhetoric: Toward the Temporal Dimension of Affect in Reader Response and Writing.* Carbondale: Southern Illinois University Press, 1996.

Keisman, Anne. "The Steinbeck Centennial." In *Dictionary of Literary Biography, Yearbook: 2002.* Ed. Mathew J. Bruccoli, George Garrett, and George Parker Anderson. Detroit: Gale, 2003, 473–76.

Kennedy, William. "'My Work is No Good.'" *New York Times Book Review*, April 9, 1989: 1, 44–45.

Kingwell, Mark. *Catch and Release: Trout Fishing and the Meaning of Life.* New York: Viking Penguin, 2003.

Kragh, Helge. *Quantum Generations: A History of Physics in the Twentieth Century.* Princeton: Princeton University Press, 1999.

Kurlansky, Mark. *The Unreasonable Virtue of Fly Fishing.* New York: Bloomsbury, 2021.

LaFontaine, Gary, with Craig J. Oberg. "One Nine-Inch Rainbow—A Last Conversation with Gary LaFontaine." *Weber Studies* 20 (Fall 2002): 8–16.

Lanigan-O'Keeffe, Martin. *Hardy's Salmon Flies: Patterns from the Fly Tying Department 1883–1969.* Machynlleth, Powys, Wales: Coch-y-Bonddu Books, 2019.

Lannoo Michael. *Leopold's Shack and Ricketts' Lab: The Emergence of Environmentalism.* Berkeley: University of California Press, 2010.

Law, Glenn. *A Concise History of Fly Fishing.* Guilford, CT: Lyons Press, 2003.

Leeson, Ted. *Jerusalem Creek: Journeys into Driftless Country.* Guilford, CT: Lyons Press, 2002.

Levy-Bruhl, Lucien. *How Natives Think.* Trans. Lillian A. Clare. London: Allen and Unwin, 1926.

Li, Luchen, ed. *John Steinbeck: A Documentary Volume.* Volume 309, *Dictionary of Literary Biography.* Detroit: Thomsen Gale, 2005.

[Lorio, Jill, ed.] *The John Steinbeck Collection: The Estate of Elaine and John Steinbeck.* Foreword by Jason Lorio. Lincoln Park, NJ: Curated Estates Auctions, 2020.

Lopez, Barry. "Steinbeck's Influence." *John Steinbeck: Centennial Reflections by American Writers.* Ed. Susan Shillinglaw. San Jose: Center for Steinbeck Studies, 2002, 57–61.

Lundy, A. L. "Scrap." In *Real Life on Cannery Row: Real People, Places and Events That*

Inspired John Steinbeck. Foreword by Thomas Steinbeck. Santa Monica: Angel City Press, 2008.

Lyons, Nick. *Full Creel: A Nick Lyons Reader*. Foreword by Thomas McGuane. New York: Atlantic Monthly, 2000.

Lyotard, Jan-Francois. *The Postmodern Condition: A Report on Knowledge*. Trans. Geoff Bennington and Brian Masumi. Minneapolis: University of Minnesota Press, 1984.

Maclean, Norman. *A River Runs Through It and Other Stories.* Chicago: University of Chicago Press, 1976.

Mallon, Thomas. *A Book of One's Own: People and Their Diaries*. New York: Ticknor and Fields, 1984.

Marks, Lester. *Thematic Design in the Novels of John Steinbeck*. The Hague: Mouton, 1969.

Marsh, John. *The Emotional Life of the Great Depression*. New York: Oxford University Press, 2019.

McElrath, Joseph R., Jesse S. Crisler, and Susan Shillinglaw, eds. *John Steinbeck: The Contemporary Reviews*. New York: Cambridge University Press, 1996.

McGuane, Thomas. *The Longest Silence: A Life in Fishing*. New York: Knopf, 1999.

McKibben, Carol Lynn. *Beyond Cannery Row: Sicilian Women, Immigration, and Community in Monterey, California, 1915–1999*. Urbana: University of Illinois Press, 2006.

McParland, Robert. *Citizen Steinbeck: Giving Voice to the People*. Lanham, MD: Rowman & Littlefield, 2016.

Meeker, Joseph. *The Comedy of Survival: Literary Ecology and a Play Ethic*. 3rd ed. Tucson: University of Arizona Press, 1997.

Moore, Harry Thornton. *The Novels of John Steinbeck: A First Critical Study*. Chicago: Normandie House, 1939.

Noble, Donald R., ed. Introduction to *The Steinbeck Question: New Essays in Criticism*. Troy, NY: Whitston Publishing, 1993, 1–7.

Nova, Craig. *Brook Trout and the Writing Life*. New York: Lyons Press, 1999.

Oborne, Marijane. "Participatory Parables: Cinema, Social Action, and Steinbeck's Mexican Dilemma." In *A Political Companion to John Steinbeck*. Ed. Cyrus Ernesto Zirakzadeh and Simon Stow. Lexington: University Press of Kentucky, 2013, 227–246.

O'Hara, David L. and Matthew T. Dickerson. *Downstream: Reflections on Brook Trout, Fly Fishing, and the Waters of Appalachia*. Foreword by Nick Lyons. Afterword by Bill McKibben. Eugene, OR: Cascade Books, 2014.

Owens, Louis. *John Steinbeck's Re-Vision of America*. Athens: University of Georgia Press, 1985.

———. *The Grapes of Wrath: Trouble in the Promised Land*. Boston: Twayne, 1989.

———. "Where Things Can Happen: California and Writing." *Western American Literature* 3, no. 4 (1999): 150–55.

Parini, Jay. Introduction to *Travels with Charley in Search of America* by John Steinbeck. New York: Penguin, 1997, vii–xxiii.

———. *John Steinbeck: A Biography*. New York: Henry Holt, 1995.

Pearson, Pauline. *Guide to Steinbeck Country*. Salinas: John Steinbeck Library, 1984.

Quigley, Edward. *In the Company of Rivers: An Angler's Stories and Recollections*. New York: Skyhorse Publishing, 2014.

Railsback, Brian. *Parallel Expeditions: Charles Darwin and the Art of John Steinbeck*. Moscow: University of Idaho Press, 1995.

———. "Dreams of an Elegant Universe on Cannery Row." Susan Shillinglaw and Kevin Hearle, eds. *Beyond Boundaries: Rereading John Steinbeck*. Tuscaloosa: University of Alabama Press, 2002, 277–94.

Raines, Howell. *Fly Fishing Through the Midlife Crisis*. New York: Doubleday, 1993.

Ransome, Arthur. *Rod and Line*. London: Jonathan Cape, 1929.

Raymond, Steve. *Rivers of the Heart: A Fly-Fishing Memoir*. New York: Lyons Press, 1998.

Ricketts, Edward F. *Breaking Through: Essays. Journals, and Travelogues of Edward F Ricketts*. Ed. Katherine A Rodger. Foreword by Susan Beegel. Berkeley: University of California Press, 2006.

———. *Renaissance Man of Cannery Row: The Life and Letters of Edward F. Ricketts*. Ed. Katherine A. Rodger. Tuscaloosa: University of Alabama Press, 2002.

Riggs, Susan F. A *Catalogue of the John Steinbeck Collection at Stanford University*. Stanford: Stanford University Libraries, 1980.

Rodger, Katherine A, ed. Introduction to *Breaking Through: Essays, Journals, and Travelogues of Edward F. Ricketts*. Foreword by Susan F. Beegel. Berkeley: University of California Press, 2006, 1–79.

Roorda, Randall. "Antinomies of Participation in Literacy and Wilderness." *Interdisciplinary Studies in Literature and Environment* 14 (Summer 2007): 71–87.

Rukeyser, Muriel. *The Life of Poetry*. New York: Current Books, 1949.

Scholnik, Robert J., ed. *American Literature and Science*. Lexington: University Press of Kentucky, 1992.

Schullery, Paul. *American Fly Fishing: A History*. New York: Nick Lyons Books, 1987.

———. *Royal Coachman: The Lore and Legends of Fly-Fishing*. New York: Simon & Schuster, 1999.

Shepard, Odell. *Thy Rod and Thy Creel*. New York: Dodd, Mead, 1931.

Shillinglaw, Susan. *A Journey into Steinbeck's California*. Photographs by Nancy Burnett. 3rd ed. Berkeley, CA: Roaring Forties, 2019.

———, ed. "*Cannery Row* Fiftieth Anniversary Edition." *Steinbeck Newsletter* 9 (Fall 1995): 1–40.

———. *Carol and John Steinbeck: Portrait of a Marriage*. Reno: University of Nevada Press, 2013.

———. Introduction to *Cannery Row* by John Steinbeck. New York: Penguin, 1994, vii–xxvii.

———. *On Reading The Grapes of Wrath*. New York: Penguin, 2014.

Simmonds, Roy S. "The Bus That Failed." Photocopy of Typed Manuscript. 125 pp. 1996–1997.

———. Correspondence with Robert DeMott. March 11, 1997.

———. *John Steinbeck: The War Years, 1939–1945*. Lewisburg, PA: Bucknell University Press, 1996.

———. "The Composition of Steinbeck's *The Wayward Bus*." In *John Steinbeck: A Centennial Tribute*. Ed. Syed Mashkoor Ali. Jaipur: Surabhi Publications, 2004, 327–49.

———. "The Composition, Publication, and Reception of John Steinbeck's *The Wayward Bus*, with Biographical Background." Serially published in 7 sections, *Steinbeck Review* 7, no. 2 (Fall 2010), through 10, no. 2 (Fall 2013).

Skues, G. E. M. *Minor Tactics of the Chalk Stream*. London: Adam and Charles Black, 1910.

Smiley, Jane. *Thirteen Ways of Looking at a Novel*. New York: Knopf, 2005.

Sontag, Susan. *On Photography*. New York: Farrar, Straus & Giroux, 1977.

Souder, William. *Mad at the World: A Life of John Steinbeck*. New York: Norton, 2020.

Springsteen, Bruce. Acceptance Speech. Quoted in Lauren Onkey, "'Not Afraid of Being Heroic': Bruce Springsteen's John Steinbeck." In *A Political Companion to John Steinbeck*. Ed. Cyrus Ernesto Zirakzadeh and Simon Stow. Lexington: University Press of Kentucky, 2013, 247–67.

Steele, Eric. *Kiss the Water*. New York: Virgil Films, 2014.

Steigerwald, Bill. *Dogging Steinbeck*. Pittsburgh, PA: Fourth River, 2012.

Steinbeck, Elaine. Foreword to *Steinbeck and the Environment: Interdisciplinary Approaches*. Ed. Susan F. Beegel, Susan Shillinglaw, and Wesley N. Tiffney. Tuscaloosa: University of Alabama Press, 1997, xi.

———. Unpublished Letter to Robert DeMott. Sag Harbor, NY. April 24, 1988.

Steinbeck, Gwyn. "'The Closest Witness': The Autobiographical Reminiscences of Gwyndolyn Conger Steinbeck." Ed. Terry Grant Halladay. Master's Thesis, Stephen F. Austin State University, 1979.

———. *My Life with John Steinbeck*. As Told to Douglas Brown. Preface by Jay Parini. Powys, Wales: Lawson Publishing, 2018.

Steinbeck, John. "Argument of Phalanx." [1933]. George Albee Papers, University of California, Berkeley.

———. *Cannery Row* (1945). *Novels 1942–1952*. Ed. Robert DeMott. New York: Library of America, 2002, 101–228.

———. *The Complete Archive of Cannery Row by John Steinbeck*. Stanford: Stanford University Libraries, 1975.

———. *Conversations with John Steinbeck*. Ed. Thomas Fensch. Jackson: University Press of Mississippi, 1988.

———. "Critics, Critics, Burning Bright." In *Steinbeck and His Critics: A Record of Twenty-Five Years*. Ed. E. W. Tedlock Jr. and C. V. Wicker. Albuquerque: University of New Mexico Press, 1957, 43–47.

———. *East of Eden* Autograph Manuscript (1951). John Steinbeck Collection. Harry Ransom Center, U of Texas, Austin. Works 1926–1966. Series 1. Box 4.

———. *East of Eden*. (1952). *Novels 1942–1952*. Ed. Robert DeMott. New York: Library of America, 2002, 307–947.

———. "Introduction by Pascal Covici." Unpublished holograph essay ms. [September 1942]. Harry Ransom Center, University of Texas, Austin.

———. *John Steinbeck on Writing*. Ed. Tetsumaro Hayashi. *Steinbeck Essay Series*, no. 2. Muncie, IN: Ball State University, 1988.

———. *Journal of a Novel: The East of Eden Letters*. New York: Viking Press, 1969.

———. Letter to George Albee. Thursday [1933]. George Albee Papers, University of California, Berkeley.

———. Letter to Joe Hamilton. October 1939. Wells Fargo Steinbeck Collection, MO 1063, box 2. Department of Special Collections and University Archives, Stanford University.

———. Letter to Lewis Gannett. December 9 [1953.] Houghton Library, Harvard University.

———. Letter to Pascal Covici, September 1942, Harry Ransom Center, University of Texas, Austin.

———. *Long Valley* ledger. Unpublished autograph notebook. 1934. Martha Heasley Cox Center for Steinbeck Studies.

———. *Murder at Full Moon*. Unpublished novel typescript. Harry Ransom Center, University of Texas, Austin. Works, M-0.

———. "My personal book." Unpublished autograph *Wayward Bus* journal. January 9, 1946–September 24, 1946. Morgan Library and Museum MA 4685.

———. "Nobel Prize Acceptance Speech." *America and Americans and Selected Nonfiction* . Ed. Susan Shillinglaw and Jackson Benson. New York: Penguin, 2002, 172–74.

———. "On Fishing." *America and Americans and Selected Nonfiction*. Ed. Susan Shillinglaw and Jackson Benson. New York: Penguin, 2002, 132–135.

———. "Rationale." *America and Americans and Selected Nonfiction*. Ed. Susan Shillinglaw and Jackson Benson. New York: Penguin, 2002, 161–62.

———, and Edward F. Ricketts. *Sea of Cortez: A Leisurely Journal of Travel and Research*. New York: Viking Press, 1941.

———. *Steinbeck: A Life in Letters*. Ed. Elaine Steinbeck and Robert Wallsten. New York: Viking Press, 1975.

———. "Suggestion for an Interview with Joseph Henry Jackson." *The Grapes of Wrath: Text and Criticism*. Ed. Peter Lisca and Kevin Hearle. New York: Viking/Penguin Critical Library, 1997, 640–643.

———. *The Forgotten Village*. New York: Viking Press, 1941.

———. *The Grapes of Wrath*. *The Grapes of Wrath and Other Writings 1936–1941*. Ed. Robert DeMott, with Special Consultant Elaine A. Steinbeck. New York: Library of America, 1996, 207–692.

———. *The Grapes of Wrath Manuscript*. Editorial Note by Jessica Nelson. Cambremer, France: SP Books-Editions des Saints Peres, 2021.

———. *The Log from the Sea of Cortez* (1951). *The Grapes of Wrath and Other Writings 1936–1941.* Ed. Robert DeMott with Special Consultant Elaine Steinbeck, New York: Library of America, 1996, 693–987.

———. "The novel might benefit by the discipline, the terseness of the drama. . . ." *Stage* 15 (January 1938): 50–51; reprinted as "The Play Novelette." *America and Americans and Selected Nonfiction.* Ed. Susan Shillinglaw and Jackson J. Benson. New York: Penguin, 2002, 155–57.

———. *The Standard Diary for 1951.* Cambridge. MA: The Standard Diary Company, 1950. Morgan Library and Museum MA 4689.

———. "The Time the Wolves Ate the Vice-Principal." *'47 Magazine of the Year* (March 1947): 26–27. Rptd in *Steinbeck Newsletter, Cannery Row* Fiftieth Anniversary Issue, ed. Shillinglaw, 10.

———. "Then My Arm Glassed Up." *America and Americans and Selected Nonfiction.* Ed. Susan Shillinglaw and Jackson J. Benson. New York: Penguin, 2002, 125–131.

———. "This Our America." Unpublished Radio Script for National Broadcasting Company, May, 1939. Annie Laurie Williams Collection, Columbia University.

———. *To a God Unknown* ledger (ca. 1932). Quoted in Nelson Valjean, *John Steinbeck, The Errant Knight: An Intimate Biography of his California Years.* San Francisco: Chronicle, 1975.

———. "The Trial of Arthur Miller." *America and Americans and Selected Nonfiction,* Ed. Susan Shillinglaw and Jackson J. Benson. New York: Penguin, 2002, 101–4.

———. *The Year 1951 Diary Book.* Holyoke, MA: National Blank Book, 1950. Morgan Library and Museum MA 4688.

———. *The Year 1952 Diary Book.* Holyoke, MA: National Blank Book Company, 1951. Morgan Library and Museum MA 4690.

———. *Travels with Charley* (1962). In *Travels with Charley and Later Novels 1947–1962.* Ed. Robert DeMott and Brian Railsback. New York: Library of America, 2007, 765–951.

———. *Un Americain à New-York et à Paris.* Paris: Rene Julliard, 1956.

———. "Un Grand Romancier de Notre Temps." *Hommage à André Gide.* Ed. by Jean Schlumberger. Paris: La Nouvelle Revue Francais, 1951. [30].

———. Unpublished Autograph Journal, November 24, 1946–June 5, 1947. Collection of SJ Neighbors.

———. Unpublished Autograph *Travels with Charley* Diary and Manuscript. Morgan Library and Museum MA 2199.

———. Unpublished Letter to Family. April 1927. Wells Fargo Steinbeck Collection, M1063, Department of Special Collections, Stanford University Libraries, Stanford, California.

———. Unpublished Letter to Esther Rodgers. June 7, 1953. Wells Fargo Steinbeck collection, M1063, Department of Special Collections, Stanford University Libraries, Stanford, California.

———. Unpublished Letter to Ritch and Tal Lovejoy. July 5, 1955. Bancroft Library, University of California, Berkeley.

———. Unpublished Letter to Graham Watson. March 29, 1966. Morgan Library and Museum MA 4952.

———. *Working Days: The Journals of The Grapes of Wrath, 1938–1941*. Ed. Robert DeMott. New York: Viking Press, 1989.

———. *Your Only Weapon Is Your Work: A Letter by John Steinbeck to Dennis Murphy*. Ed. Robert DeMott. San Jose: Steinbeck Research Center, 1985.

Steinbeck, John IV, and Nancy Steinbeck. *The Other Side of Eden: Life with John Steinbeck*. Amherst, NY: Prometheus, 2001.

Steinbeck, Thom. Interview with author. Hempstead, NY. March 22, 2002.

———. [Untitled recollection of his father]. *John Steinbeck: Centennial Reflections by American Writers*. Ed. Susan Shillinglaw. San Jose: Center for Steinbeck Studies, 2002, 88–92.

———. "My Father, John Steinbeck." In *John Steinbeck: A Centennial Tribute*. Ed. Stephen K. George. Westport, CT: Prager, 2002, 3–12.

Stewart, Susan. *On Longing: Narratives of the Miniature, the Gigantic, the Souvenir, the Collection*. 1984. rptd. Durham, NC: Duke University Press, 1993.

Stodola, Sarah. *Process: The Writing Lives of Great Authors*. New York: Amazon, 2015.

Stow, Simon. "Introduction: The Dangerous Ambivalence of John Steinbeck." In *A Political Companion to John Steinbeck*. Ed. Cyrus Ernesto Zirakzadeh and Simon Stow. Lexington: University Press of Kentucky, 2013, 8–16.

Strehle, Susan. *Fiction in the Quantum Universe*. Chapel Hill: University of North Carolina Press, 1992.

Swan, Kenneth D. "The Merit of John Steinbeck: A Wide-Ranging Debate." In *Steinbeck's Prophetic Vision of America: Proceedings of the Bicentennial Steinbeck Seminar*. Ed. Tetsumaro Hayashi and Kenneth D. Swan. Upland, IN: Taylor University for The John Steinbeck Society of America, 1976, 56–84.

Swensen, James R. *Picturing Migrants: The Grapes of Wrath and New Deal Documentary Photography*. Norman: University of Oklahoma Press, 2015.

Szalay, Michael. *New Deal Modernism: American Literature and the Invention of the Welfare State*. Durham, NC: Duke University Press, 2000.

Tamm, Eric Enno. *Beyond The Outer Shores: The Untold Odyssey of Ed Ricketts, the Pioneering Ecologist Who Inspired John Steinbeck and Joseph Campbell*. New York: Four Walls Eight Windows, 2004.

Tatum, Stephen. "Topographies of Transition in Western American Literature." *Western American Literature* 32 (1998): 310–52.

Tedlock. E. W., and C. V. Wicker, eds. "Introduction: Perspectives in Steinbeck Criticism." In *Steinbeck and His Critics: A Record of Twenty-Five Years*. Albuquerque, University of New Mexico Press, 1957, xi–xli.

TeMaat, Agatha. "John Steinbeck: On the Nature of the Creative Process in the Early Years." PhD diss. University of Nebraska, 1975.

Timmerman, John H. *John Steinbeck's Fiction: The Aesthetics of the Road Taken*. Norman: University of Oklahoma Press, 1986.

———. *Searching for Eden: John Steinbeck's Ethical Career*. Macon, GA: Mercer University Press, 2014.

Traver, Robert [John D. Voelker]. *Traver on Fishing*. Ed. Nick Lyons. Guilford, CT: Lyons, 2001.

Trodd, Zoe. "Star Signals: John Steinbeck in the American Protest Literature Tradition." In *A Political Companion to John Steinbeck*. Ed. Cyrus Ernesto Zirakzadeh and Simon Stow. Lexington: University Press of Kentucky, 2013, 49–76.

van Gelder, Robert. "Interview with a Best-Selling Author: John Steinbeck." *Cosmopolitan* (April 1947); reprinted in *Conversations with John Steinbeck*. Ed. Thomas Fensch. Jackson: University Press of Mississippi, 1988, 43–48.

Valenti, Peter. "Steinbeck's Ecological Polemic: Human Sympathy and Visual Documentary in the Intercalary Chapters of *The Grapes of Wrath*." In *Steinbeck and the Environment: Interdisciplinary Approaches*, eds. Susan F. Beegel, Susan Shillinglaw, and Wesley N. Tiffney. Tuscaloosa: University of Alabama Press, 1997, 92–112.

Veggian, Henry. "Bio-Politics and the Institution of Literature: An Essay on *East of Eden*, Its Critics and Its Time." In *East of Eden: New and Recent Essays*. Ed. Michael J. Meyer and Henry Veggian. Amsterdam: Rodopi, 2013, 87–121.

Viking Press. "Memorandum of Agreement." September 12, 1938.

———."Memorandum of Agreement." April 10, 1945.

Wagner-Martin, Linda. *John Steinbeck: A Literary Life*. London: Palgrave Macmillan, 2017.

Waldmeier, Joseph. "John Steinbeck: No Grapes of Wrath." In *A Question of Quality: Popularity and Value in Modern Creative Writing*. Ed. Louis Filler. Bowling Green, OH: Bowling Green State University Popular Press, 1976, 219–228.

Walton, Izaak. *The Compleat Angler Or, The Contemplative Man's Recreation, with Instructions How to Angle for a Trout or Grayling in a Clear Stream*. By Charles Cotton. Introduction by Howell Raines (5th edition, 1676); New York: Modern Library, 1996.

Watson, Graham. *Book Society*. New York: Atheneum, 1980.

Weeks, Edward. *Fresh Waters*. Boston: Little, Brown, 1968.

Wert, Hal Elliott, *Hoover the Fishing President: Portrait of the Private Man and His Life Outdoors*. Mechanicsburg, PA: Stackpole, 2005.

Wetherell, W. D. *One River More*. New York: Lyons Press, 1998.

———. *Vermont River*. New York: Lyons Press, 1984.

———. "Why Fish." *Upland Stream: Notes on the Fishing Passion*. Boston: Little, Brown, 1991, 184–204.

Whitelaw, Ian. *The History of Fly-Fishing in Fifty Flies*. Illustrations by Julie Spyropoulos. New York: Stewart Chabori and Chang, 2015.

Wickstrom, Gordon. *Notes from an Old Fly Book*. Boulder: University Press of Colorado, 2001.

Willis, Lloyd. *Environmental Evasion: The Literary, Critical, and Cultural Politics of "Nature's Nation."* Albany: SUNY Press, 2011.

Wilson, Edmund. *The Boys in the Back Room: Notes on California Novelists*. San Francisco: Colt, 1941.

Woit, Steve. *Fly Fishing Treasures: The World of Fly Fishers and Collecting*. Lexington, MA: Privately Printed, 2018.

Wollum, Rick. Interview with author. Livingston, MT. August 2005.

Wyse, Lowell. *Ecospatiality: A Place-Based Approach to American Literature.* Iowa City: University of Iowa Press, 2021.

Zane, Nancy. "The Romantic Impulse in Steinbeck's *Journal of a Novel: The East of Eden Letters* (1969)." *Steinbeck's Posthumous Work: Essays in Criticism.* Ed. Tetsumaro Hayashi and Thomas J. Moore. Steinbeck Monograph Series 14. Muncie, IN: Ball State University/Steinbeck Research Institute, 1989, 1–11.

INDEX

ABOUT THE AUTHOR

Robert DeMott is the Edwin and Ruth Kennedy Distinguished Professor of English Emeritus at Ohio University in Athens, where he taught American literature and creative writing from 1969 to 2013 and where he received half a dozen graduate and undergraduate teaching awards and supervised twenty-one PhD dissertations. He is a former acting director of San Jose State University's Steinbeck Research Center (1984–1985) and a founding staffer on the original *Steinbeck Newsletter* (1968) and *Steinbeck Quarterly* (1969–1993), and he has been a longstanding member of the editorial boards of San Jose State's *Steinbeck Newsletter* and *Steinbeck Studies* (1994–2005) and, since 2016, a member of the editorial board of *Steinbeck Review*. He consulted on and appeared in the Learning Channel's Emmy-nominated documentary film on *The Grapes of Wrath* (2000). For significant contributions to Steinbeck studies he was awarded a Burkhardt Prize from Ball State University (1987) and the National Steinbeck Center's Trustees Award (2006). A lifelong fly-fisherman, DeMott is a Federation of Flyfishers International certified casting instructor and a life member of both Trout Unlimited and the Northern Kentucky Fly Fishers. His recent books are a memoir, *Angling Days: A Fly Fisher's Journals* (2016, enlarged edition, 2019); interviews, *Conversations with Jim Harrison: Revised and Updated* (2019); and prose poems, *Up Late Reading Birds of America* (2020). He lives in Athens, Ohio, with the writer Kate Fox.

www.ingramcontent.com/pod-product-compliance
Lightning Source LLC
Chambersburg PA
CBHW031255090426
42742CB00007B/471